IMAGES
of America

CHASE CITY

ON THE COVER: Chase City was a proud town, hosting five or six parades each year. People from all over Southside, Virginia, came to help in the celebration of its prosperity. This photograph is of a parade in the late 1940s. Pictured here is the Camp Pickett, Virginia, military marching band. They participated in each of Chase City's parades starting after World War II until after the Korean conflict was over. (South Central Fair Association, Inc.)

IMAGES
of America

CHASE CITY

John Caknipe Jr.

ARCADIA
PUBLISHING

ISBN 978-0-7385-5339-9

Published by Arcadia Publishing
Charleston, South Carolina

Printed in the United States of America

Library of Congress Catalog Card Number: 2007935846

For all general information contact Arcadia Publishing at:
Telephone 843-853-2070
Fax 843-853-0044
E-mail sales@arcadiapublishing.com
For customer service and orders:
Toll-Free 1-888-313-2665

Visit us on the Internet at www.arcadiapublishing.com

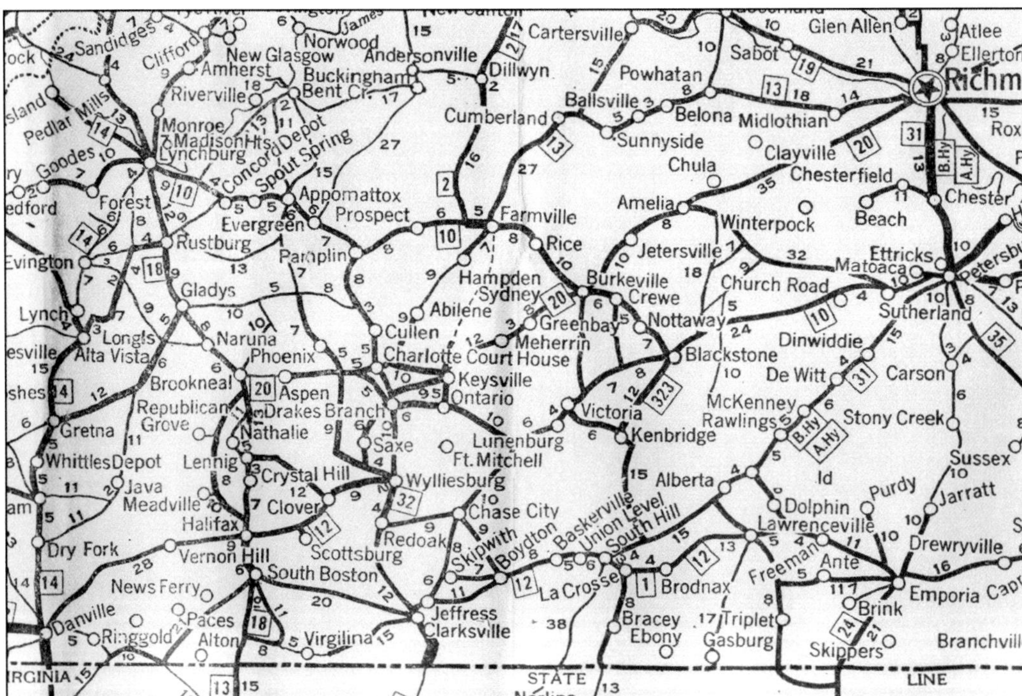

This cut-out portion of a 1920 Virginia state highway map printed and given to customers by First National Bank of Chase City shows the location of Chase City in the Southside community. Drawing a line a little below Virgilina through Drakes Branch illustrates the Virgilina Gold District. The vein was surveyed and the survey was published as "Geology of the Ore Deposits of the Virginia and North Carolina," *Virginia Geological Survey Bulletin*, Plate I, by F. B. Lancy in 1917. (Glen and Lisa Gillespie.)

Contents

Acknowledgments

There are many special thanks deserved by individuals who helped to bring this text to print. My committee was Charles Rockwell (retired, Coca-Cola), Tommy Emory (retired county librarian), Debbie Blue (Mecklenburg Electric Cooperative), Tina Wood (MacCallum More Museum), and Janet Flynn (Chase City Chamber of Commerce, director). I am very grateful to editor Nicholas Elmes and *News-Progress* for opening their archives to me and giving me assistance, support, and encouragement. I'm grateful to Hugh Lankford for immediately coming forward with the photographs that allowed me to submit the proposal and to Bill Gregory for going the extra mile, copying numerous photographs from his collection for my use. I'm thankful to the Town of Chase City and to town manager Ricky Reese for allowing me access to its records and photographs and to the South Central Fair Association, Inc., for literally taking all its photographs off the walls and handing them to me.

James Lewter spent hours advising me; Charles Queensberry ran all over town collecting old newspapers and other papers for my research; and Debbie Blue proofread the text, encouraged my liaison with Mecklenburg Electric, and even tried to read my handwriting (sorry). Special thanks goes to literally hundreds of current and former residents of Chase City for photographs, stories, encouragement, and support in attempting to preserve this small portion of Chase City's history.

Lastly, special thanks go to (my "sweetie") Betty K. McKinney Caknipe for her patience, encouragement, and tolerance of both me and the computer. She is my inspiration, support, and foundation.

Legend for courtesy lines:

GLG—Glen and Lisa Gillespie
BML—Butler Memorial Library
BML/HJ—Butler Memorial Library, Harvey Jeter
SVHP—Southside Virginia Historical Press
CC—Town of Chase City
WCG—William C. Gregory
MWC—Mildred Wilson Caknipe
CCPO—Chase City Post Office, Teresa Inge, postmaster
SCFA—South Central Fair Association, Inc.
HL—Pozie "Hugh" Lankford
JL—James Lewter Jr.
PC—Presbyterian Church, Katheryn Routt
JG—James C. Gurley
RS—Ruth S. Scott
JC—John Caknipe Jr.
EM—Eugene Morris
NP/SA—*News Progress*, Shirley A. Andrews
DT—Dorothy Bridges Tuck
KW—Elena "Kitty" Johnson Williams
JRL—James R. Lenhart
JAY—J. Andy Young
LLE—Lucy Lind Emory
MMMG—MacCallum More Museum and Gardens
IMB—Irene Morgan Brooks
CDS—Carolyn Duke Shearin
LB—Lorraine Benson

INTRODUCTION

A divided nation and a conquered land, the South was under martial law—it was called Reconstruction. The little village of Christiansville, Virginia, fell prey to the carpetbaggers of the North and would be no more. The property surrounding the crossroads village and the plantations became platted parcels for sale because of the enormity of taxes levied by the U.S. government to repay its war debt.

The demise of Christiansville would be followed by a new, vibrant community—Chase City, named for the controversial U.S. Supreme Court chief justice Salmon P. Chase. The name was chosen by the new regime, as Salmon Chase was a friend of John Boyd and George Endly, the founders of the new town. All three men were from south-central Ohio and knew each other during the days when Chase was governor of Ohio. As chief justice, Chase was responsible for the impeachment proceedings against Pres. Andrew Jackson, but early in the proceedings, Chase suffered a heart attack. In 1873, he came to Richmond, Virginia, to visit a friend. The constituency from Christiansville visited him to ask permission to use his name for the new city. He granted permission, but in less than a month (May 1873), he expired, never having seen his namesake. He knew Chase City was strategically located in Mecklenburg County, Virginia. Two major roads in the area intersected in Chase City (they were later named Highways 46 and 49). Chase City was situated in the middle of the Virgilina Gold Vein, which runs from six miles south of Virgilina to six miles northeast of Drakes Branch. Tiny Chase City became a stop along the Mecklenburg-Richmond Railroad, which ran from Keysville, Virginia, to Durham, North Carolina, in 1873. With the opening of the rail lines, the citizens of Chase City responded to the mine owners, stockholders, and professionals by building several rooming houses. Because of its central location, gaming facilities, and full-service support of its guests, Chase City became a very desirable destination.

The grand opening of the Mecklenburg Mineral Springs Hotel and Sanitarium (or hospital) drew people from all over the East Coast for its lavish entertainment and state-of-the-art curative hydrotherapy techniques. Visitors came for treatment and respite, and it was the ideal surroundings for mining executives to deposit their families while they went off to take care of the day-to-day business in the raucous mining communities.

Gold, silver, and tungsten brought companies and investors from New York, Pennsylvania, Ohio, and New Jersey to reopen the mines, which had been discovered in the 1850s but abandoned in favor of the California Gold Rush. This cash-laden group wanted fineries. Chase City provided them. Small, dug spring baths with curative lithia-calcium water (common in Virginia), entertainment for all occasions, recreation of all types, and sports beyond imagination were available.

With many distilleries in operation, Chase City's fame was actually its apple cider—later cider from a variety of fruits. The countryside was lush with vegetation and farming. Adjacent to the village were at least two dairies. Vegetables and fruits were abundant, but the primary income sources have always been tobacco, cotton, and timber. With Reconstruction, farming changed. The Sharecropper Law of 1869 made small farms profitable without the farmer investing in the land. Severe taxes were levied on tobacco, cotton, and distilled spirits, and with the taxes, one could only sell his wares to a licensed U.S. agent. Tobacco and cotton warehouses sprang up all over the tobacco region. By 1890, Chase City had four.

As Chase City continued to grow, it became the shopping destination not only for area residents and tourists but also for neighboring residents of Lunenburg and Charlotte Counties. In the off-season, the warehouses became social, entertainment, and recreational facilities, hosted evangelists and speakers, dances, "boxbowling," skating, and basketball. Many stalls of goods, produce, and prepared foods were located adjacent to or in the alleyways surrounding the warehouses. Several millinery shops, numerous dry goods stores, two large hardware stores, a furniture factory with stores, a wagon and spoke factory with two stores, gristmills, rolling mills, ice plants, and farm supply stores with a host of support services and shops dotted the landscape and began to form a town. The population nearly doubled every decade from 1870 through 1920. The new settlers after 1900 came from the mountains of Virginia, North Carolina, South Carolina, and Georgia for the rich and cheap farmlands surrounding Chase City—the plantations were all but a memory.

Chase City's history is richly punctuated with many firsts in the state and nation. The list includes the first hydrotherapy sanitarium in the United States; the first licensed female pharmacist in Virginia and the first female graduate of the Medical College of Virginia Pharmacy Program; the first recipient of the Congressional Medal of Honor in Virginia; the first meeting place for the Virginia–North Carolina Fox Hunters Association; the first area in the United States to breed English Thoroughbreds; and in 1850, the county was listed as the wealthiest county and one of the largest counties in Virginia. The April 24, 1873, edition of *Southside Virginian* in Boydton, Virginia (with a widespread distribution to England), titled Chase City as "the wealthiest Northern town in the South."

In 1907, several of the mines closed. More closed in 1908, and the hotels in Chase City began to suffer with more staff than guests. In April 1909, the grand Mecklenburg Mineral Springs Hotel and Sanitarium, heavily insured, burned. An effort to rebuild was launched by the manager, Col. William T. Hughes, and by 1927, the stock sales continued to be good, but the 1929 Depression closed the chapter.

The following pages are the result of exhaustive research through numerous resources and current citizens of Chase City's community. They present a photo journal overview of an era that is fading quickly from the memories and photographic collections of our ancestors. Ten of the people interviewed for this book have died since May 2007. Chase City's history is quietly fading away.

One

The Development of a New Town
Chase City before 1910

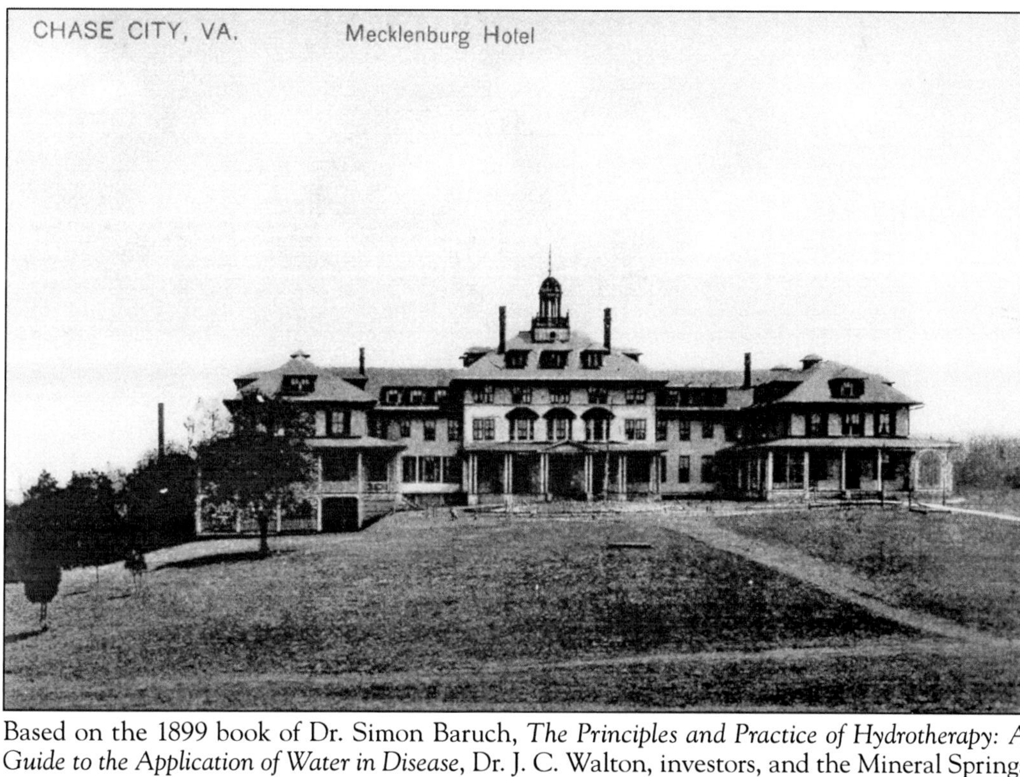

Based on the 1899 book of Dr. Simon Baruch, *The Principles and Practice of Hydrotherapy: A Guide to the Application of Water in Disease*, Dr. J. C. Walton, investors, and the Mineral Springs Corporation of Chase City built the first hotel/sanitarium of its kind in the United States. After three years of construction, it opened in 1903 and contained 150 guest rooms along with rooms and separate quarters for patients. Attracting guests such as John Phillip Sousa among many others, the hotel/sanitarium attended to the finer needs of the well-to-do. The hotel offered a men's club, private baths, lecture rooms, laundry, bowling alley, and private physicians with full medical staffing. The hotel was surrounded by 45 acres of lawn and timber with livery and riding stables. There was a children's playground in the backyard along with ponies and carts for pleasure rides or lessons. All rooms had outside windows, were steam heated, and had electric lights. (BML.)

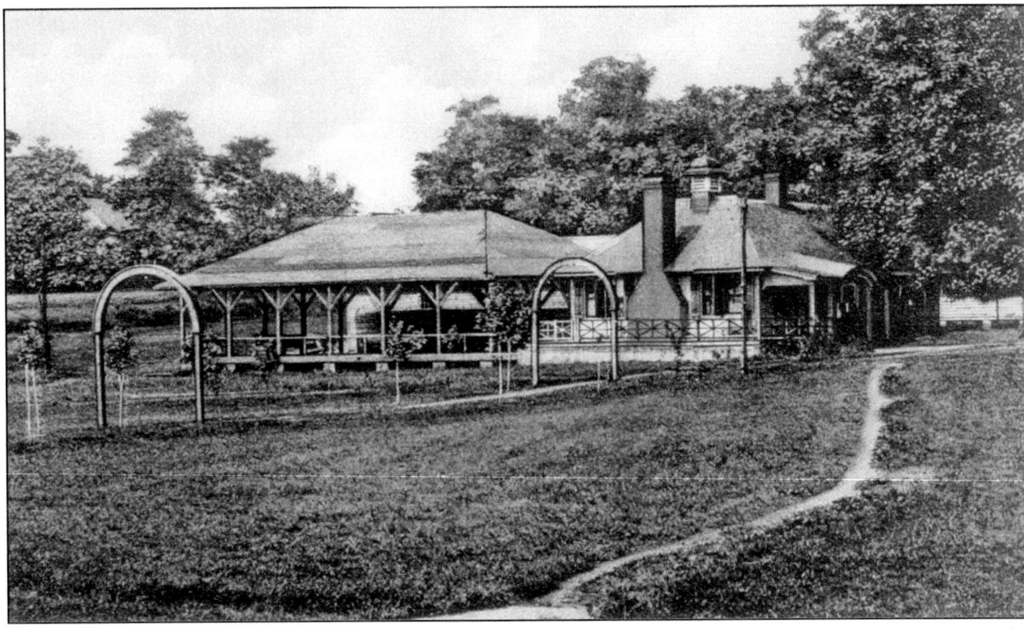

Mineral springs on the property contained lithia and chloride calcium waters that won a medal and certificate from the Columbian Exposition in Chicago and the World's Fair Grand Prize medal in 1904. The springs were reported to prove beneficial in the treatment of a host of conditions. The water was served liberally to guests. It was bottled and shipped all over the country until 1915. The sanitarium also used the water for spa therapy, baths, exercises, massages, and hot-pack applications. (SVHP.)

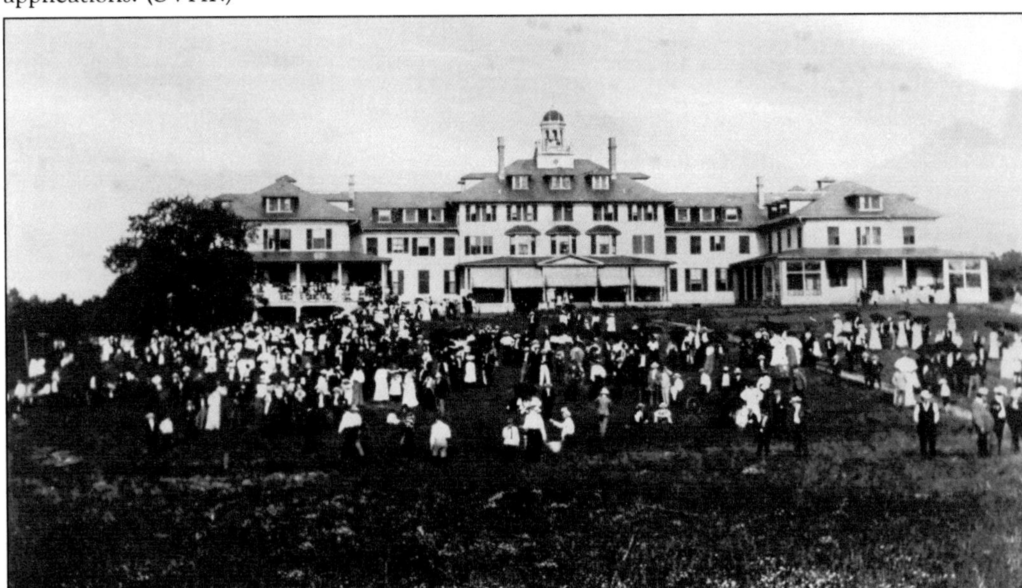

The Mecklenburg Mineral Hotel/Sanitarium offered the guests billiard and pool rooms, a gymnasium, tennis courts, several porticos, and a nine-hole golf course. It quickly became home to many conferences and conventions. By 1908, several of the mines closed, and hydrotherapy had fallen out of favor with the medical community. The hotel suffered. This 1902 photograph shows the hotel near completion. (CC.)

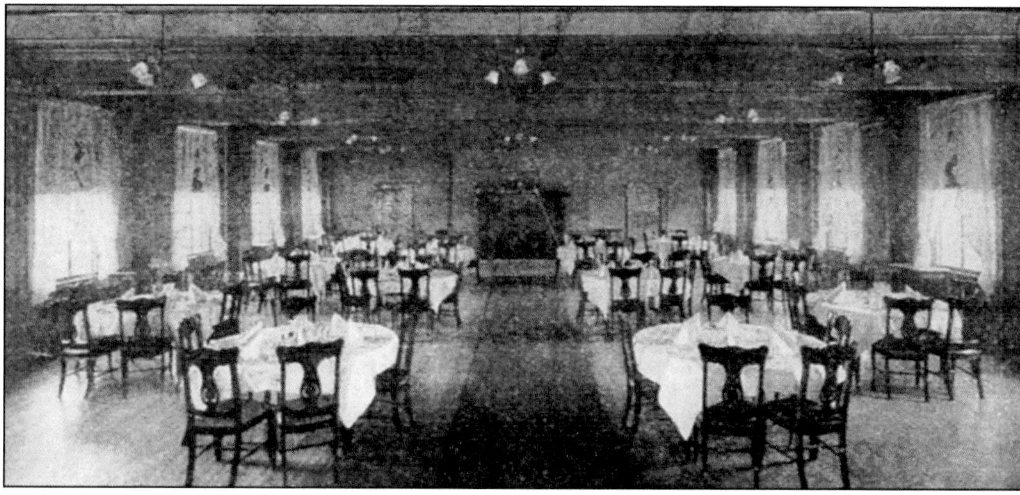

This is the main dining room with the finest china and linens. The hotel featured a gourmet menu complete with pastries and the finest cigars. The dining room had the capacity to serve 100 guests at a sitting. (WCG.)

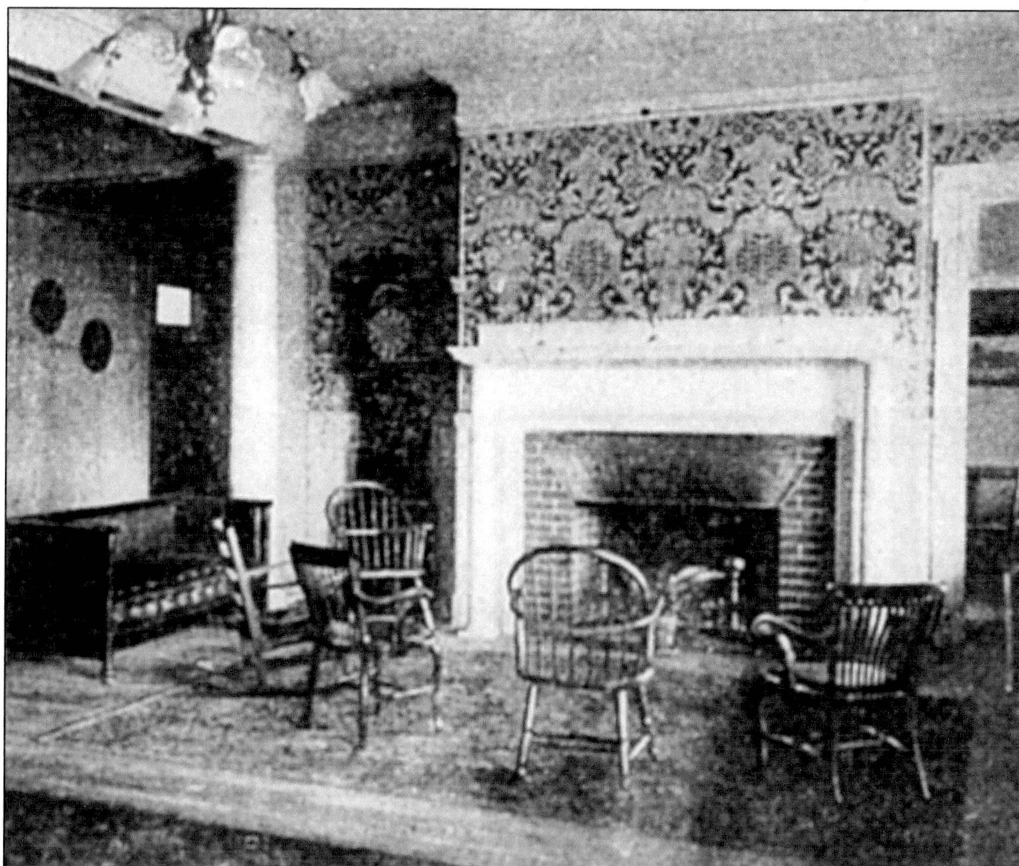

This is the south rotunda of the hotel. It was a favorite place to meet and greet friends and other guests. (WCG.)

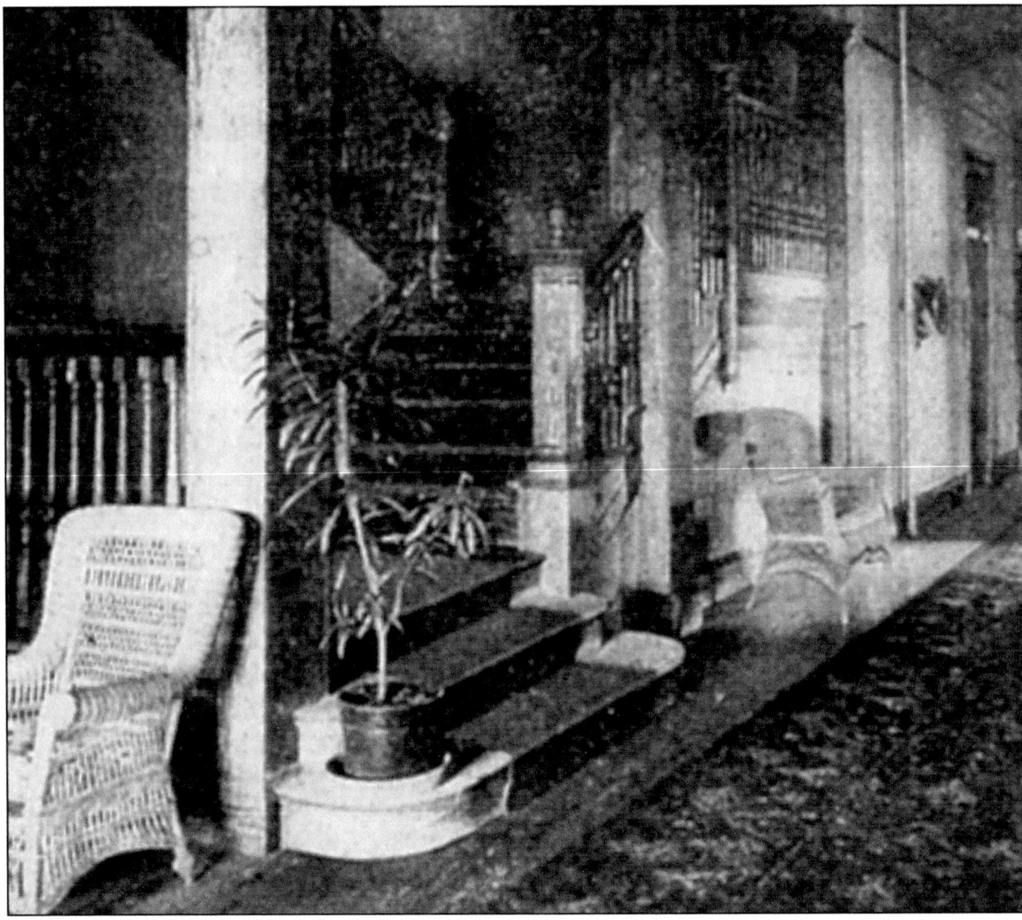

The north stairway led to the suites with private baths. This wing's rooms all had windows overlooking Chase City. (WCG.)

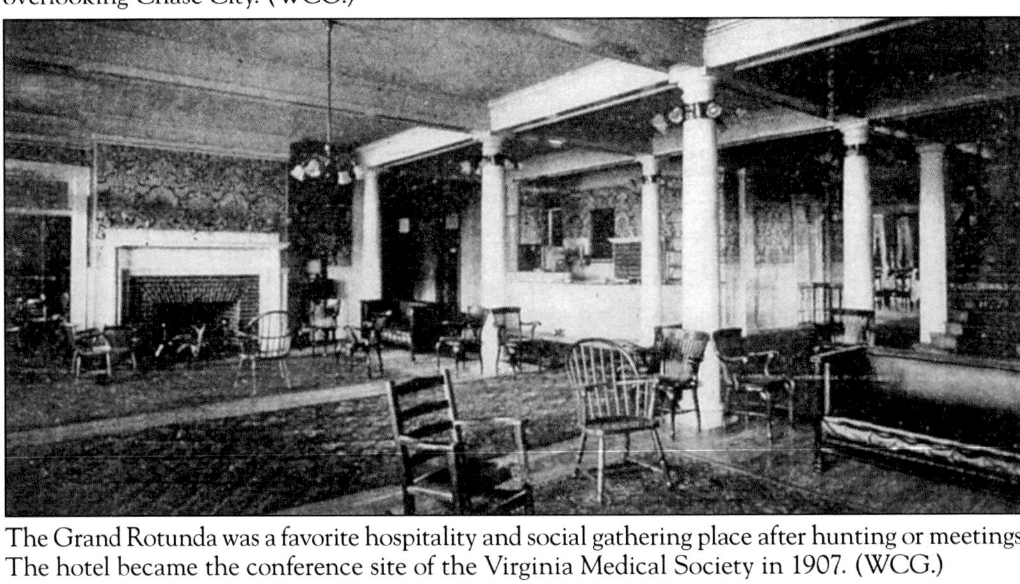

The Grand Rotunda was a favorite hospitality and social gathering place after hunting or meetings. The hotel became the conference site of the Virginia Medical Society in 1907. (WCG.)

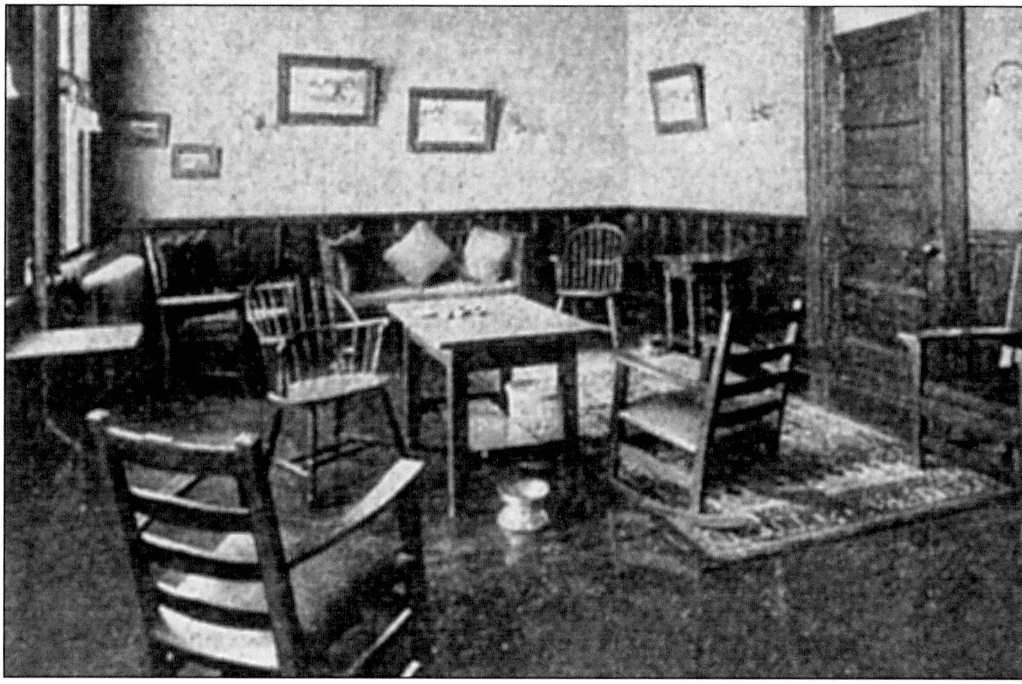

This is a photograph of one of the smoking parlors. The smoking parlors also served as hunting strategy meetings and for occasional games of cards. (WCG.)

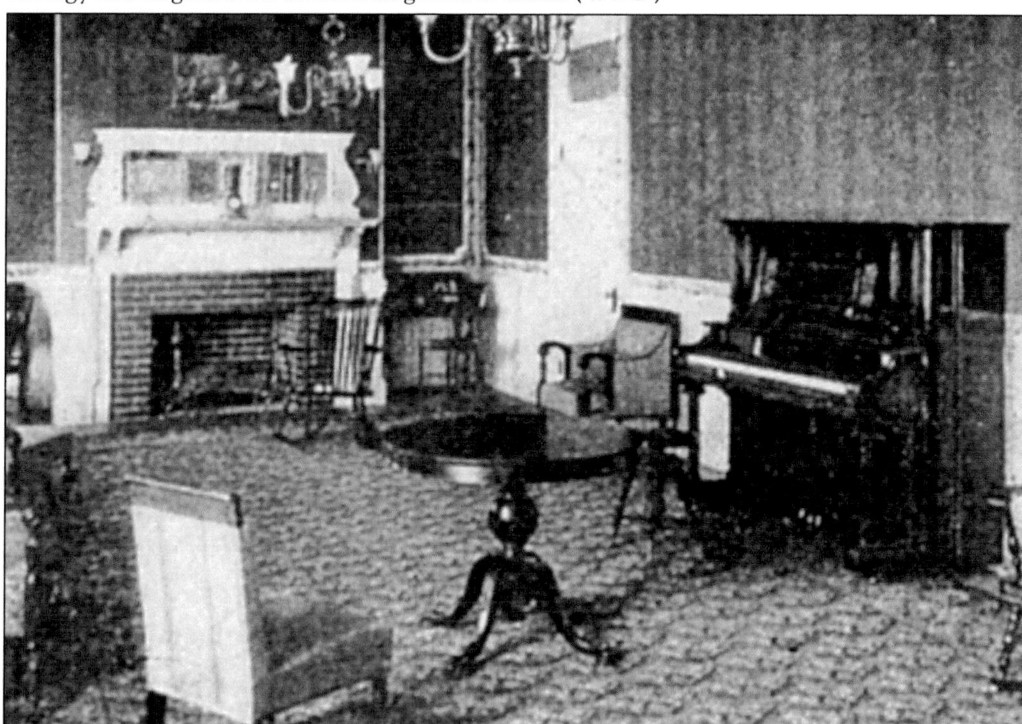

Pictured here is one of the small meeting parlors, which were used for informal groups and light entertainment. (WCG.)

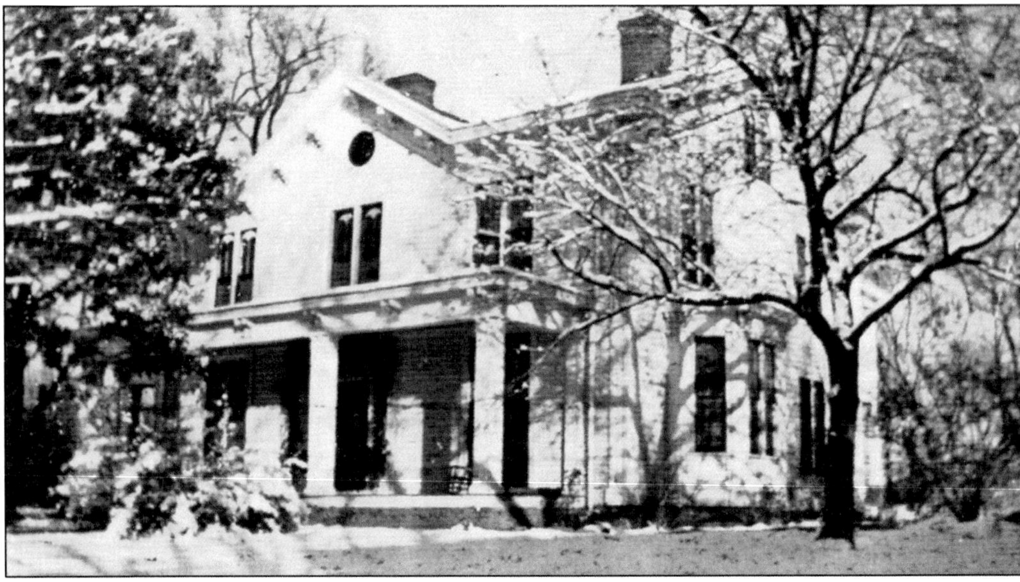

The Richard C. Puryear estate was 1,325 acres. In 1868, George A. Endly, a former banker from Pittsburgh, purchased the estate, called Shadow Lawn, including the home, which was built before 1819. Endly had a federal appointment to head the county board of supervisors from 1869 to 1873. In 1872, Endly had Shadow Lawn remodeled by Edward Holt, and in 1900, he sold the home to the Mecklenburg Mineral Springs Corporation. Endly died on July 8, 1912. (MWC.)

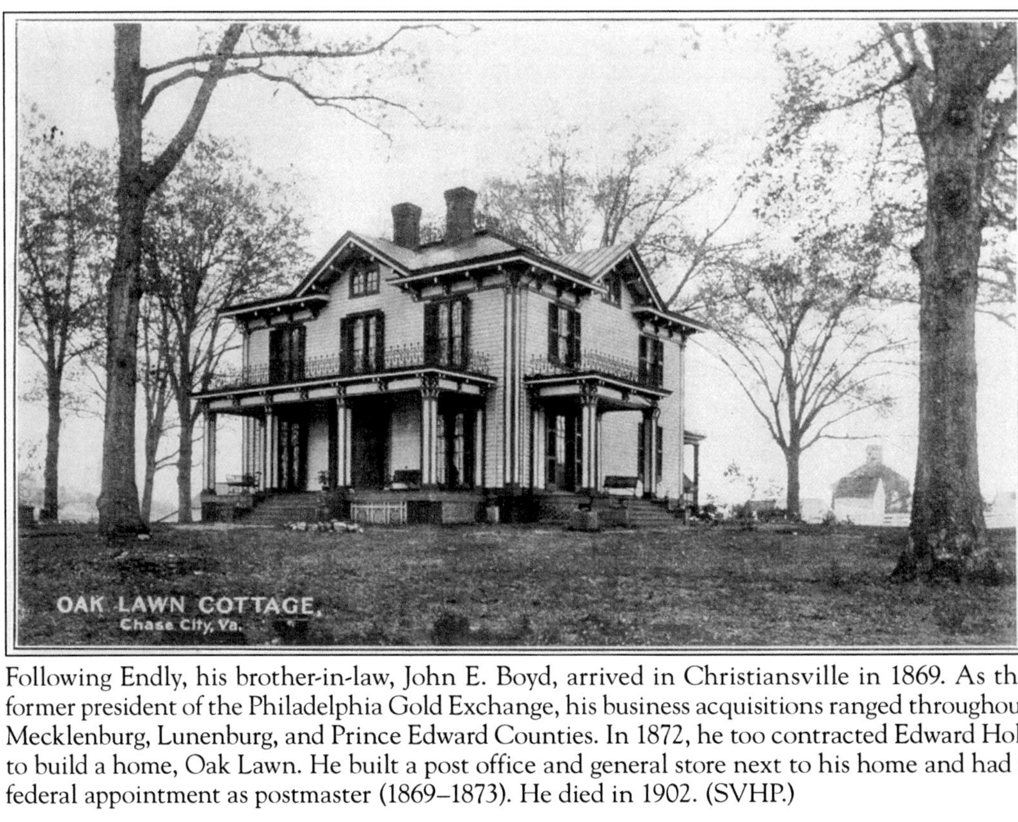

Following Endly, his brother-in-law, John E. Boyd, arrived in Christiansville in 1869. As the former president of the Philadelphia Gold Exchange, his business acquisitions ranged throughout Mecklenburg, Lunenburg, and Prince Edward Counties. In 1872, he too contracted Edward Holt to build a home, Oak Lawn. He built a post office and general store next to his home and had a federal appointment as postmaster (1869–1873). He died in 1902. (SVHP.)

In 1871, a platted Christiansville was advertised in Ohio and Pennsylvania. Cummings C. Riddick (born May 8, 1833) was one of the first to arrive. Formerly a private in the 16th Ohio Infantry from 1862 to 1865, he came to town as a carpenter and received a federal appointment to postmaster, but only for five months in 1879. By 1885, he had acquired a copper mine, lumber mill, three farms, two homes in town, and several other enterprises with his sons. (CCPO.)

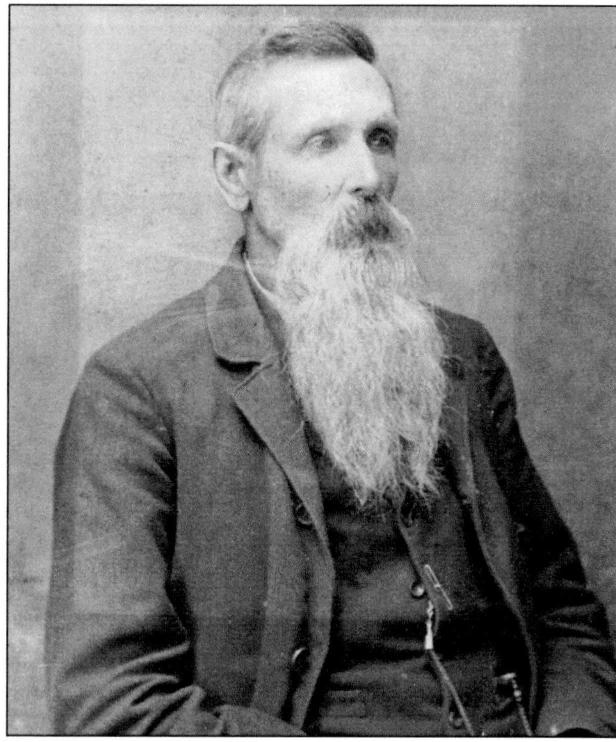

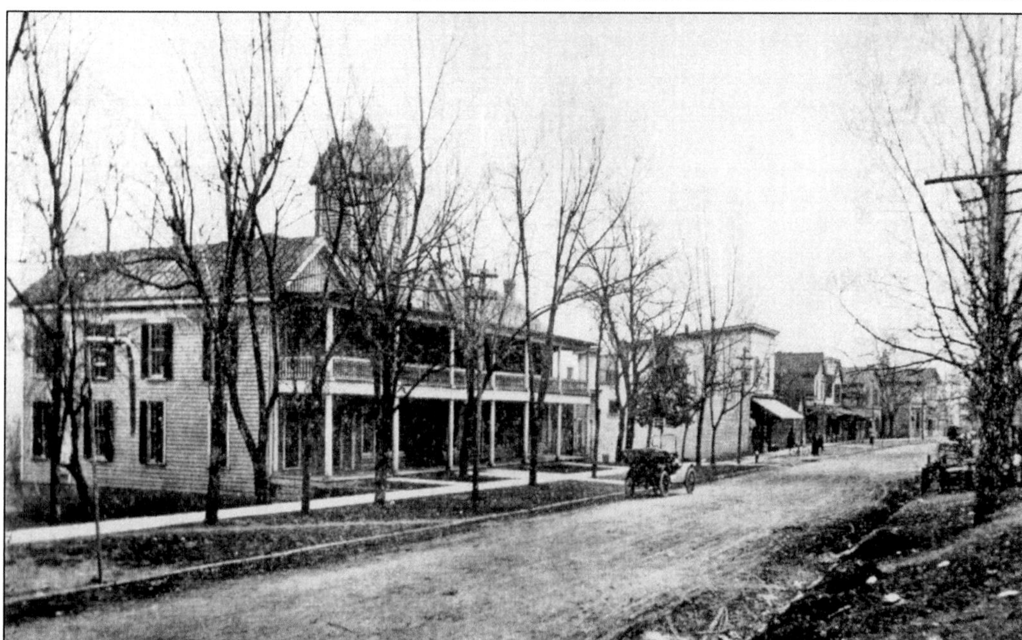

The mineral springs attracted tourists, and in 1883, a new hotel was built. The hotel was named the Mineral, which changed in 1909 to the Little Mecklenburg. Its manager, M. William Blair, retired in 1912 and received a proclamation from the town. The hotel was also called the Blair House (later the Dair House). The building next door is the J. M. Williams home, which was moved in 1895, and next to that is the home and drugstore of Dr. W. H. Saunders. (SCFA.)

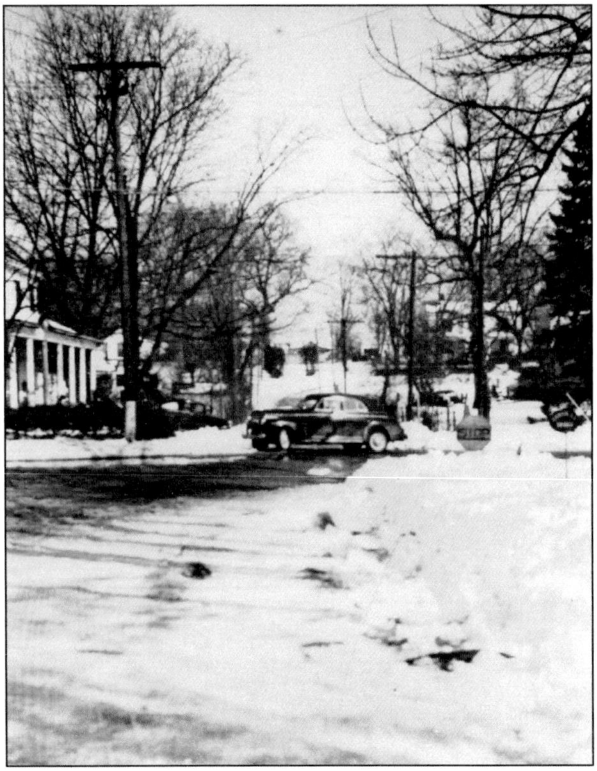

The 1880s was a period of rapid growth. Many shops, rooming houses, and businesses grew up, especially along Fifth Street from the train station to Main Street. In 1887, at the northeast corner of Fifth and Main, the Jackson Hotel (a boardinghouse) was built and stayed in operation until 1947. The first hotel in town was the little City Hotel, located in the middle of Third Street between Main and Marshall Streets in 1881. It too became a boardinghouse. (HL.)

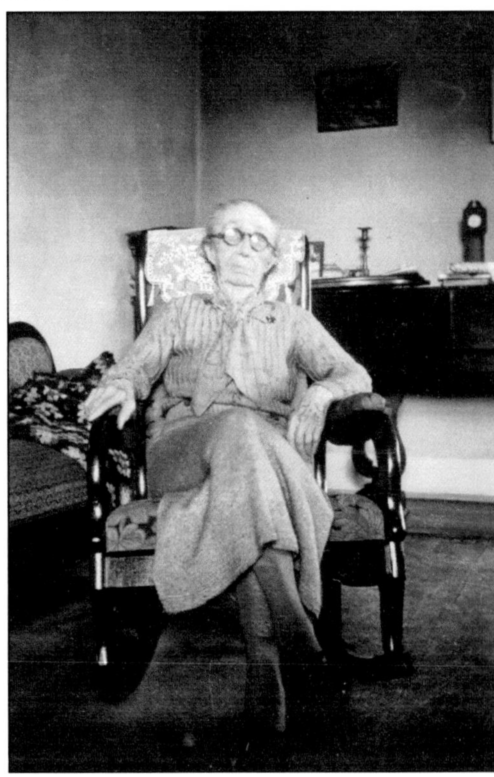

Two doors down from the Mineral Hotel was the home and drugstore of Dr. W. H. Saunders, which opened for business on February 3, 1888. The store was operated by his wife, Adelia A. Saunders, who was the first woman to be registered as a pharmacist in Virginia. Pictured here after her retirement in 1932, she died in 1937 at the age of 93. Her great-niece continued to operate the A. A. Saunders Drug Store until her death in 1942. In 1945, the store became Chase City Flower Shop. (JL.)

This 1895 image is reported to show Lucius Gregory and his wife in their carriage passing by the Bank of Chase City (opened for business in 1882), where he worked as first vice president under George Endly. (GLG.)

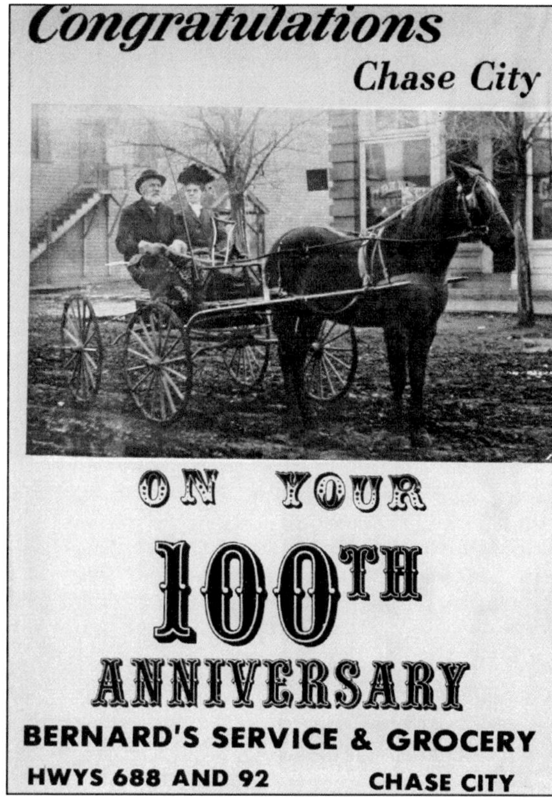

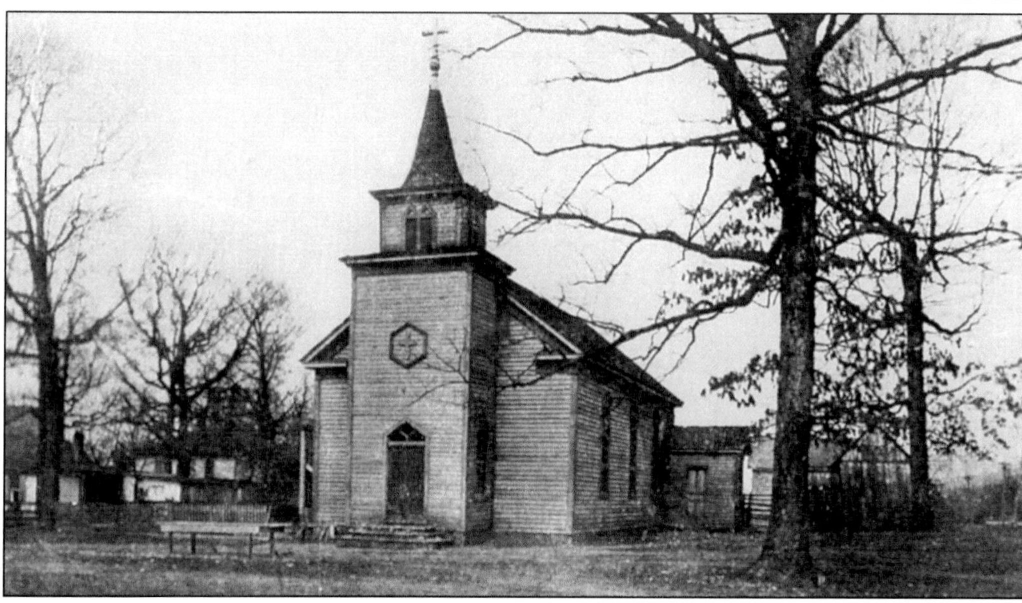

Several churches were built for the citizens and tourists. Chase City always had a reputation for being a church town, and the first church in Mecklenburg County was the *c.* 1761 St. John's Episcopal Church. The church also served as the county courthouse until Lunenburg built a new one in 1765. Moved several times, the church had a permanent home in 1888 at Fourth and Marshall Streets. The foundation is from the foundation of the original church. (WCG.)

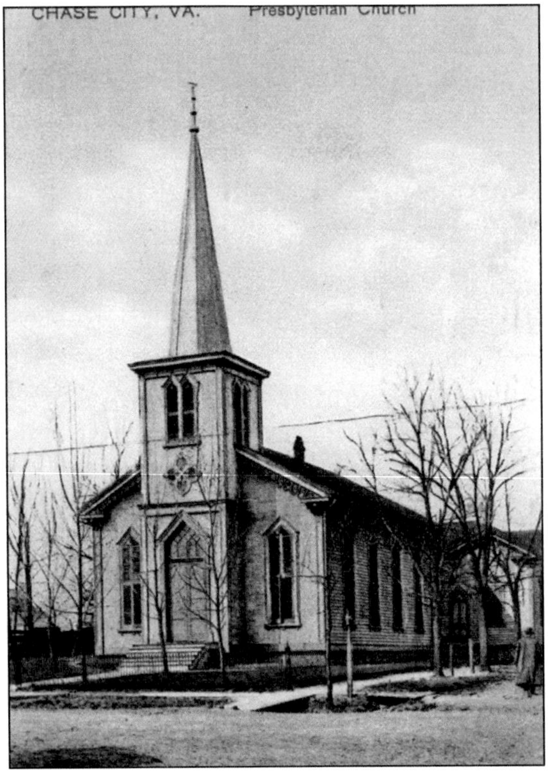

The next church in Christiansville (Chase City) was the Presbyterian Church, built in July 1869 with George Endly as its first elder. This church was affiliated with the Southern Presbyterian Church and had several names, but since 1875, it was simply the Presbyterian Church. The church was built by Edward Holt's father and brother. The most well-known pastor was Dr. Thomas Drew of Melcombe, Regis, England, who served from 1871 to 1884 and from 1891 to 1916. His daughter, Hortense, 17, of Cornwall, England, arrived with him and started the Christian Girls School in her home. (PC.)

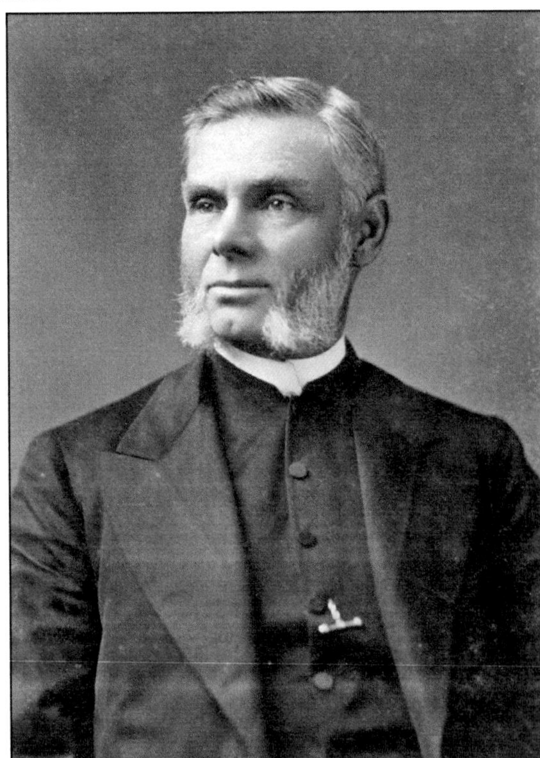

This photograph of Dr. Drew in 1895 has appeared in most publications about Chase City. Dr. Drew was noted for riding his bicycle about town and helping the volunteer fire department. He died on October 12, 1923. Hortense remained part of the church until her death at the age of 83. The church was originally at Third and Main Streets but was moved to North Main Street. (PC.)

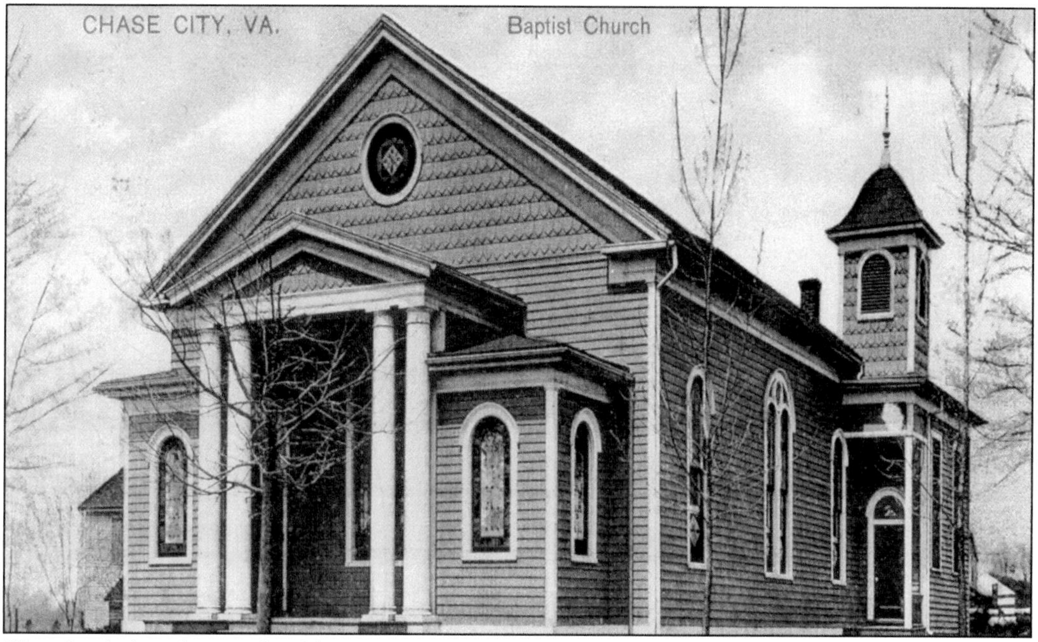

The third church was the Christiansville United Presbyterian Church (1872–1884), begun by Rev. J. Y. Ashenhurst of Ashland, Ohio, who was charged with building a church for the town and a boarding school for the African Americans. Learning of the desire by the Baptists to have a church in town, he sold the building. The First Baptist Church held its first service August 6, 1884, with a congregation of 15. It became part of the Concord Baptist Association. (JG.)

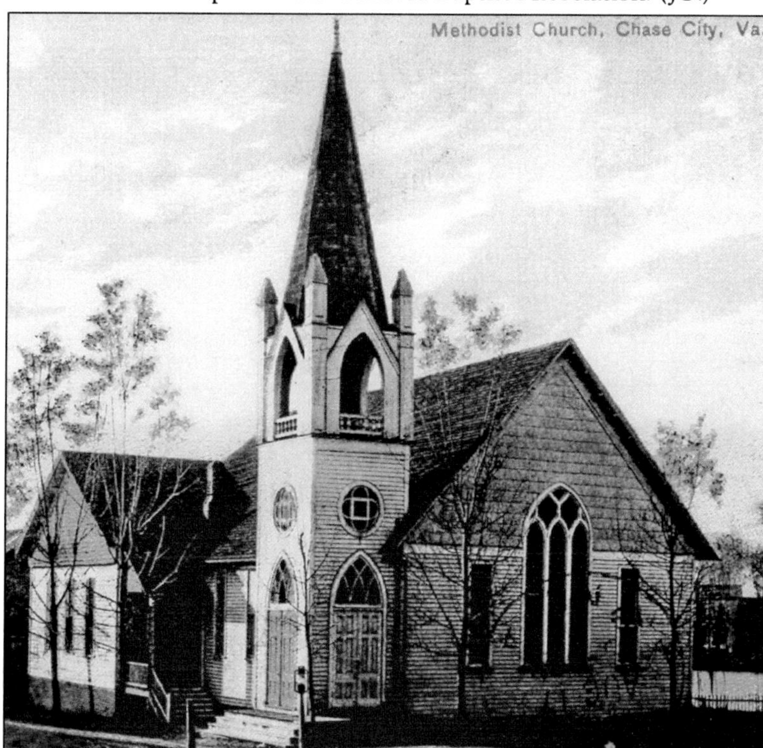

The third oldest religion in Chase City was Methodism (1840), with a small meetinghouse south of town at the fork of the Boydton Plank Road. In 1875, they built a new meetinghouse, but with a lot from Endly, a new church was begun in 1885 at Third and Marshall Streets. A parsonage was built on Main Street near Third Street, but this was moved behind the church in 1901 to make way for the new Gregory Hotel. (RS.)

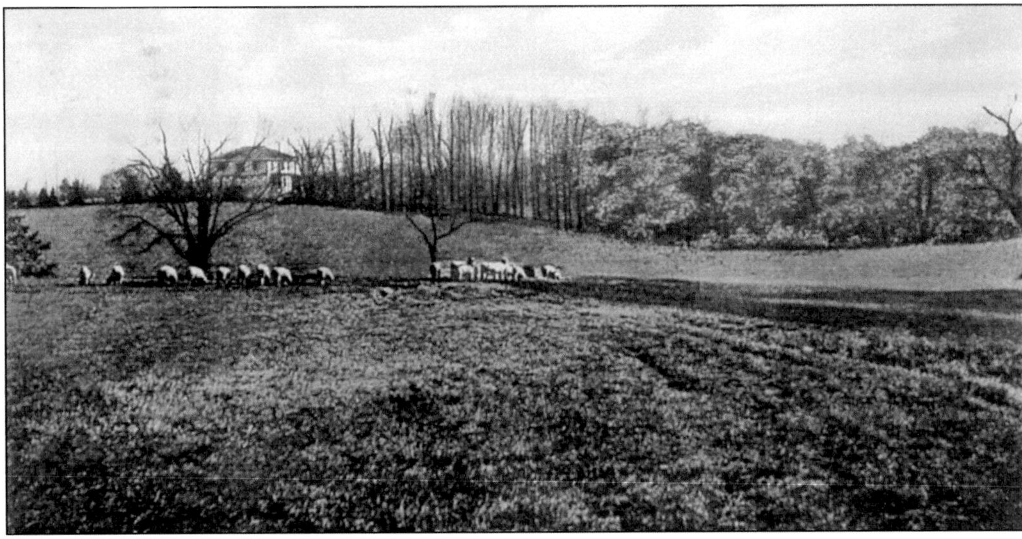

This 1908 postcard of the Mecklenburg Hotel shows the front yard serving as pastureland for local cattle and sheep farmers per lease for $2.50 per month. To the right in the distance is the stately home and school of Hortense Drew. In 1908, she closed her school and began teaching in the newly formed Chase City School District. (WCG.)

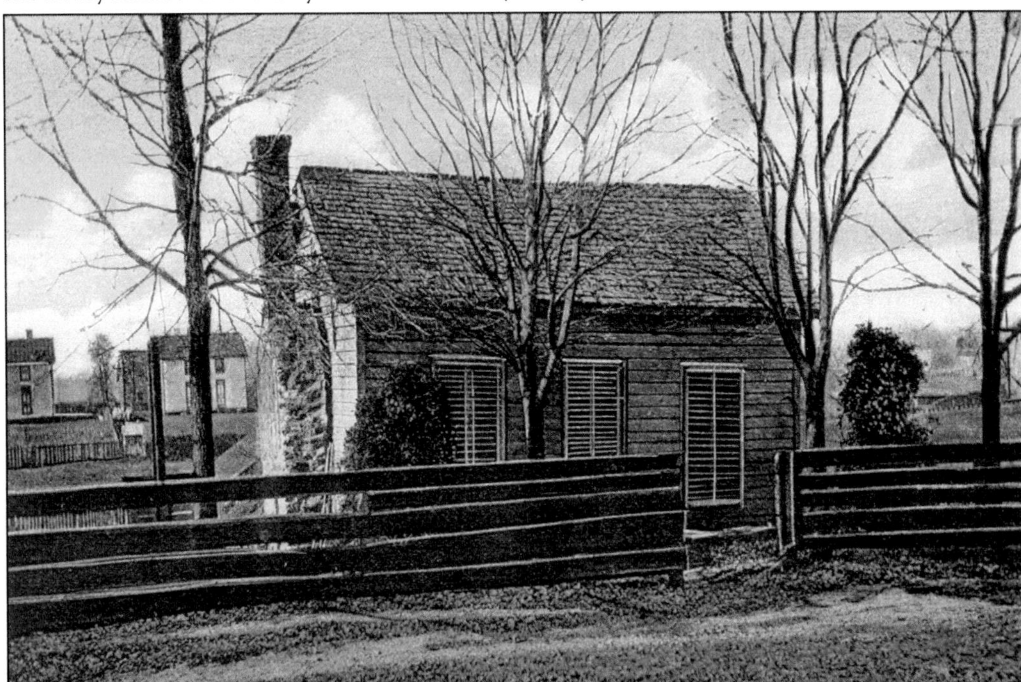

Housing was booming in the early 1900s. This photograph shows typical Federal homes and plantation cabins. Between streets were alleyways where citizens built privies and disposed of garbage. The alleys were trenched, and the town water wagon washed the waste into the nearest stream. By 1900, this had to be done twice per week; it was so bad in 1903 that a "night soil" tax was passed to purchase a special wagon and hire a night soil collector, who took the soil 800 yards outside the town limits. (SVHP.)

Most homes either went to a public well in town or had a 20- to 30-foot well dug on their property, such as this remodeled well. The water was obtained by lowering a bucket attached to a rope, filling the bucket, retrieving it, and pouring the water into a container. (LB.)

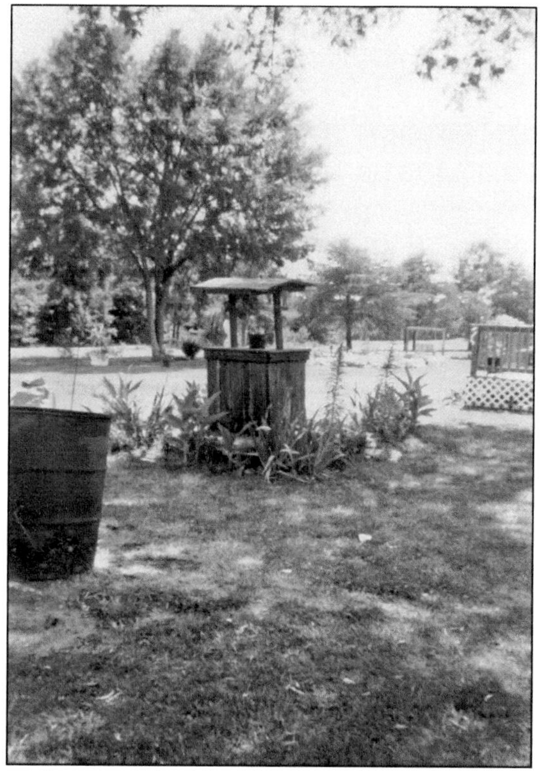

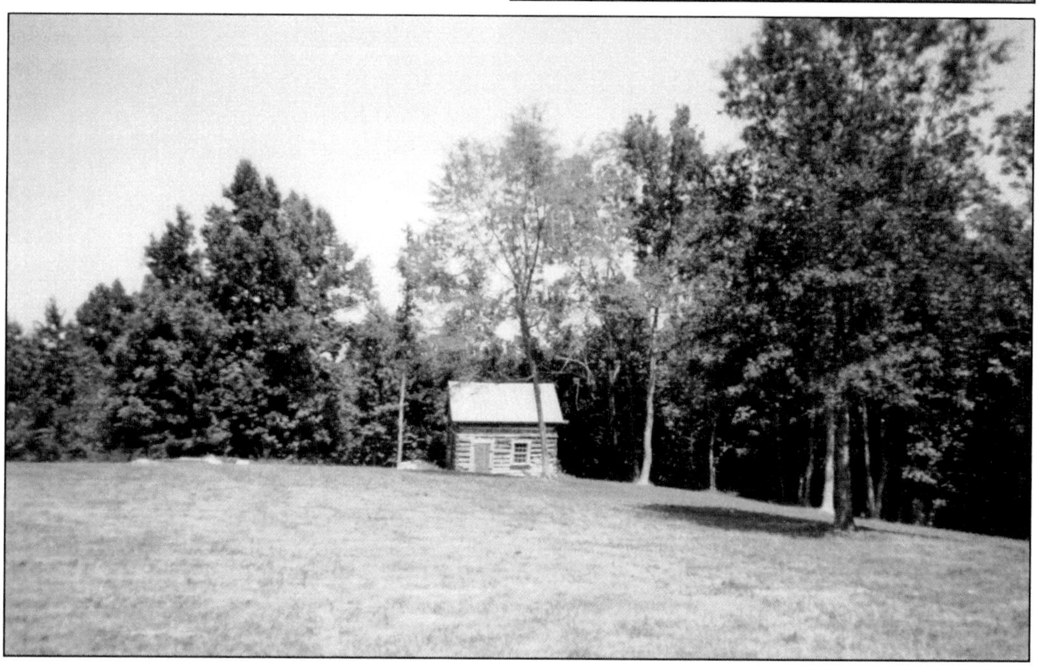

Many cabins still dot the landscape and are often referred to as slave quarters. In fact, many were first homes, laborer cabins, lumbermen cabins, sharecropper cabins, and retreats. Most were built in the simplistic style of cutting logs, notching the ends, and overlapping them. The cracks were filled with mud to seal. (LB.)

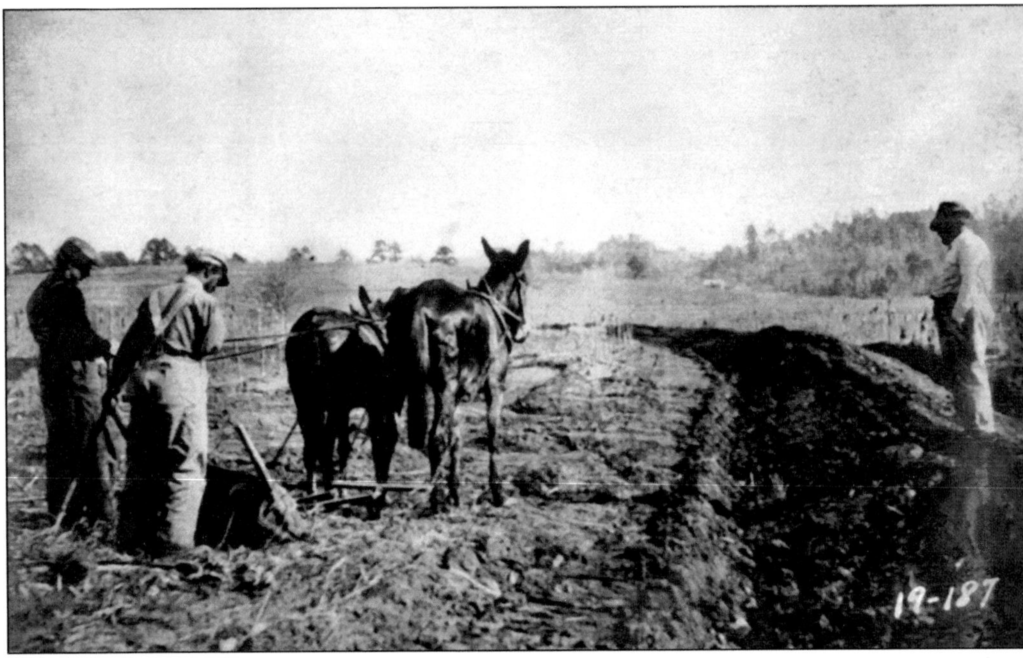

There was an art and science to trenching. This photograph depicts what John Gee did for Chase City from 1872 until about 1917. A trenching pan was pulled by two mules to cut a deep trench on either side of the alleyway. The large mule would walk in the trench with the smaller on top to keep the pan moving straight and level. By 1914, parts of Chase City had a sewage system, but it failed in 1918. (EM.)

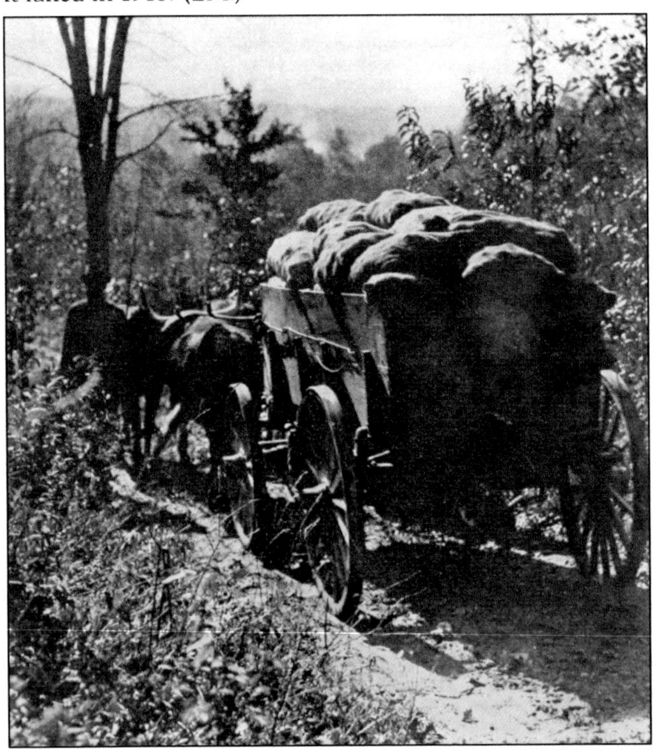

Many local farmers favored oxen for their temperament and load capacity. With horses, oxen, and people in town, the dirt streets were filthy and either muddy or dusty. By the late 1890s, gravel began to be spread and sidewalks were built of concrete. The old plank sidewalks and streets had no durability. Cement blocks had to be placed at crossings for people to get across the street. This 1932 photograph shows that oxen were still abundant in the area. (GLG.)

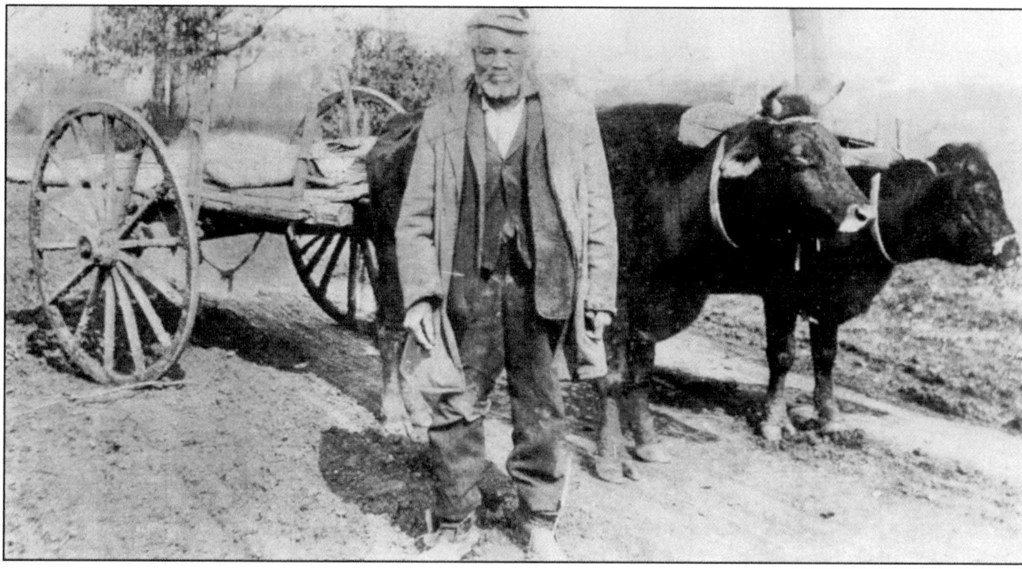

This famous photograph from 1880 of Uncle Gilbert bringing his produce to town depicts the times. Uncle Gilbert, a slave, had been given to Betsy Smith Brame in 1827 by her father, Capt. Robert Smith. A freeman after the Civil War, he continued to live in Chase City with his family. (SVHP.)

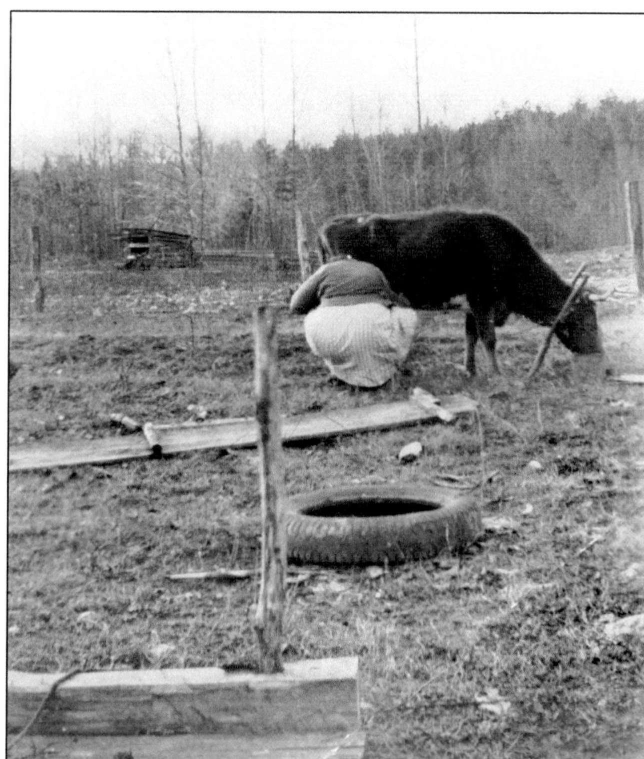

Cattle were a necessary part of Chase City's economy for beef, milk, and butter. There were at least two milking stations in town where farmers would bring the cows and sell the fresh milk daily. One station was at Fifth and Main Streets, the other next to Shadow Lawn. Without refrigeration, milk would not last more than two or three days. After the first day, the cream would rise, then the milk would sour, then the milk would curdle. (DT.)

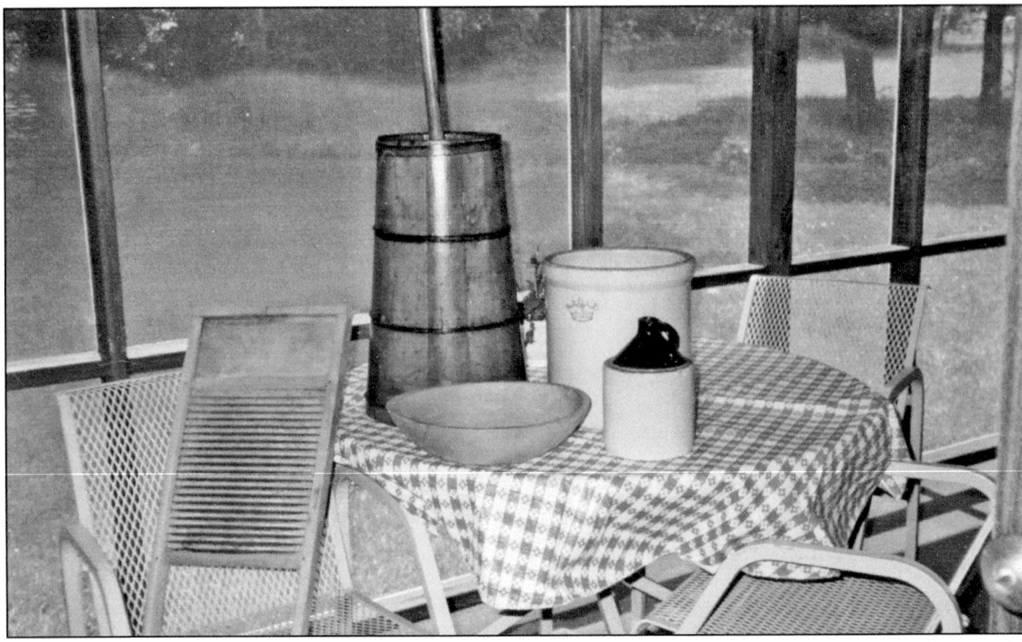

This is a contemporary photograph of a well-stocked kitchen in 1900, including a cider jug for fermenting juices, a crock for aging cabbage, a mixing bowl for dough, a washboard for laundry, and a butter churn. (KW.)

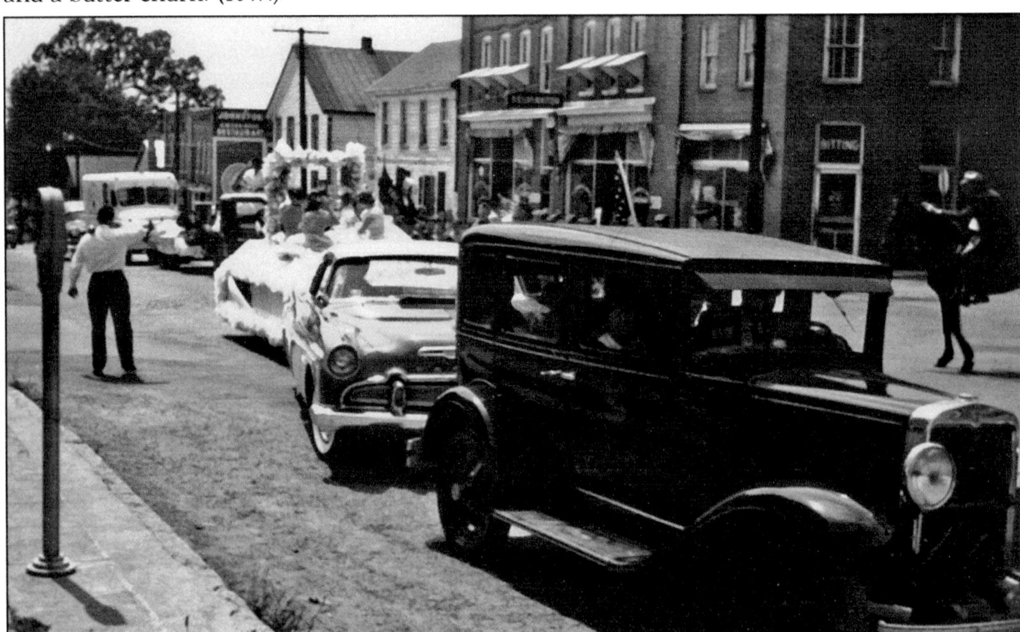

From the train station to Main Street became the first business district. In this 1948 photograph taken in front of the Chase City Progress building, the first store on the right is L. W. Bitting and Sons Company (general merchandise, hay, and grain). The next two doors are F. B. Roberts' Chase City Hardware Company, and the next building is the Davis Café. The last building is the Robertson-McCall Furniture Company (an outlet for Nicholson Furniture Manufacturing, and in 1924, it sold dry goods), and upstairs is the Goode, Roberts, and Wells Auction House. (JRL.)

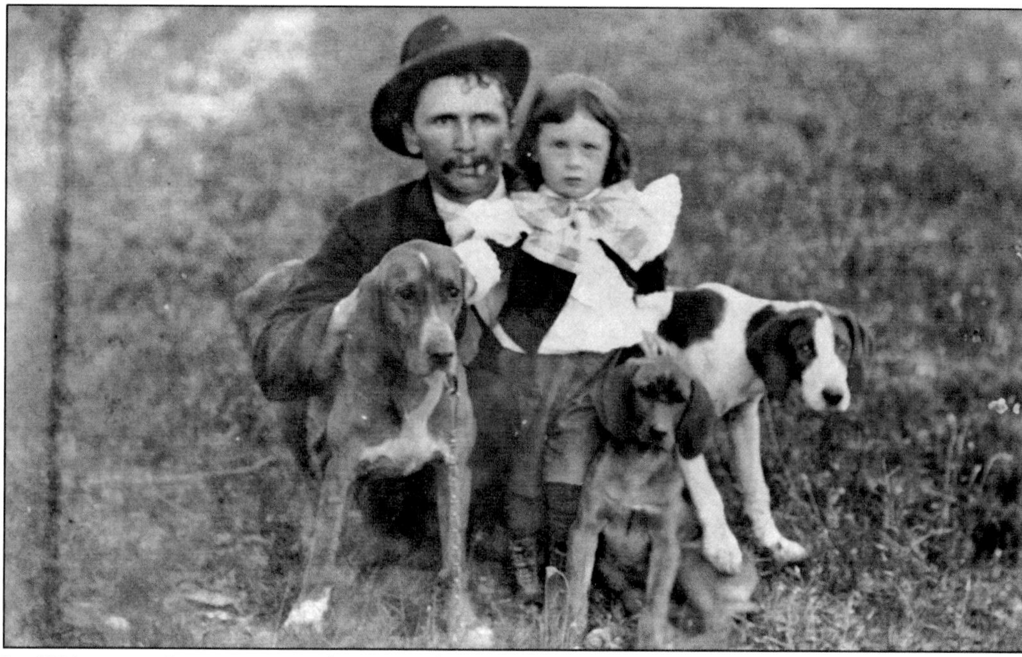

In 1891, a new physician arrived in town, having recently graduated from the College of Physicians and Surgeons in Baltimore. Beginning practice in Chase City before his 21st birthday was Dr. Clarence H. Saunders (1870–1934), son of Dr. W. H. and Adelia Saunders. In this 1890s photograph, he is shown with his two loves—children (his nephew Harold) and animals. He went on all calls by horseback or carriage, knowing many would not be paid for. Suffering many acquired illnesses, he died at age 64. (JL.)

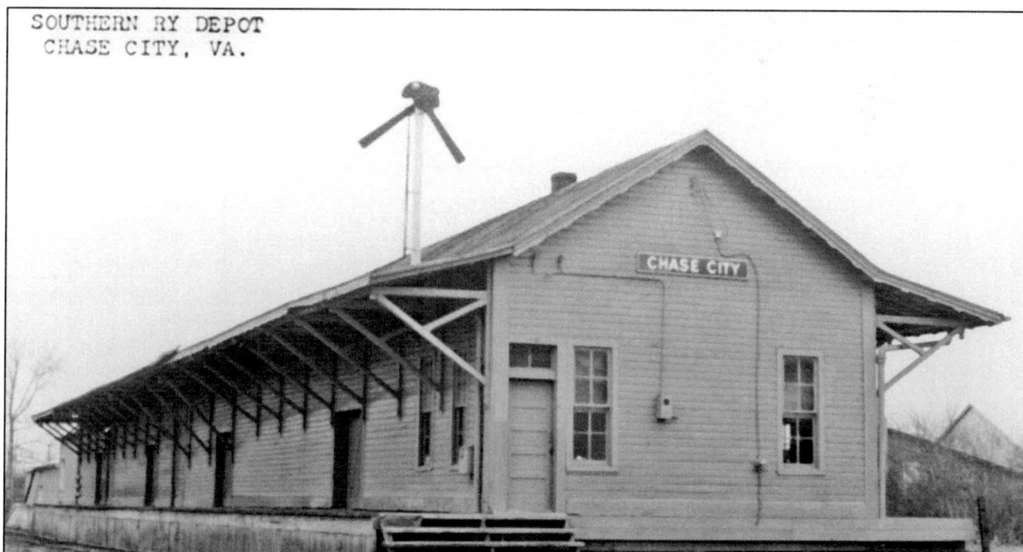

The Mecklenburg Richmond Railroad (founded in 1882) was a main attraction to townspeople. Everyone listened for the steam engines and the whistle on its three passenger stops daily. No photographs were found of the original freight and passenger terminals, but after being seized in 1917 by the U.S. government to help with the war effort, they were sold back to Southern Railroad in 1921. The freight terminal was rebuilt after that time. (JAY.)

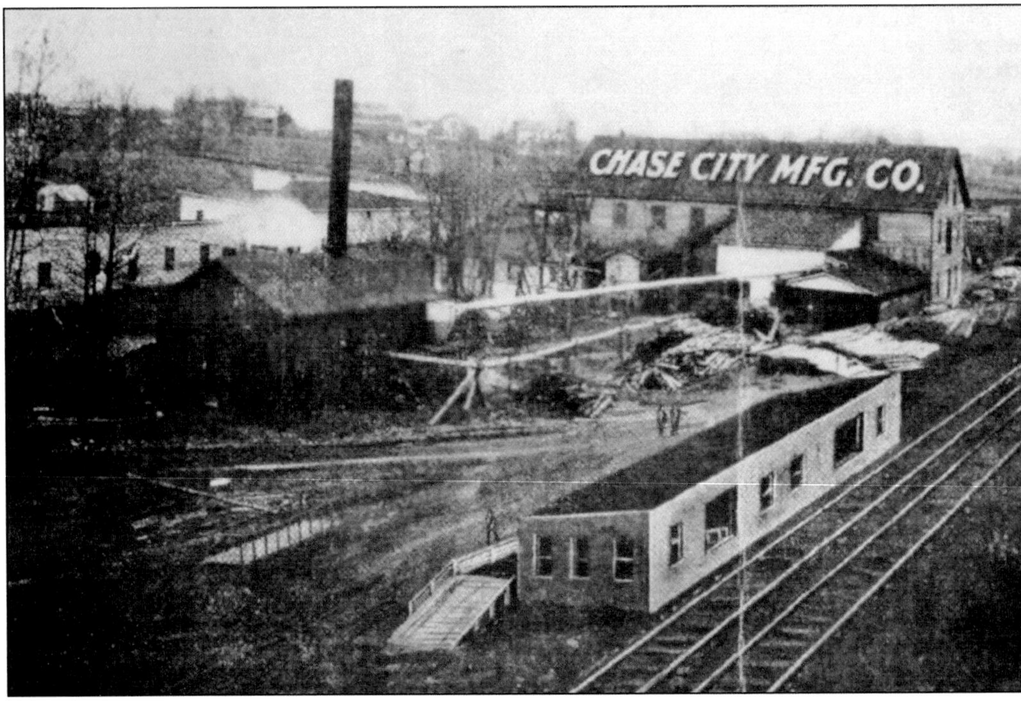

Besides farming and lumber, the largest business in Chase City in 1895 was Chase City Manufacturing. This company made spokes, axles, wheels, wagons, and custom wagons such as the night soil wagon. Owned by Lucius Gregory and treasurer Eugene S. Emory, in 1917, it began making wooden crates for the war effort. Closed in 1926, it was purchased by W. A. Butler. (NP/SA.)

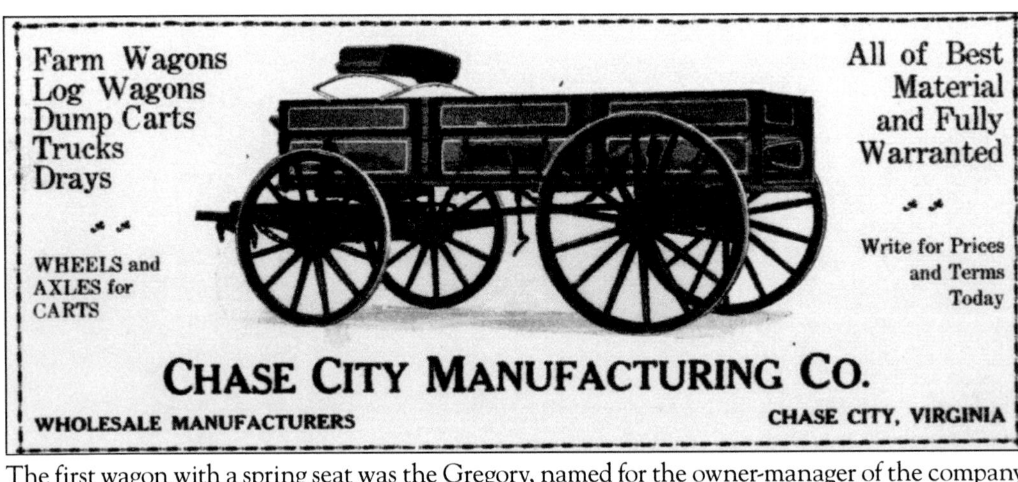

The first wagon with a spring seat was the Gregory, named for the owner-manager of the company. Other wagons were named Our King and Little Giant. It was considered one of the finest wagon companies in the South, and in 1938, it was reported that the wagons were still in good use. (WCG.)

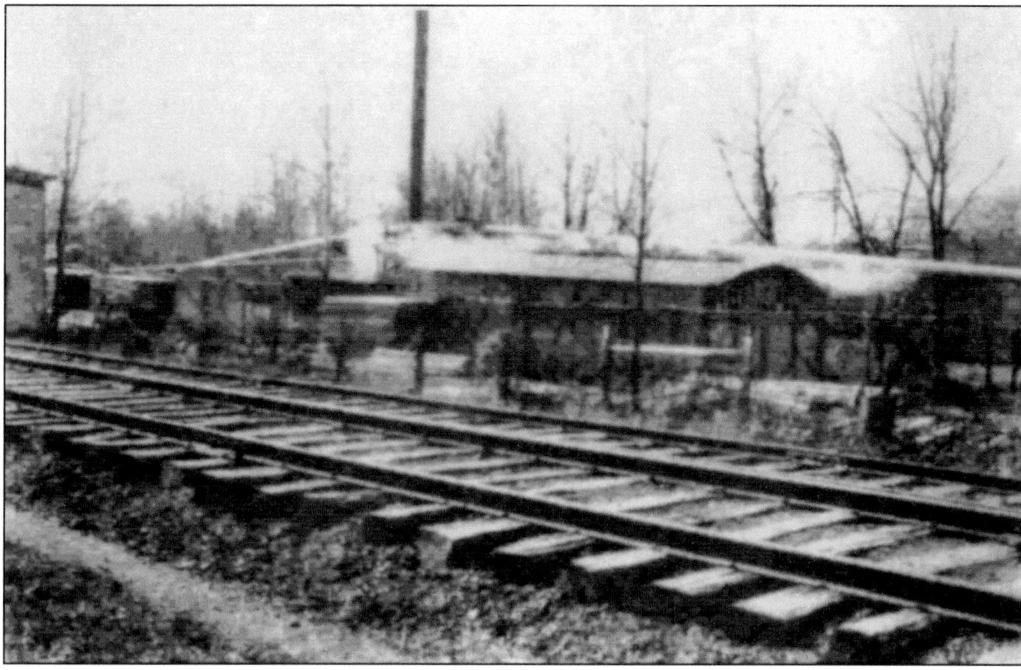

The company had built such a reputation that by 1900, it had a spur track for both its wholesale business from the factory and its retail business, located across Factory Street (renamed B Street) next to the company/community general store. (NP/SA.)

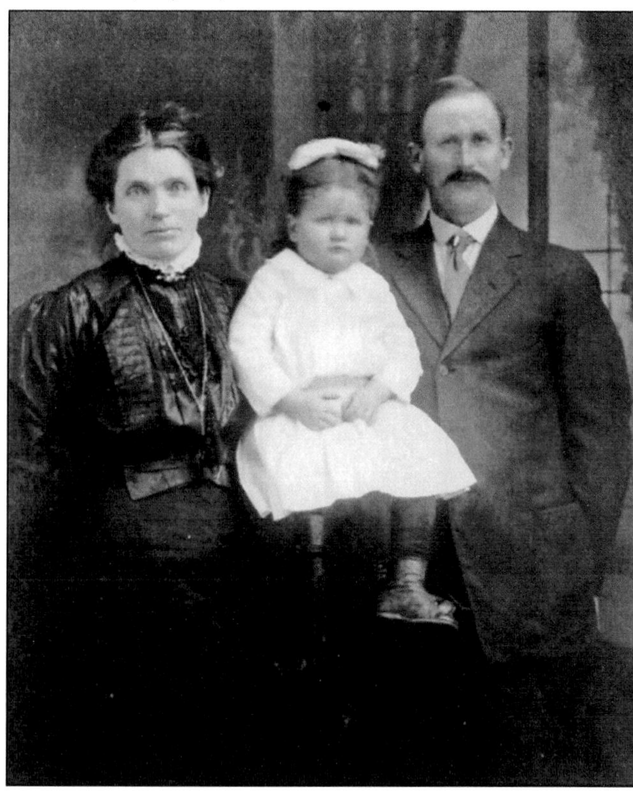

Like their parents, Charles T. Eggleston and his wife, Anna Eudora Inge, were born in Chase City (both in 1874). Pictured with their daughter Martha Jane (Smith) in 1913, Charles Eggleston began work with Chase City Manufacturing at the age of 17 and was foreman for the wagon division. He and his family lived in company housing. Lucius Gregory had developed Factory and High Streets for his employees. They had the option to purchase or rent. (Harvey Smith.)

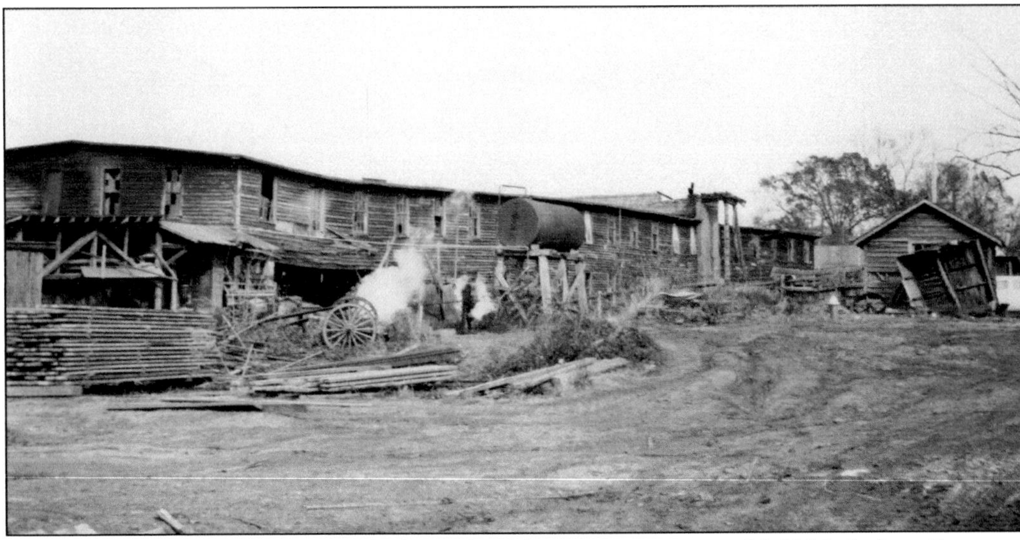

At the opposite end of town, one block north of the train station, was M. K. Nicholson Furniture factory, which began operation in 1895. With wholesale, retail, and auction outlets, it became a large operation with a spur track. During World War I, it also built wooden crates. The two factories shared their lumberyard. (LLE.)

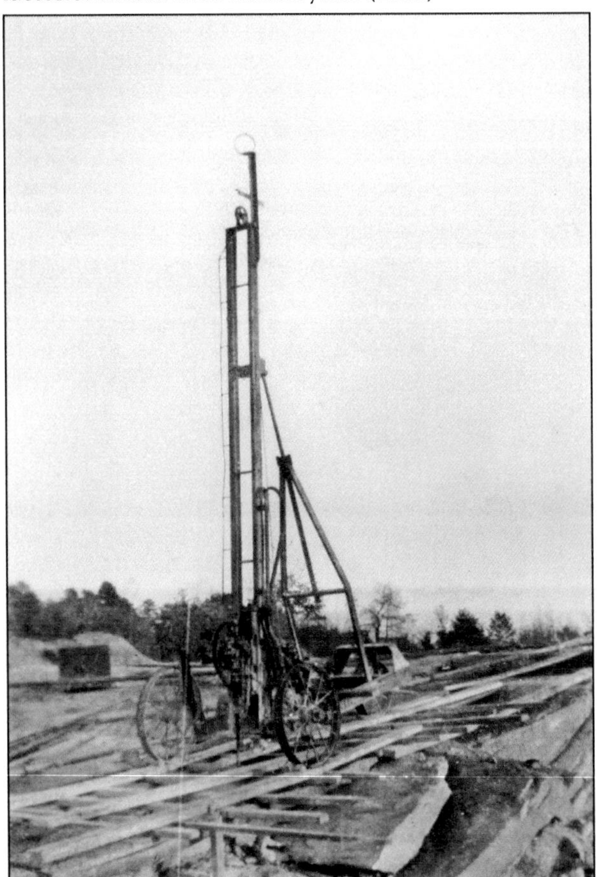

With the need for so many spur tracks across the country, a drill press was invented in 1890. Pictured here is a rail tie drill used to install spur lines. (Nannie Clardy family.)

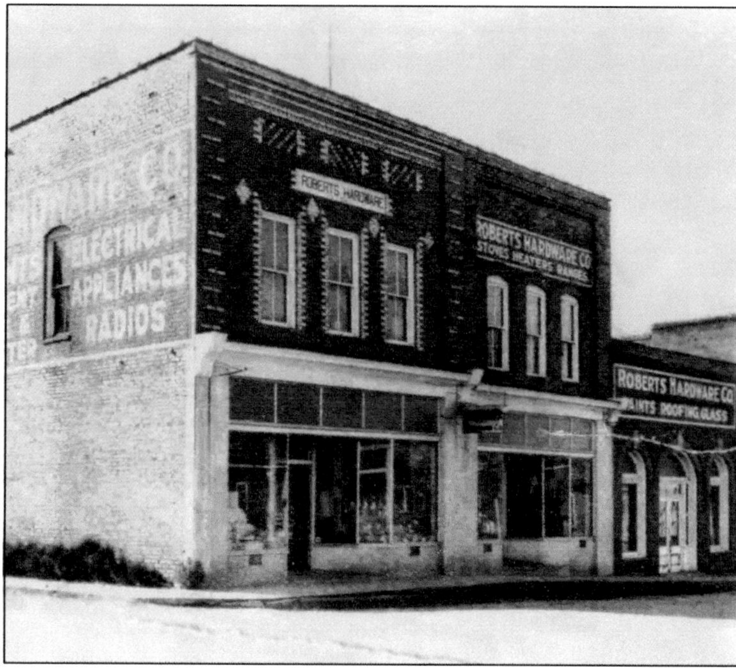

The Roberts family was an entrepreneurial group in Chase City during the 1880s and later. The second of their hardware stores was located at the corner of Main and Sycamore Streets (the busy corner of Abbeyville Road). It boasted a sales staff of four, two in management, a livery, and two warehouse buildings across the street for farm implements and Indian motorcycles. It was owned by T. E. Roberts. (NP/SA.)

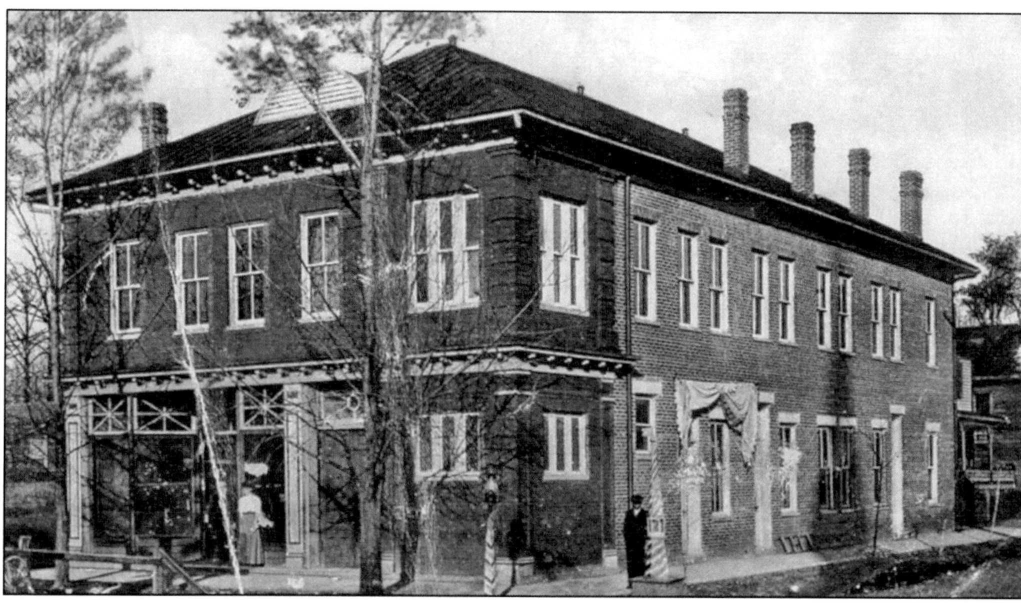

In 1900, a town hall was proposed, designed, and funded. It was completed in February 1903 at the corner of Third and Main Streets. The town hall is at right, with the town sergeant's office in the rear, and next door is the post office. Behind the post office was a barbershop. Upstairs were city chambers. The building soon became a meeting and entertainment house. In October 1903, the town purchased 300 chairs for the hall from Andrews School Furniture in Racine, Wisconsin. (HL.)

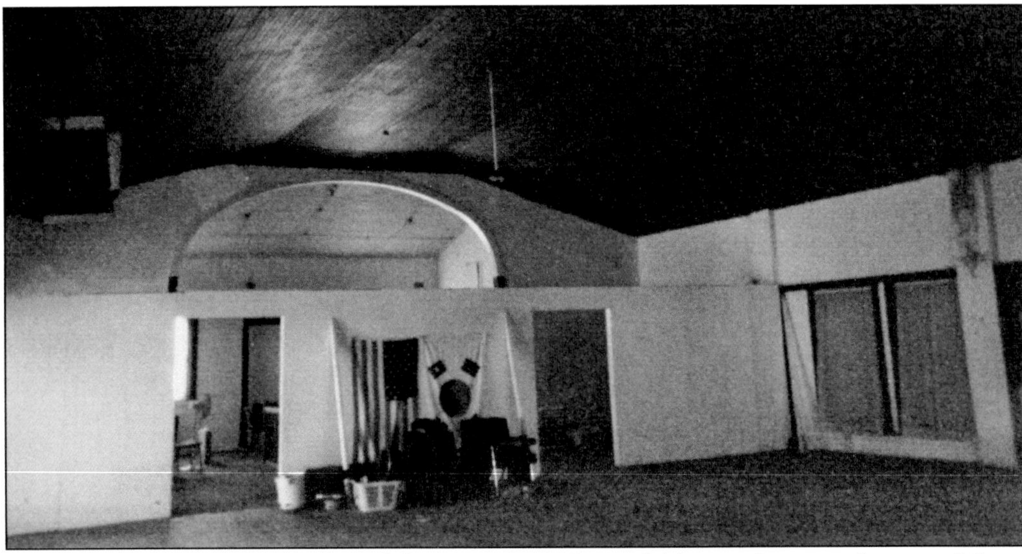

This photograph shows the second floor as it was. Beautiful knotted pine ceilings and floors still exist. The meeting room was used by the YMCA, the Virginia Volunteers, and traveling shows. B. A. Roberts sold tickets. In 1905, a piano was purchased, and in 1908, the chairs got new cushions. That same year, two special police officers had to be hired for each event at the "Opera House" (as it was called) because of the lawlessness of "Virginia City" (the nickname of Chase City). (JC.)

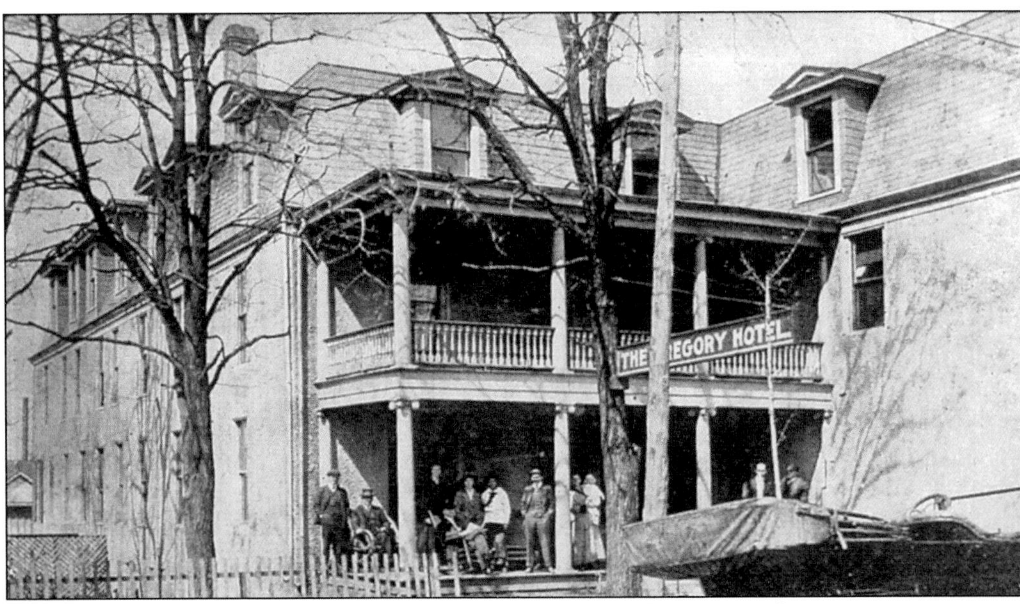

Across the street, Pearl W. Gregory opened the Gregory Hotel in 1903 with a restaurant, tearoom, and the Chase City Bakery. The W. J. Gregory family was transferred to Chase City in 1901 by the railroad with their son Earle. W. J. Gregory was the local telegrapher and dispatcher. The Gregorys liked living in a boardinghouse so much that they built one on the former site of the Methodist parsonage. In 1932, the top floor caught fire, and it became a two-story hotel instead of the three-story hotel pictured here. (WCG.)

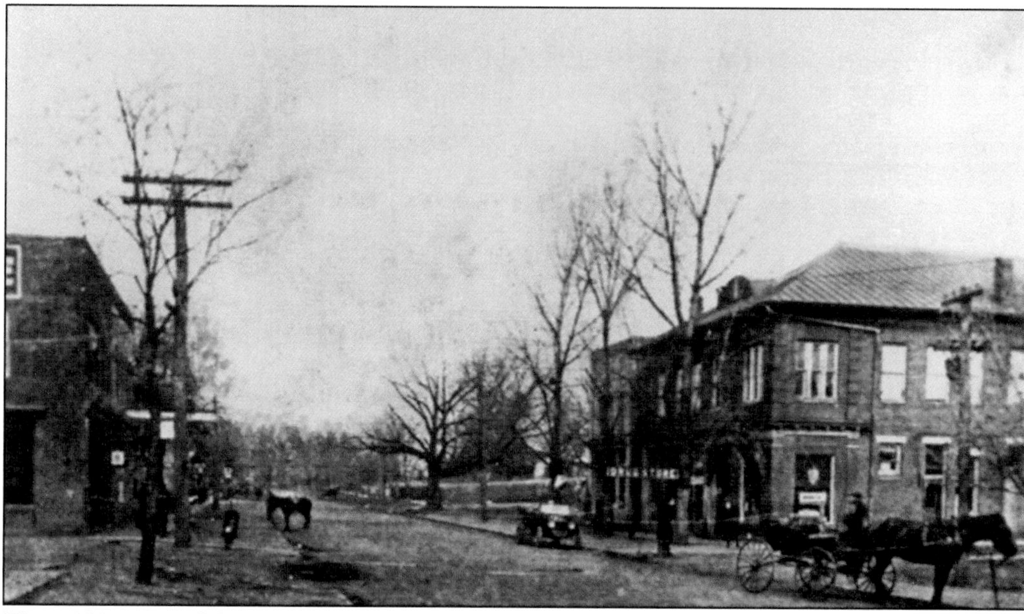

This 1909 postcard shows Main Street north from town hall. In June, Dr. H. L. Burwell leased the former town hall to open a pharmacy. On June 5, the Opera House was leased by R. E. Stearms for $100 per year and hosted a picture theater one or two nights per week. In August 1920, it was leased by C. E. Geoghegan as a movie theater until he could get his built. Besides town hall, the building contained the barbershop of J. A. Winfield upstairs. (Wyatt Garrett.)

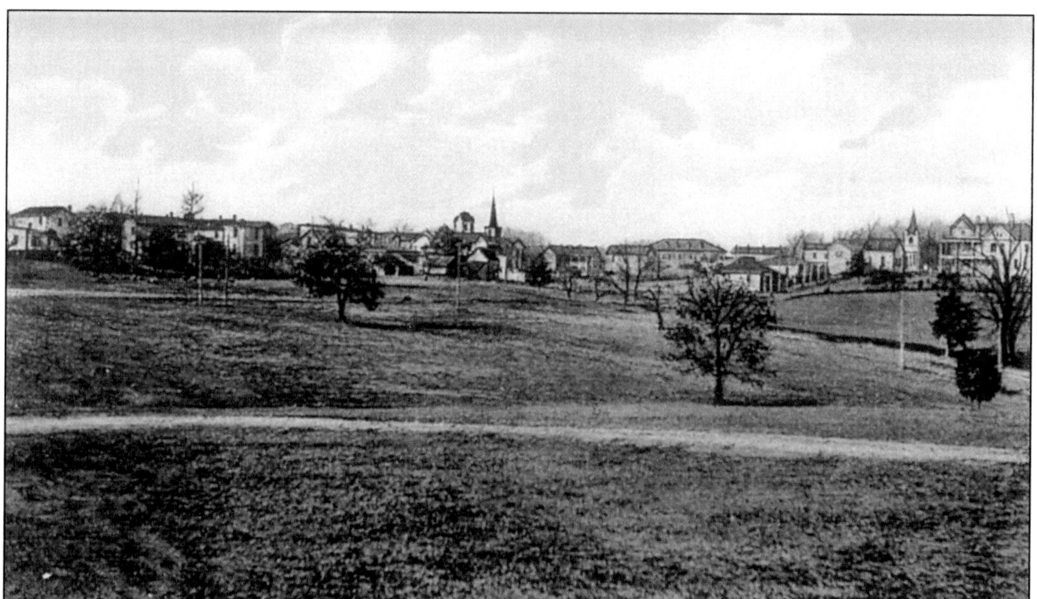

Taken from the front porch of the Mecklenburg Hotel in 1905, this is a panoramic view of Chase City. Pictured are the stately Dr. R. A. Dodd home (right), Centenary Methodist Church, the Gallion home (closest), town hall (largest building), Little Mecklenburg Hotel, Presbyterian church steeple, several businesses, and the Men's Club (left). The front yard is the nine-hole golf course. (WCG.)

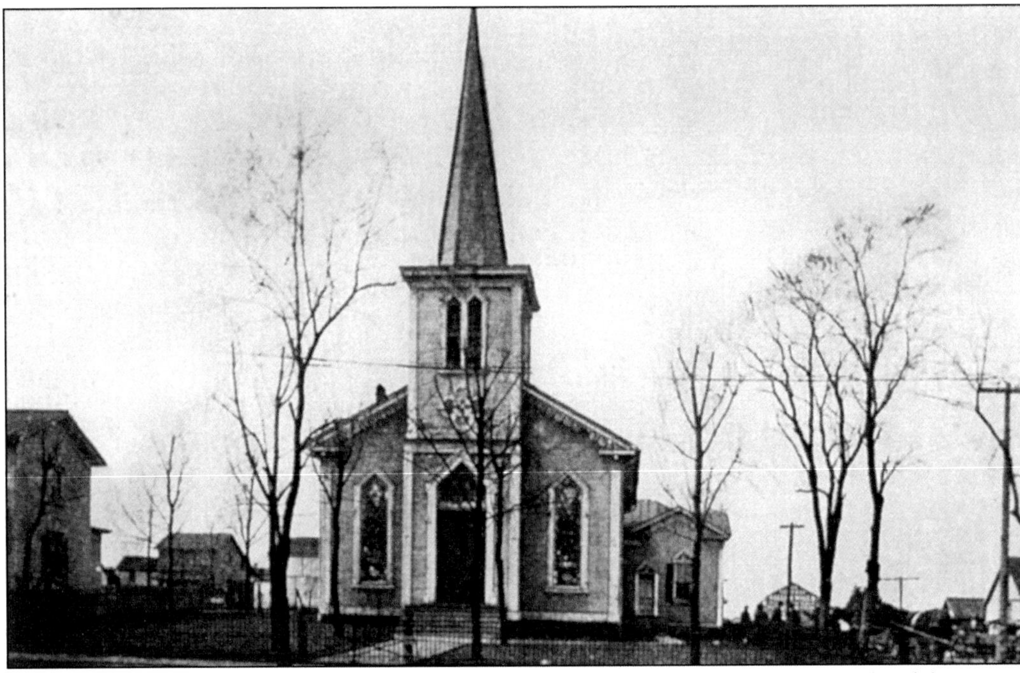

In the left distance is the Holloway house, Chase City's first public elementary school from 1885 to 1900, when it became a private school run by Frances Compton Maddox. To the left of the school is the Barnett Hotel (opened in 1888), purchased by the Mecklenburg Mineral Springs Corporation in 1900. To the right of the church in the distance is Willis and Willis, a company that provided livery, blacksmithing, and hauling. The white roof at far right is the Star Warehouse (opened 1883), a parachute factory from 1941 to 1945. (WCG.)

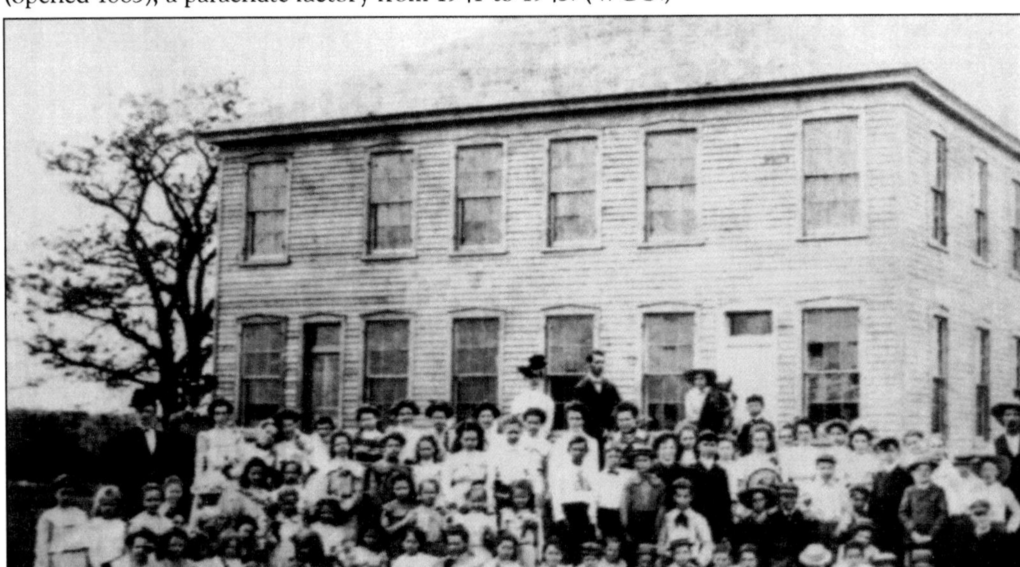

The Chase City High School was located at Third and Randolph Streets near the Standard Oil Company storage facility from 1885 to 1908. This school offered grades four through seven. The school charged tuition until 1930. A new high school was begun in 1905 and completed in 1909. (Donald and Virleen Moss.)

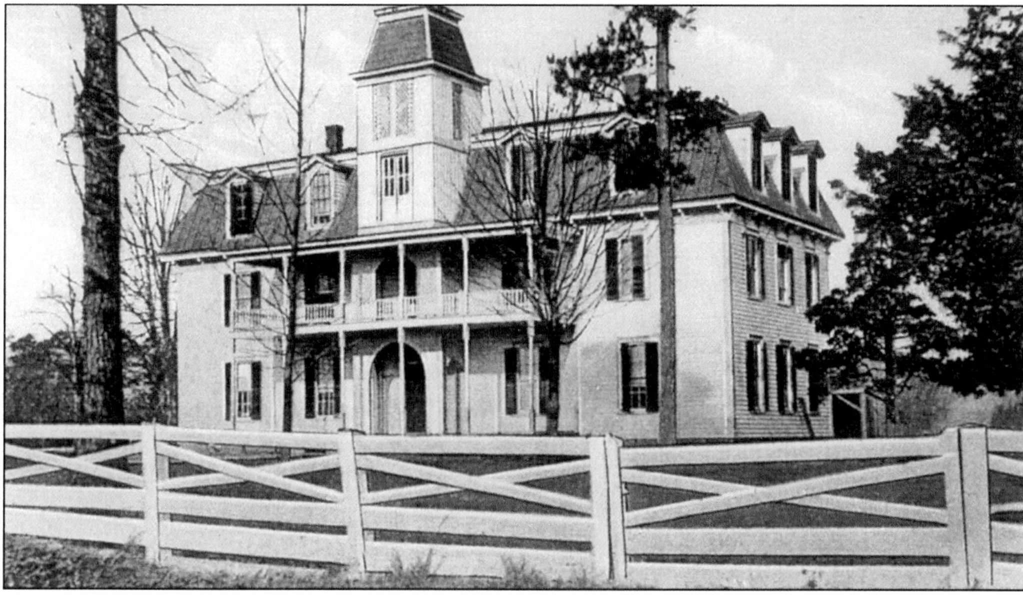

Children whose families could afford higher tuition attended the military Southside Male Academy at Academy Lane and Boyd Street, which opened in October 1889. By 1892, the school became coeducational, and in 1900, the school had 110 students with a male dormitory of 16 rooms next door. By 1910, it had become a girls' boarding school but allowed young men to attend classes, although they could no longer board there. (JAY.)

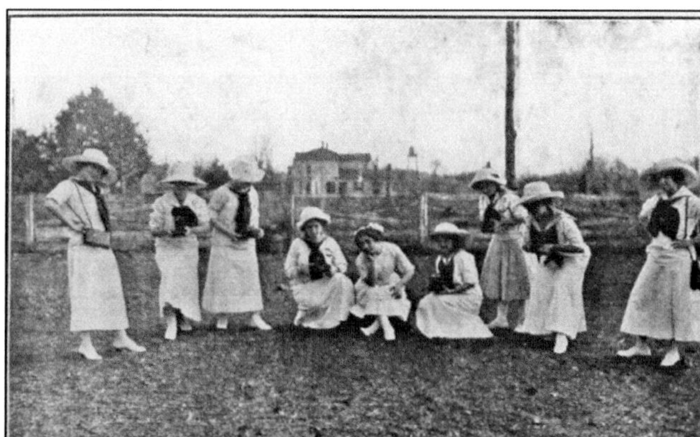

Kodak Club

MOTTO

"To see ourselves as others see us"

Officers

EDITH BRATTON.............President
DELMA JONES.............Secretary and Treasurer

Members

EDITH BRATTON	GLADYS FLETCHER
MAYNIE CREDLE	LETA HESTER
BERTHA CARTER	DELMA JONES
LILLIAN COATES	BERTIE YANCEY

In 1910, photography was quite popular in the academy. The Kodak Club of the school is posing for a photograph on the front lawn overlooking the pasture and the home of S. E. Spaulding in the distance. The Jeffreys-Spaulding Lumber Company is less than two blocks north on Boyd Street and began operation 1910. (JAY.)

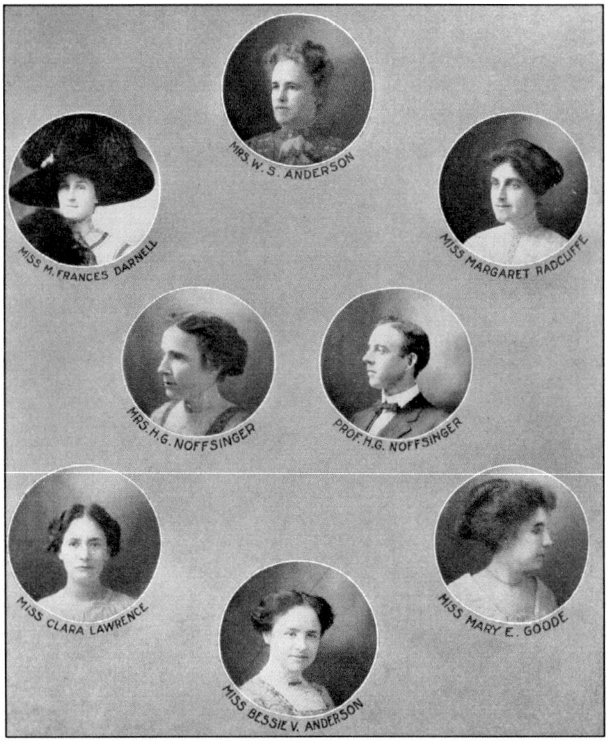

This is a 1911 photograph of the staff of the academy. By 1914, the Southside Academy had become a normal school (teachers college) during summers for Richmond College of Richmond, Virginia. The student teachers that came during the summers stayed in local homes. In 1912, town council voted to not charge these homes a license fee. (JAY.)

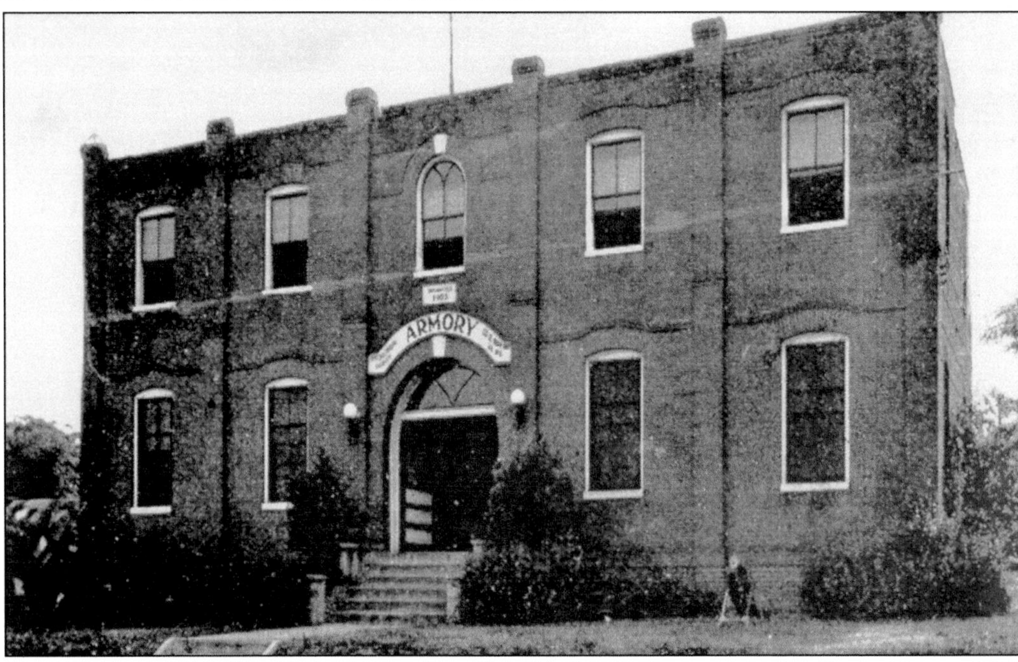

In 1903, the Mecklenburg Guard was formed and held its meetings in the Opera House. With rigorous recruitment, it needed its own building. With support from the town, county, and fundraisers, a building was begun in 1907 and completed in the spring of 1909. Situated on Main Street next to the First National Bank building, the armory became the new home of town hall, the fire department, and Chase City's first library. (SVHP.)

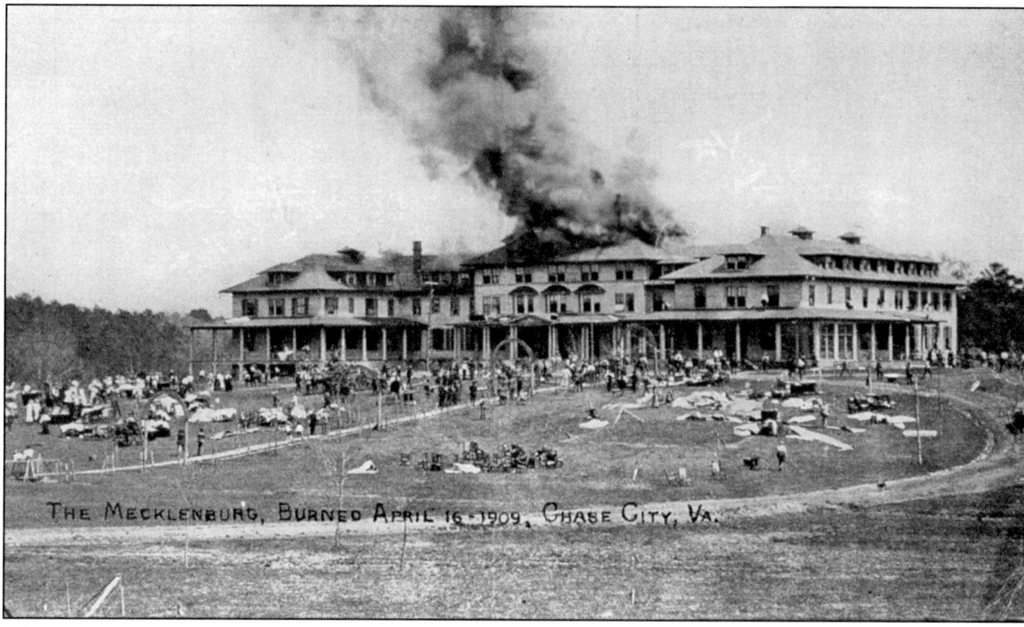

Almost four full city blocks of Chase City burned in 1903. The town had been plagued with fires. The night of April 15, 1909, brought a devastating blow to Chase City's economy with the fire that destroyed the heavily insured Mecklenburg Hotel. The few guests and staff were joined by workers from Emory's Mill to remove all they could from the hotel to try and keep the fire from spreading, but to no avail. (SVHP.)

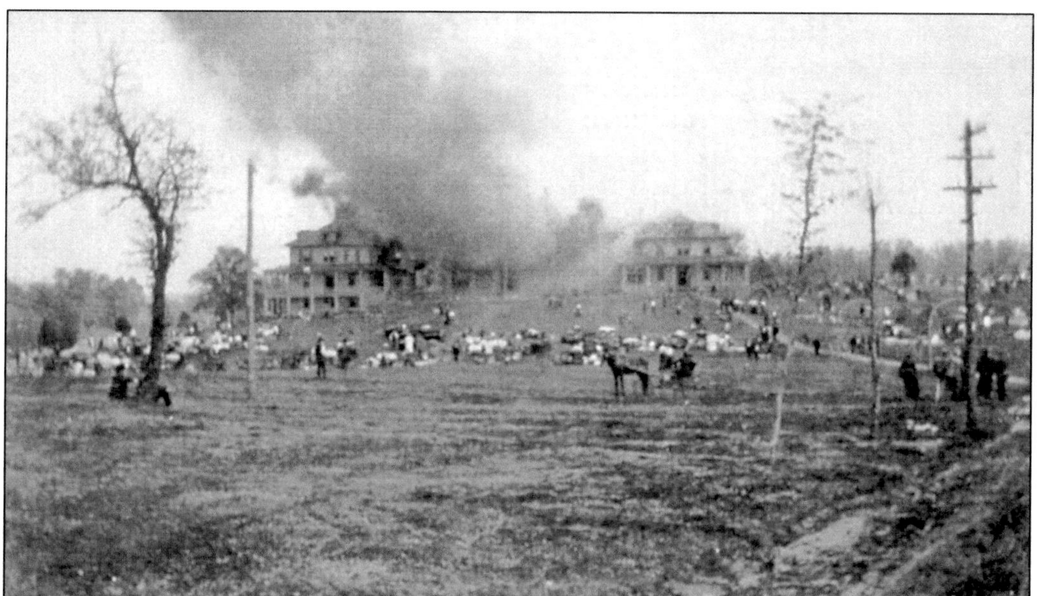

The entire community came to assist, but the fire was too large for the small volunteer fire department to handle. The citizens and guests were helpless but to watch as the hotel eventually became totally engulfed in flames. The fire is reported to have begun in the kitchen, and there were no reported fatalities, but recently this has come to question, as descendants of one of the bakers (a Russian) reports he was killed in the fire. (WCG.)

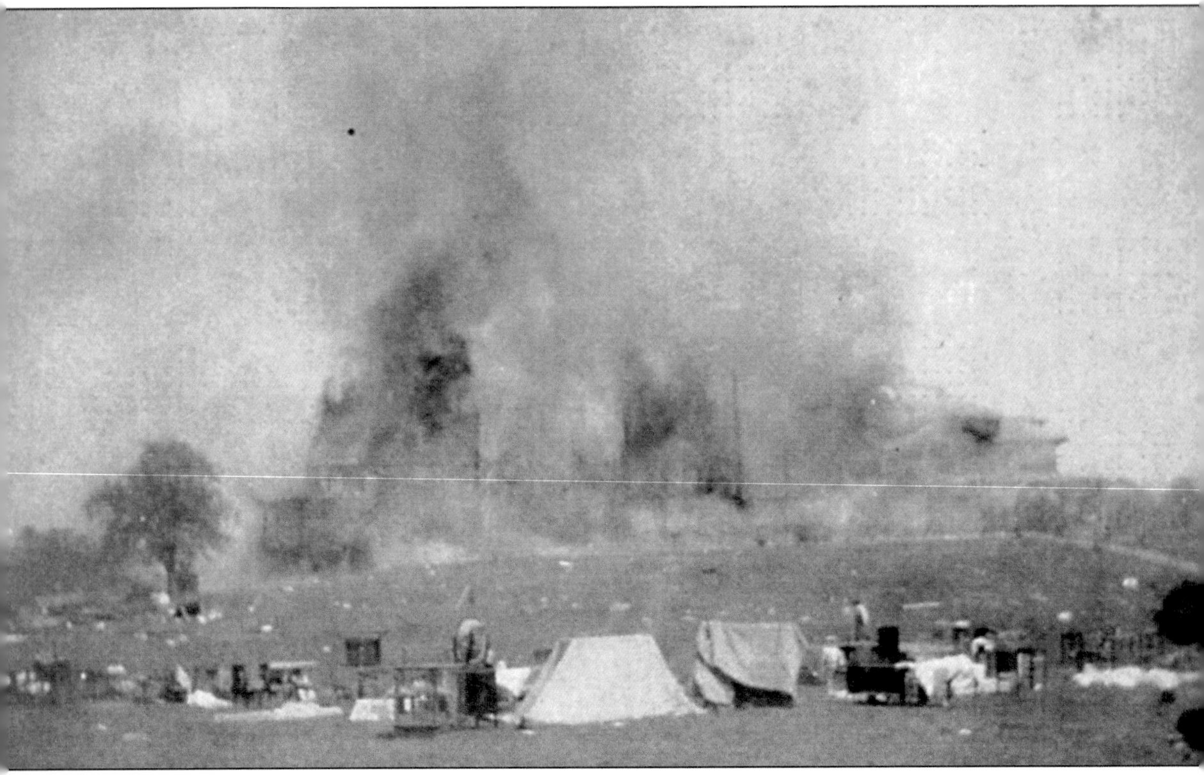

By mid-afternoon on April 16, everyone had left, the remains of the hotel were scattered about the lawn, and much had been covered to protect it against smoke, embers, and weather. Many of the items were moved to the Little Mecklenburg and the Barnette Rooming House (formerly the Barnett Hotel), but many are in the possession of Chase City's citizens, antique collectors, and dealers far and wide. There is a good collection also at the MacCallum More Museum. (WCG.)

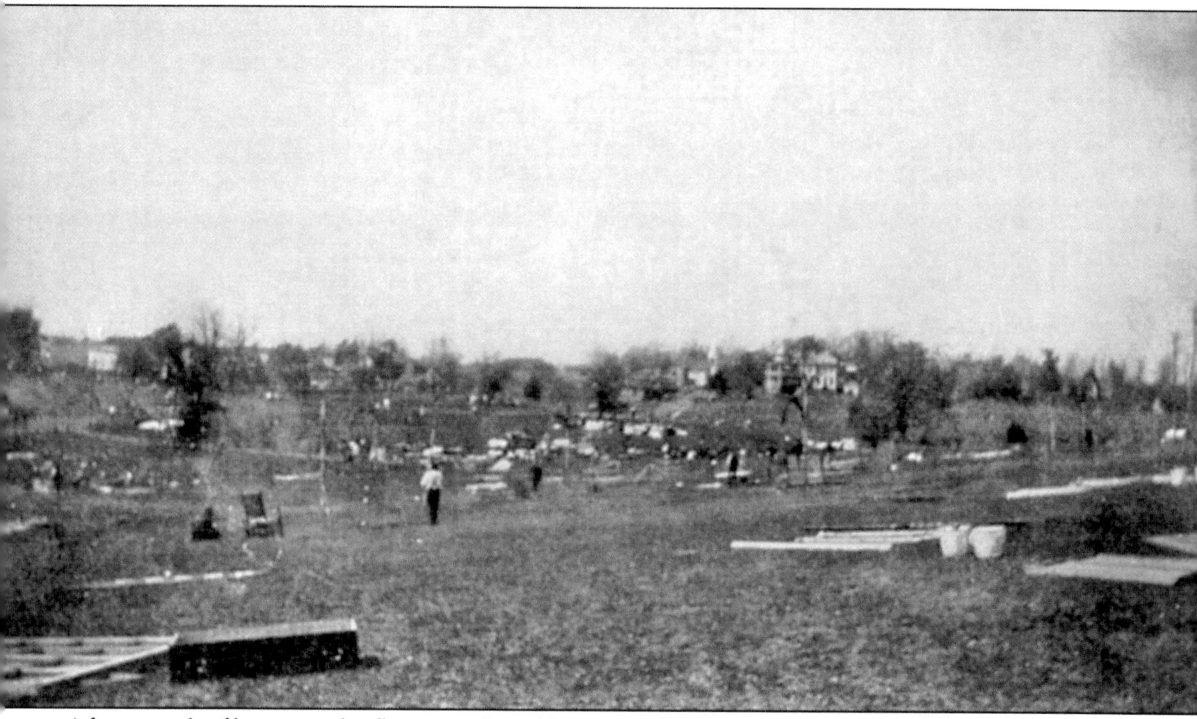

After a week of burning, the flames and smoldering ash had subsided, and cleanup began. Efforts were underway to sell stock and rebuild, and even in the 1920s, stock sales continued, but with increasing costs, 15 acres of the grounds were sold in 1927, with the remainder being sold at auction in 1946. (WCG.)

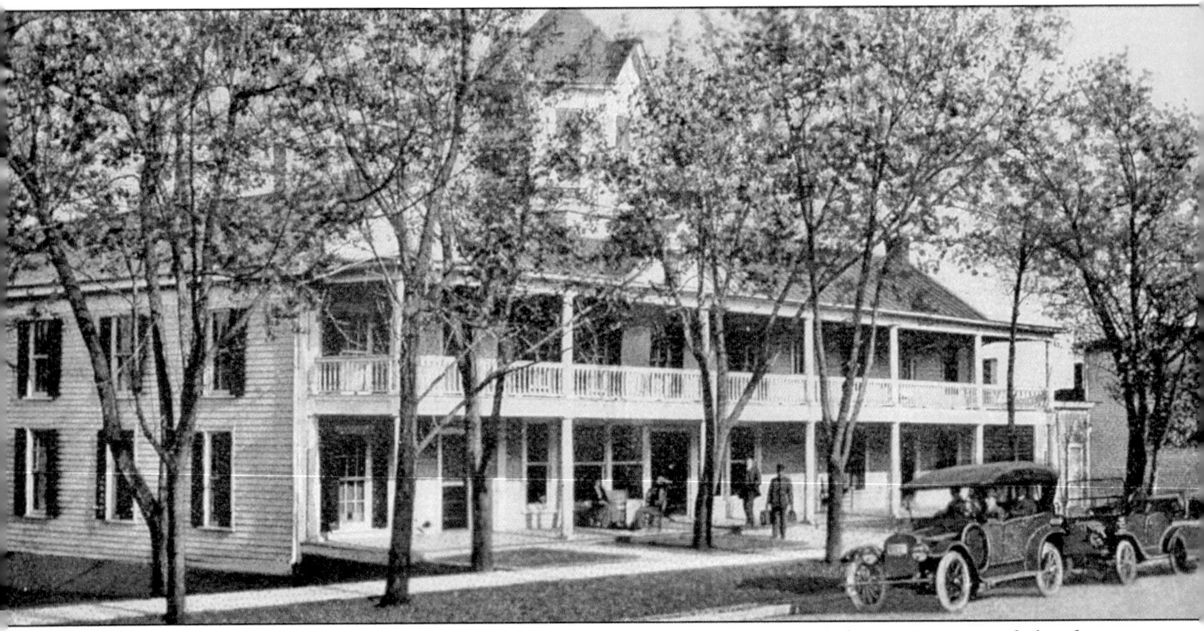

The Little Mecklenburg was remodeled and advertised many of the amenities of the former Mecklenburg Mineral. It also had a new manager, M. William Blair. When Blair retired in October 1912, he was so well liked that the city issued a proclamation in his honor. Later the hotel was often referred to as the Blair and the Dair House. (SVHP.)

Two

CHASE CITY
FROM 1910 THROUGH 1928

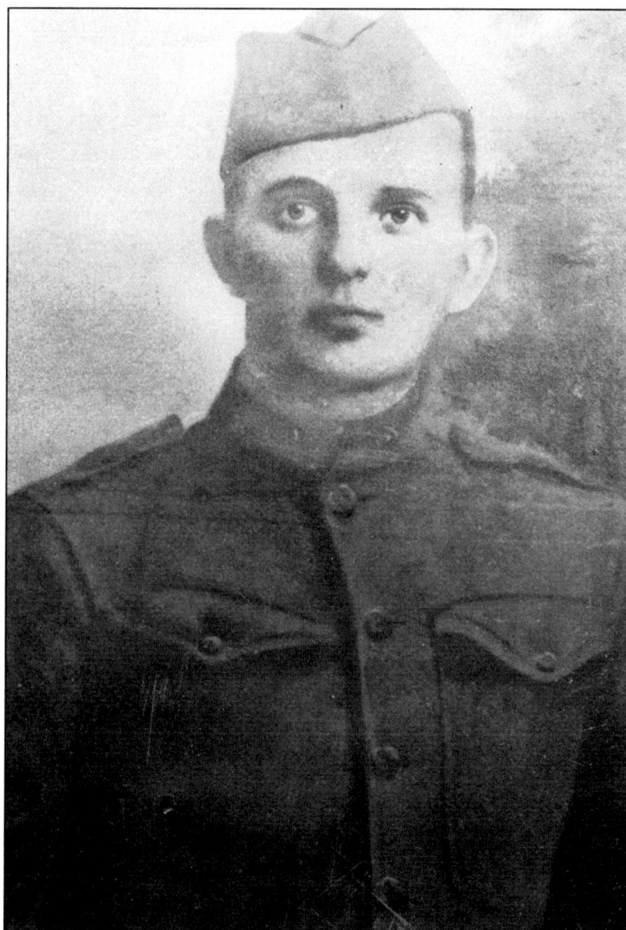

This *c.* 1914 painting of Earle Davis Gregory illustrates his enthusiasm for military service. Born in Clayville, Virginia, on October 18, 1897, he arrived in Chase City at the age of three. In 1912, he entered Fork Union Military Academy, which he attended until the summer of 1915. During his senior year, he held the rank of first lieutenant. On July 14, 1914, he joined Company E, 2nd Virginia Volunteers, in Chase City, and he was appointed first sergeant a month before his 21st birthday. The 2nd was activated into the Virginia National Guard in 1916, and from July 1916 to February 1917, Earle served on the Mexican border. On April 6, 1917, the United States entered World War I, and Company E was sent to Camp McClellan, Alabama. Earle became platoon sergeant of a trench mortar platoon. On October 8, 1918, his unit was sent into combat in France. In his first day of battle, Sergeant Gregory charged a machine gun nest and destroyed it, capturing three enemy soldiers. (Ronnie A. Bugg.)

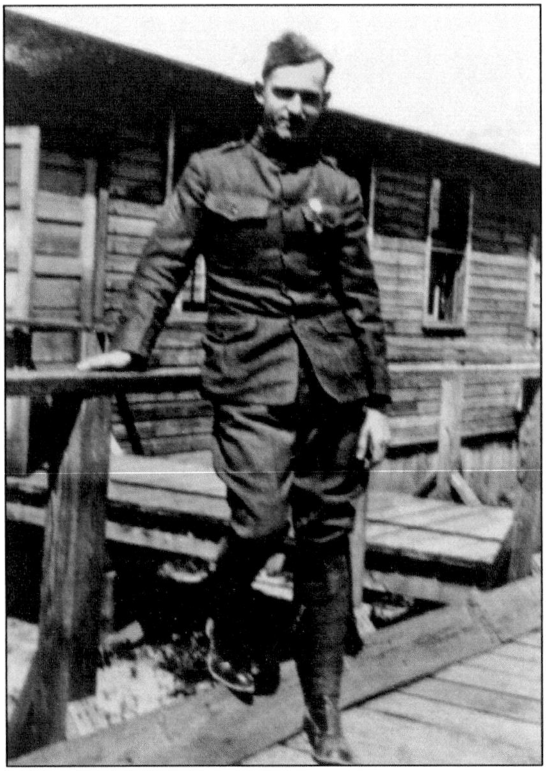

Before the first day was over, Earle had attacked an enemy holding area and captured 20 more enemy soldiers. Three days later, he was seriously wounded and returned to the Camp Lee, Virginia, hospital, where he stayed for six months. He was honorably discharged on April 25, 1919. This photograph was taken shortly after he was awarded the Congressional Medal of Honor on April 29, 1919, the first Virginian to receive this honor. (Ronnie A. Bugg.)

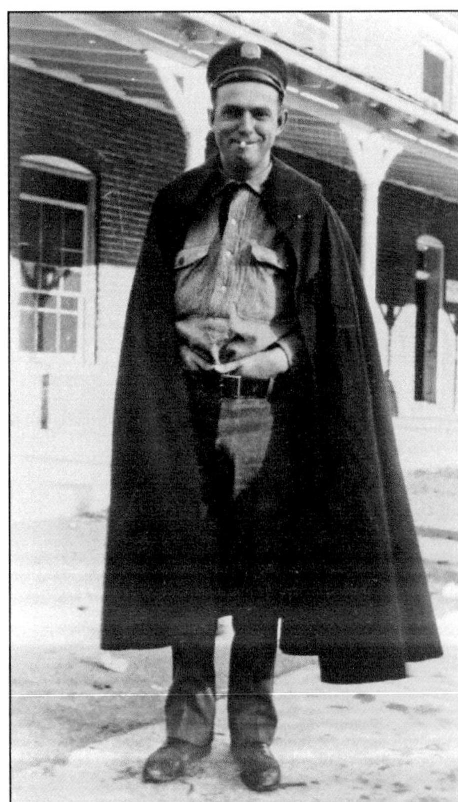

In September 1919, Earle Gregory entered Virginia Polytechnic Institute (VPI) under the disabled veterans program. He was elected class president twice and president of the student body his senior year. He began working for the American Red Cross, and in 1932, he went to work for the Veterans Administration in recreational services, from which he retired. This 1925 photograph was taken at a VPI class reunion. (Virginia Tech University Libraries, Digital Library and Archives.)

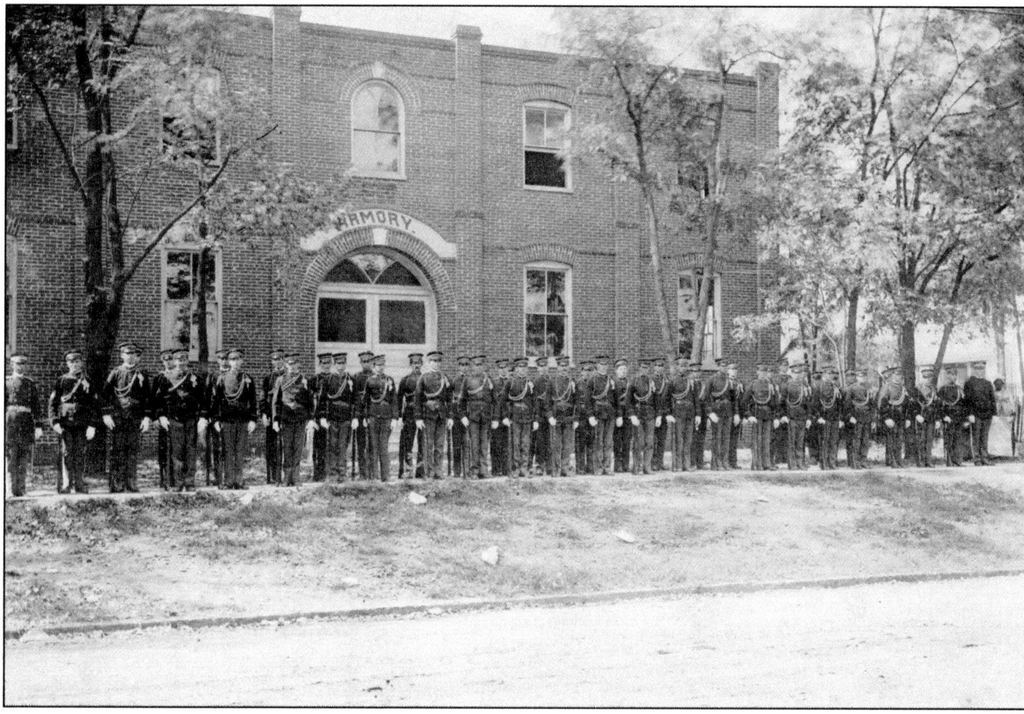

Company E, 2nd Virginia Volunteers, prepares to escort Secretary of State William J. Bryant, who is to speak at the Mecklenburg fairgrounds in 1913. They are in formation in front of the Chase City Armory. Capt. J. E. Brame is the commander. (Town of Chase City, Charles Queensberry.)

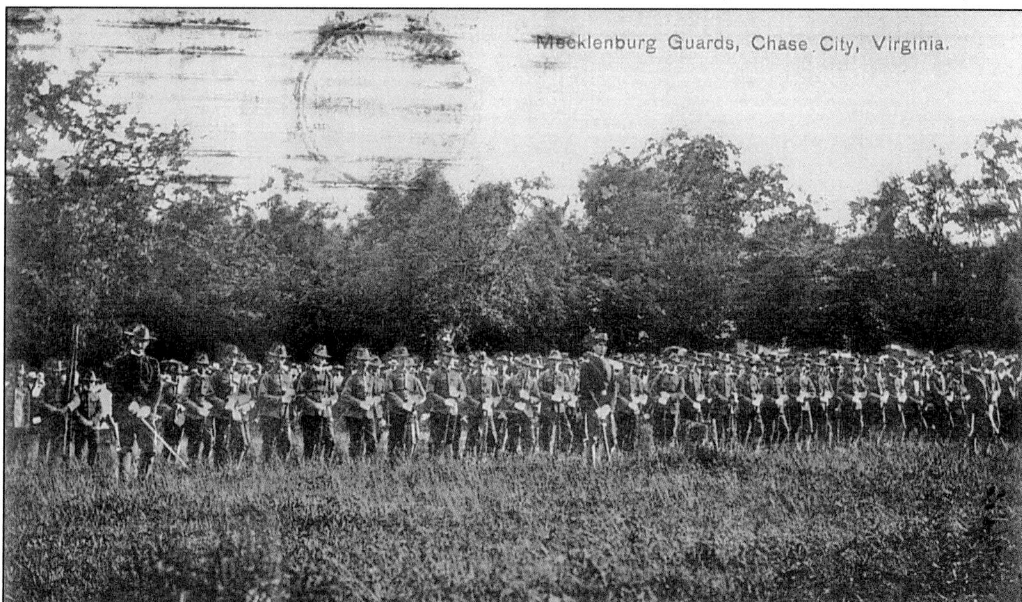

Here Company E volunteers are practicing not only for training but also for the citizens. The sessions were respectable entertainment and helped with recruitment. Capt. J. E. Brame was commander for several years and was also president of the South Central Fair Association, Inc., for several years. (WCG.)

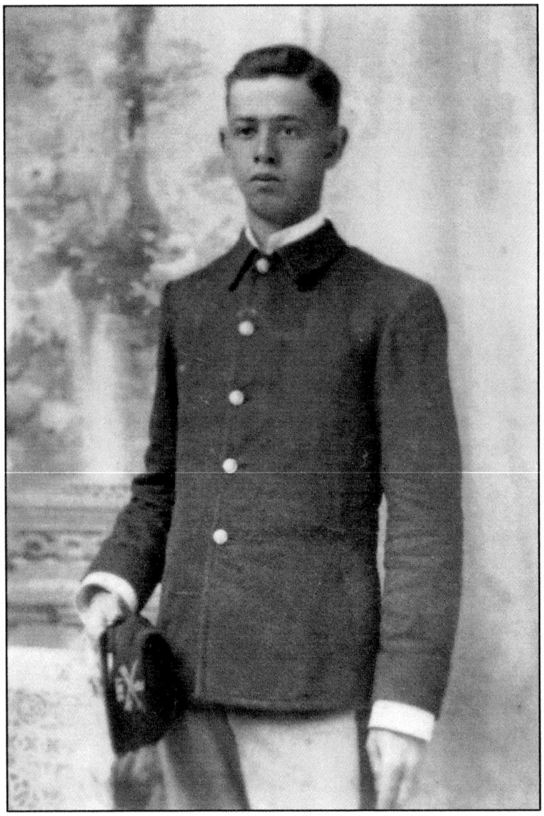

John Ellis Brame Sr. was born in Chase City on September 3, 1875, attended VPI, and returned to Chase City in 1917. He taught agriculture for 37 years and was instrumental in having a public school of agriculture in town with an adjoining cannery, which opened in 1919. He assisted with the development of the Virginia and the national Future Farmers organizations. He is pictured here around 1892. (Ray and Betty Brame Wallace.)

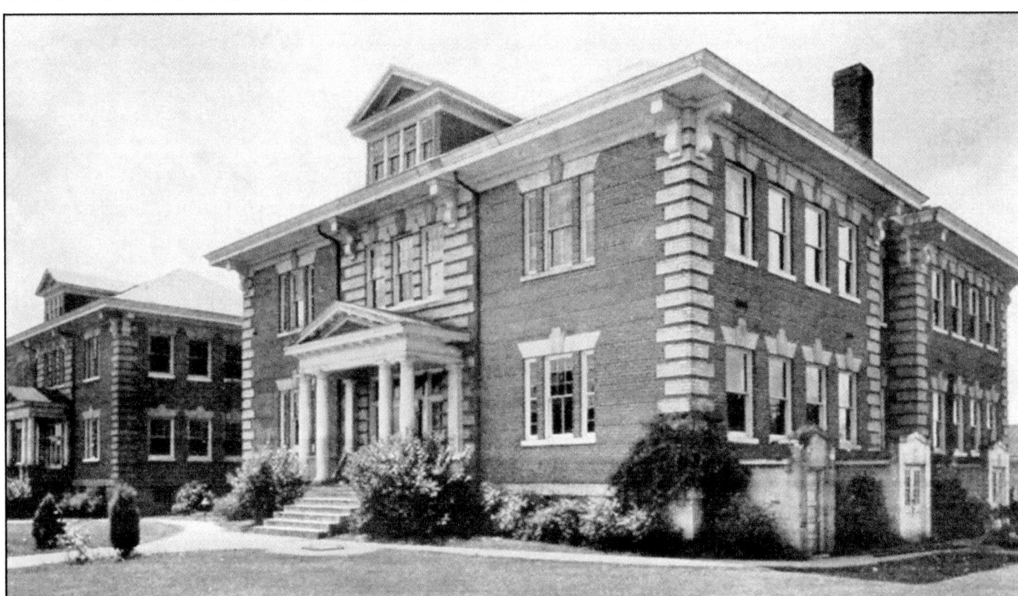

This photograph shows the first new Chase City High School, completed in 1909 (right), and the Chase City Elementary School, completed in 1917 (left). In the bottom right corner is the roofline of the school of agriculture, with the top floor serving as a school of home economics. Next door, a cannery building was planned. These two additions were completed in 1919. (Wyatt Garrett.)

The Bank of Mecklenburg, founded in 1891, was taken over by First State Bank in November 1903. Above was the Southern Telephone and Telegraph Company, founded in 1900. Also on the second floor were a barbershop and an insurance sales office. Next door is the 1912 opening of the new Bigger and Company dry goods store in the old Collins stall. The store offered groceries, hats, men's and ladies' dry goods, millinery, and material. (WCG.)

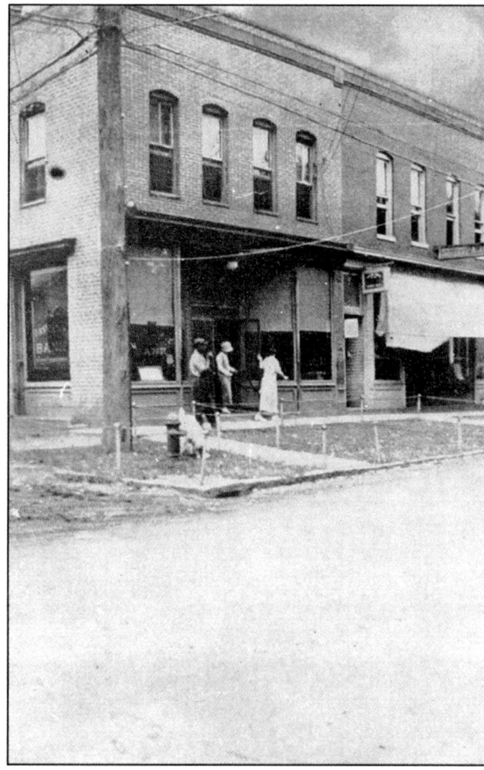

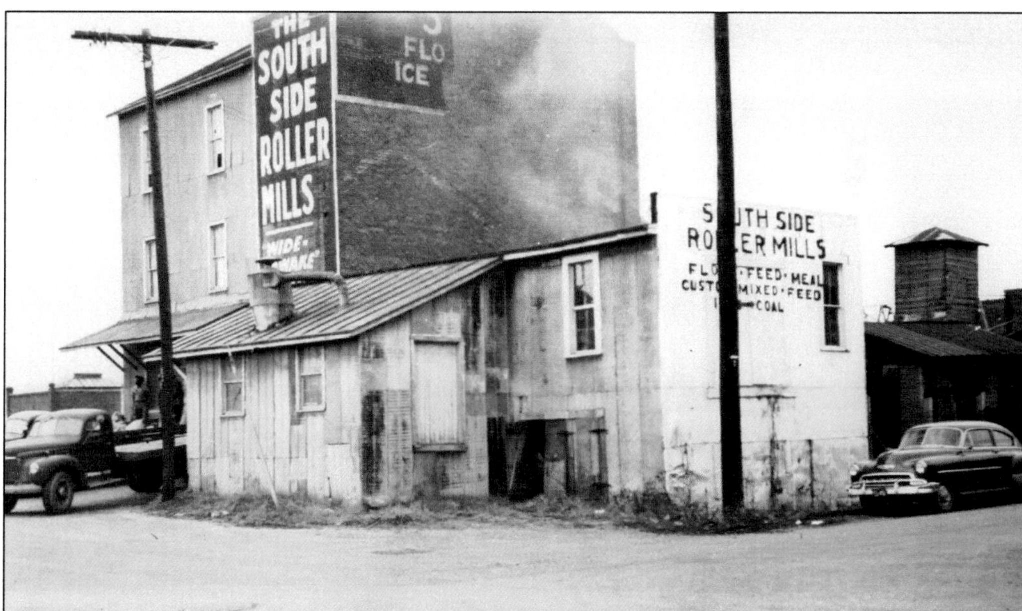

Third Street continued to develop from Main Street to the railroad tracks, a distance of three and a half blocks. At Third and Randolph Streets, Southside Supply Company began an aggressive business project. First was Southside Roller Mills (1912), which could produce 400 pounds of flour per hour. The flour was packed in 200-pound barrels or 100-pound flour sacks. Their trade brand was Wide Awake Flour. (LLE.)

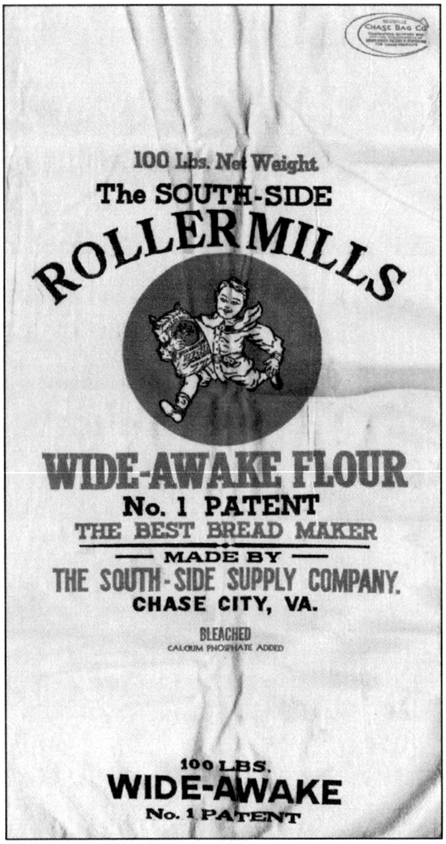

This flour sack was used starting around 1920 and continued until the mill closed in 1981. The mill also had an original set of stone grinding wheels for cornmeal. Unable to obtain parts to repair the grinder, they stopped making cornmeal in 1970. Southside Supply Company was begun by Charles Boswell as its first president and Judd A. Robertson. In 1915, R. L. Emory became secretary and manager of operations, becoming its president in 1934. He died on September 19, 1946, at the age of 60. (LLE.)

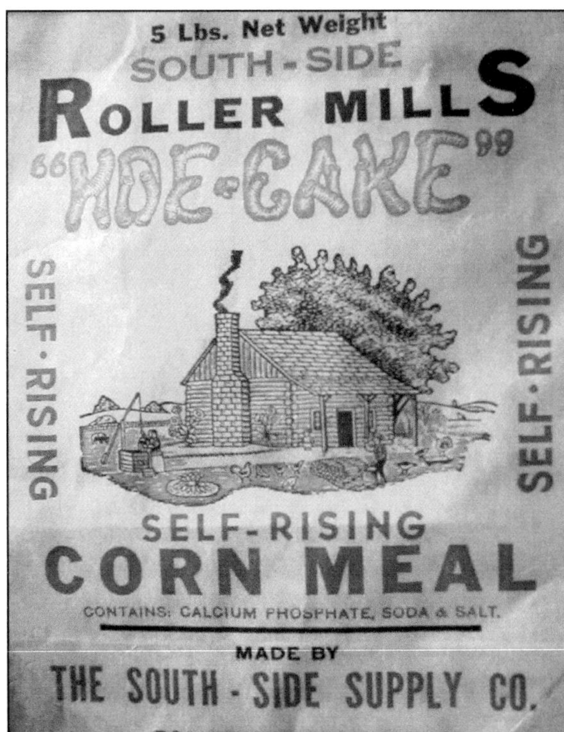

The trade name for the cornmeal was Hoe-Cake, and it was sold in bulk or paper bags. When the hopper broke, the company was unable to find an antique replacement part. This part of the operation had to shut down. (LLE.)

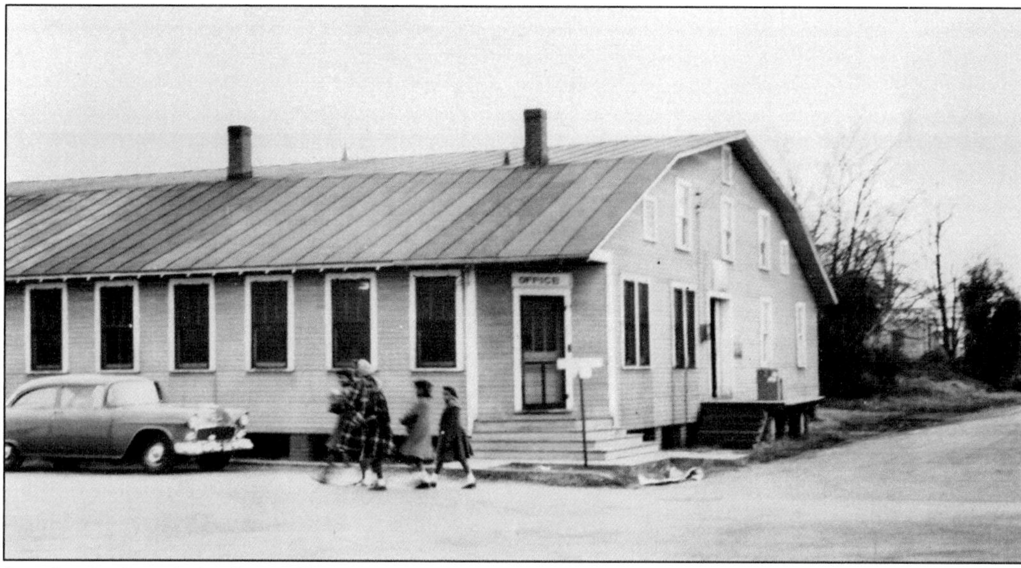

Southside Supply had its offices on Boyd Street at Third Street, across from Willis and Willis. The second president of the company was A. H. Robertson. Along with the roller mill, Southside Supply sold coal starting in 1912, and in 1913, their primary contract was with the Chase City Power Plant, situated only one block away. (LLE.)

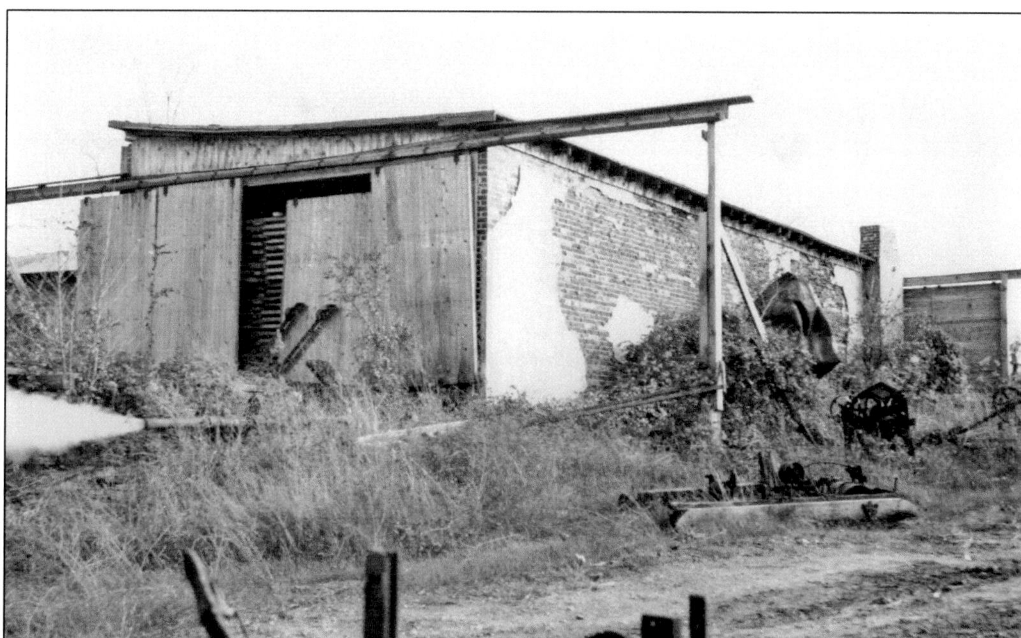

Southside was begun by Charles Boswell, its first president, and Judd A. Robertson. This 1950 photograph shows a kiln for the grain. Located on Endly Street, it was abandoned in 1941 and, as shown here, has fallen into disrepair. (LLE.)

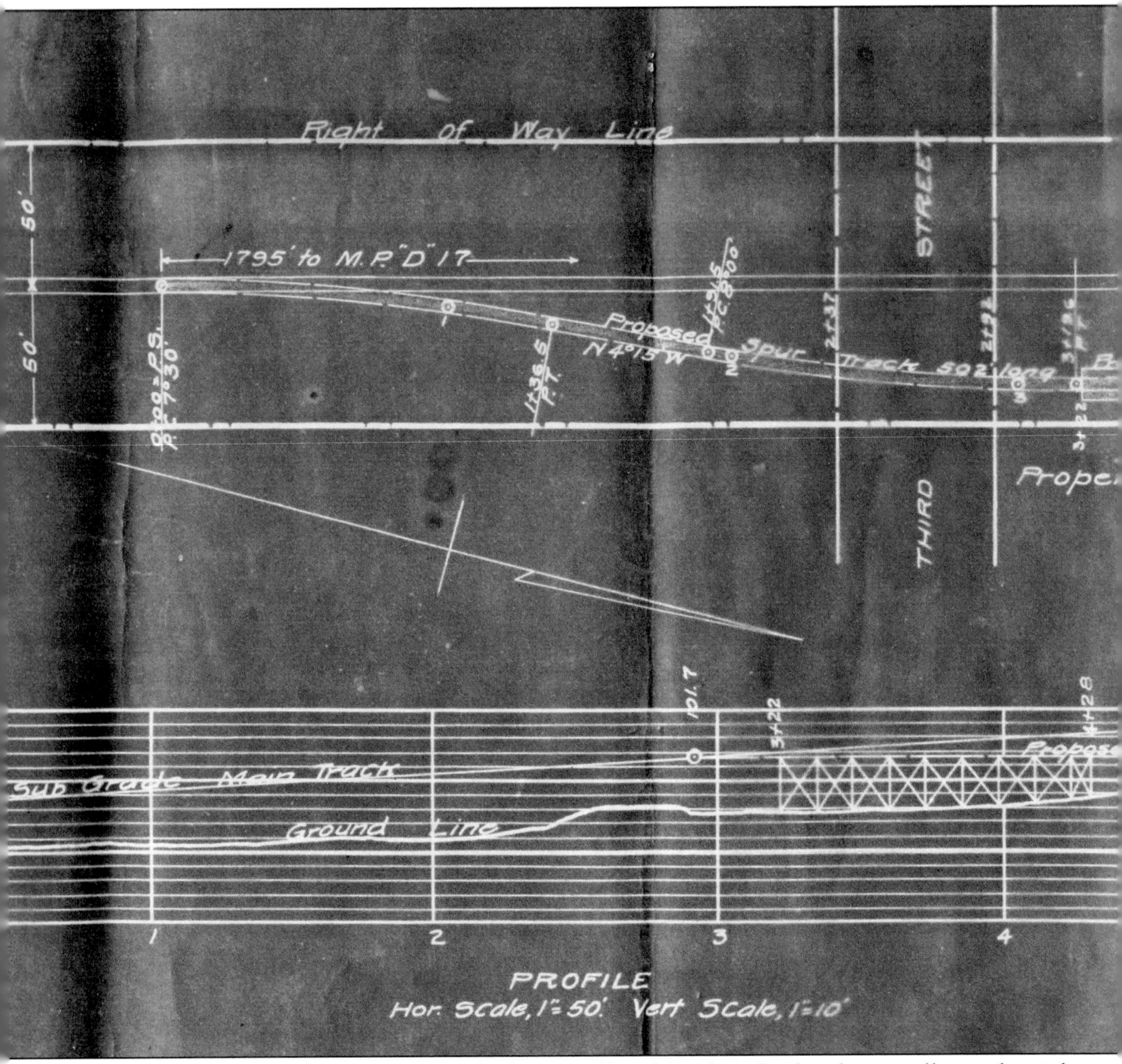

A contract was negotiated between Charles Boswell and Southern Railroad to install an industrial spur track next to Southside Roller Mills on June 10, 1912. The cost was $1,841. Since this was one block from the Chase City Coal Power Plant, the town agreed to pay $500 toward the spur.

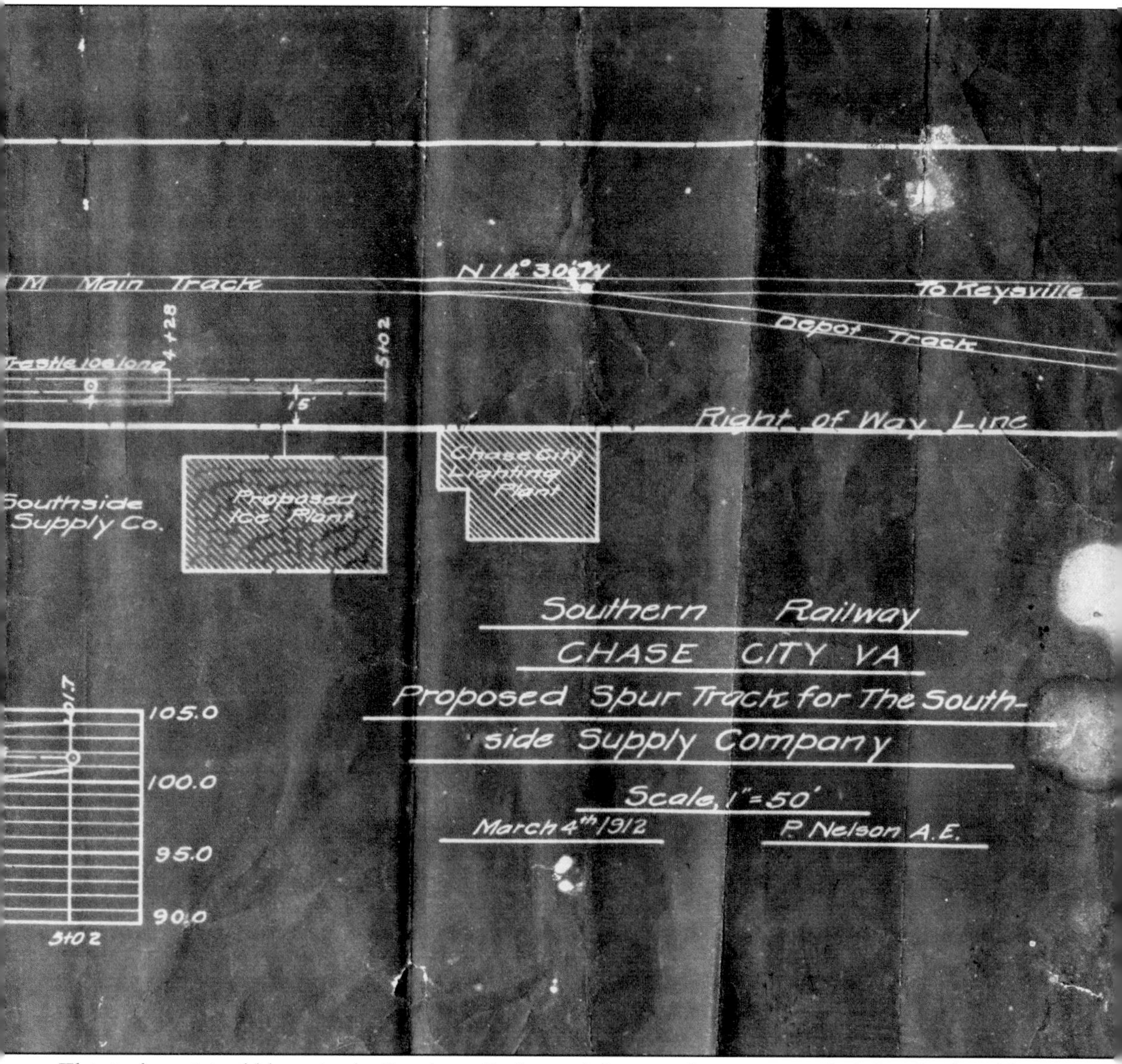

This is the original blueprint by Southern Railway of the spur that was installed. Southside sold coal until 1985. (LLE.)

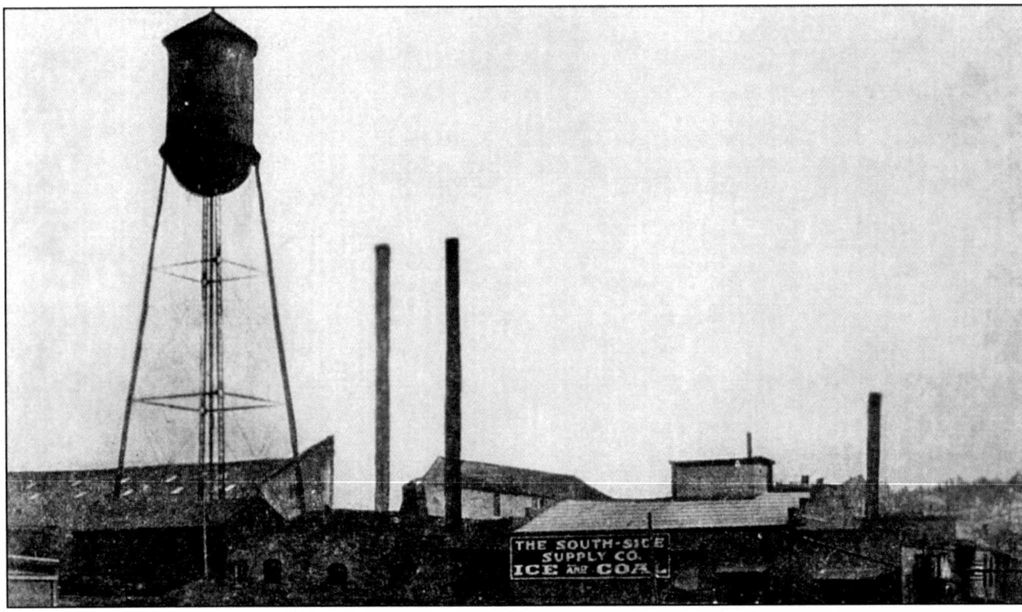

Next to the roller mill at 310 Randolph Street was the icehouse, which was needed by the town citizens and the train. The old icehouse, owned by Dr. Tyree Finch near Mills Store, had been condemned in April 1910 and had to be moved. With this new icehouse, a new trend began in Chase City on August 1, 1910: the sale of ice cream. The icehouse operated until 1965 next to the Chase City Power Plant in the old cannery building at Fourth and Boyd Streets. (WCG.)

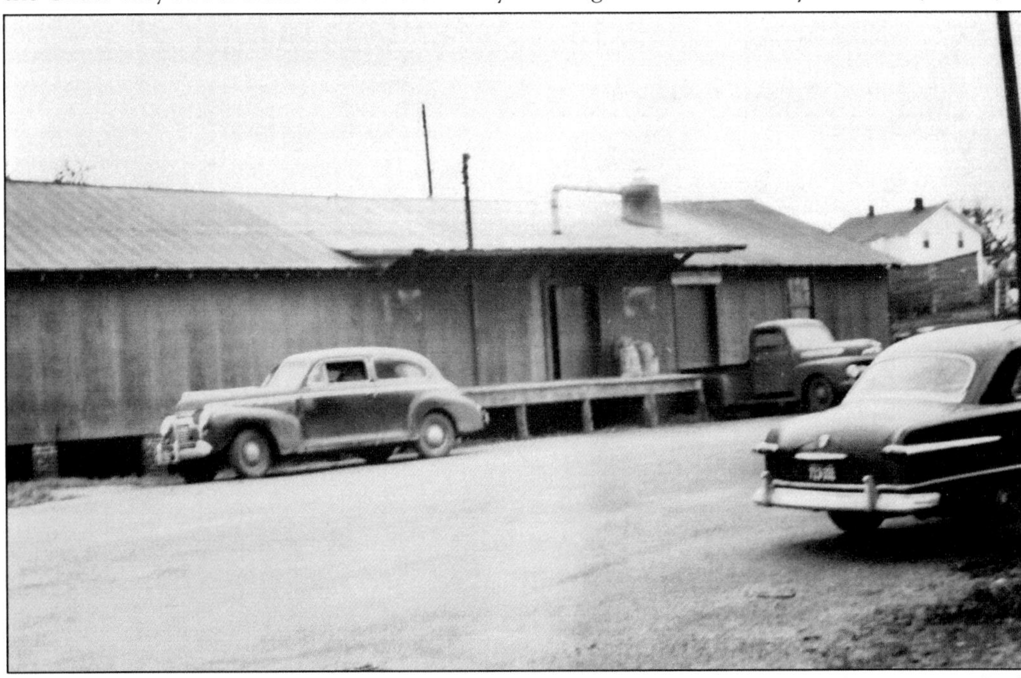

At 240 Randolph Street was the hammer mill. This mill processed grains for farmers into feeds for chickens, cattle, and other livestock. Each breed of animal needed a blend of ground grain to aid with digestion and nutrition. The mill operated from 1912 through 1985, the last of Southside Supply's enterprises to close. (LLE.)

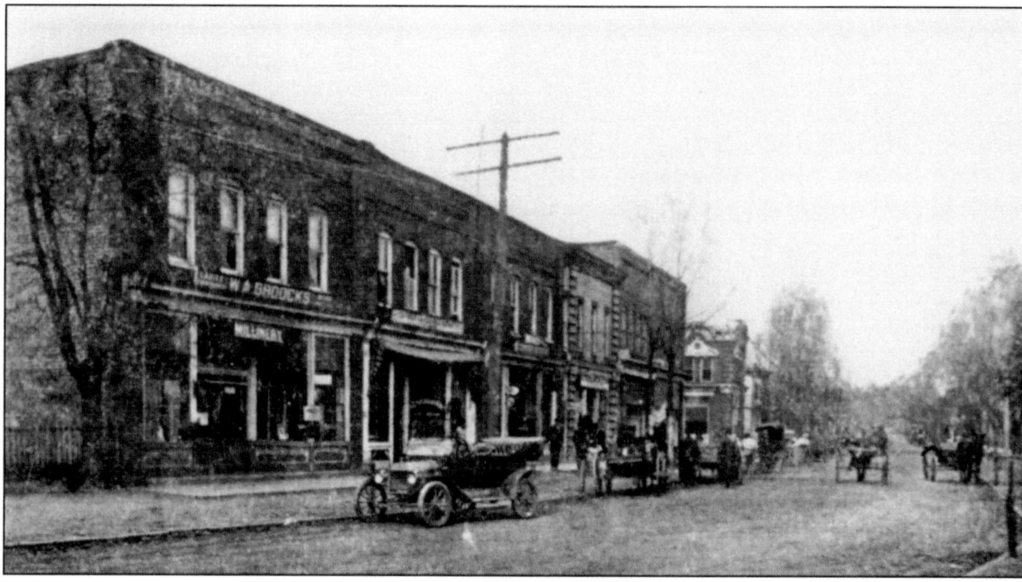

This photograph of the west side of the 100 block of Main Street from 1912 shows partial sidewalks. The stores are W. A. Broocks General Store and Millinery (founded 1900), Chase City Hardware Store (founded 1903), Williams 5-and-10¢ Store (founded 1912), and Hardy and Company, "The Peoples Store" (opened in 1908 but not incorporated until 1927). Williams Store and Hardy and Company were both purchased in 1945 by Leggets Department Store. The electric company is in the process of installing poles on this end of town. (Wyatt Garrett.)

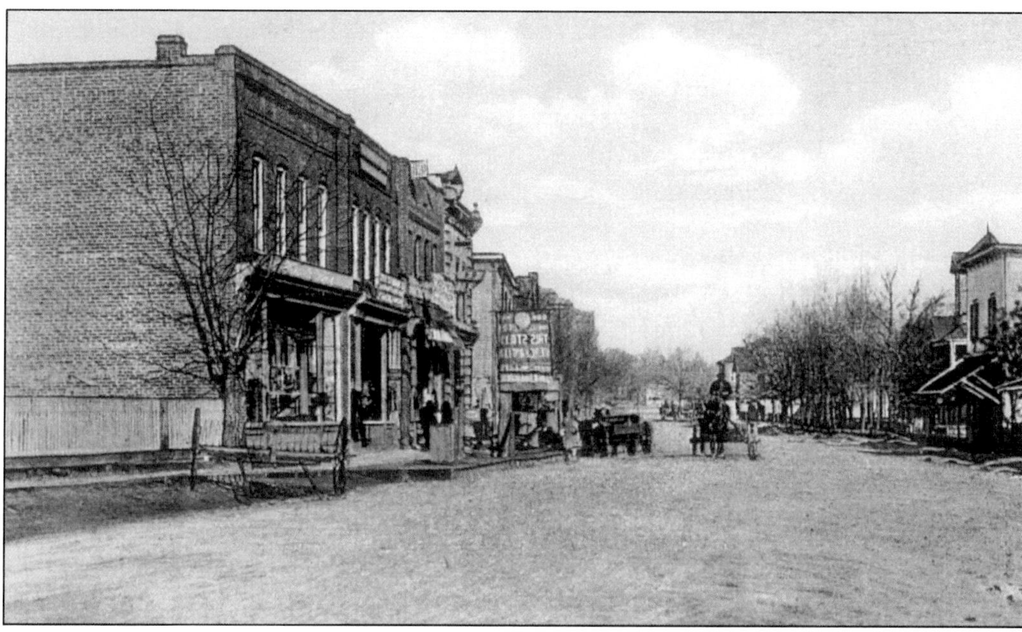

The same location is seen two years earlier in this reverse-image photograph. A sign is shown over what became Williams Store. The sign states "This Store has moved." Across the street is the home and drugstore of A. A. Saunders, and in the distance at right is the Little Mecklenburg Hotel, with its tree-lined front. The light-colored building on the far left is the Bank of Chase City. (Wyatt Garrett.)

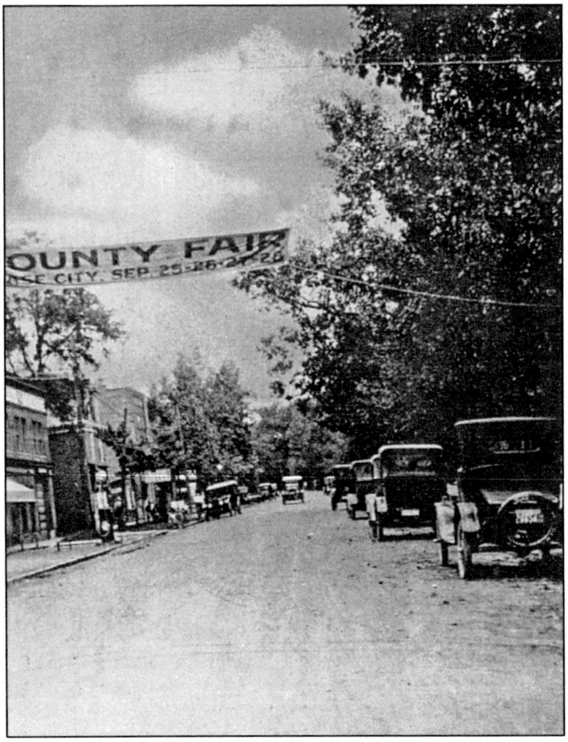

This 1915 photograph of North Main Street's 300 block shows the west side of the street across from town hall nearly completely developed, including the three new buildings of the Chase City Department Store. This company was begun by Sarah Lipsitz in 1915 and remained family owned and operated for nearly 70 years. The trees lining the streets obscure most of the town's buildings. The end building is the new P. H. Maddox Drug Store, also opening in 1915. (WCG.)

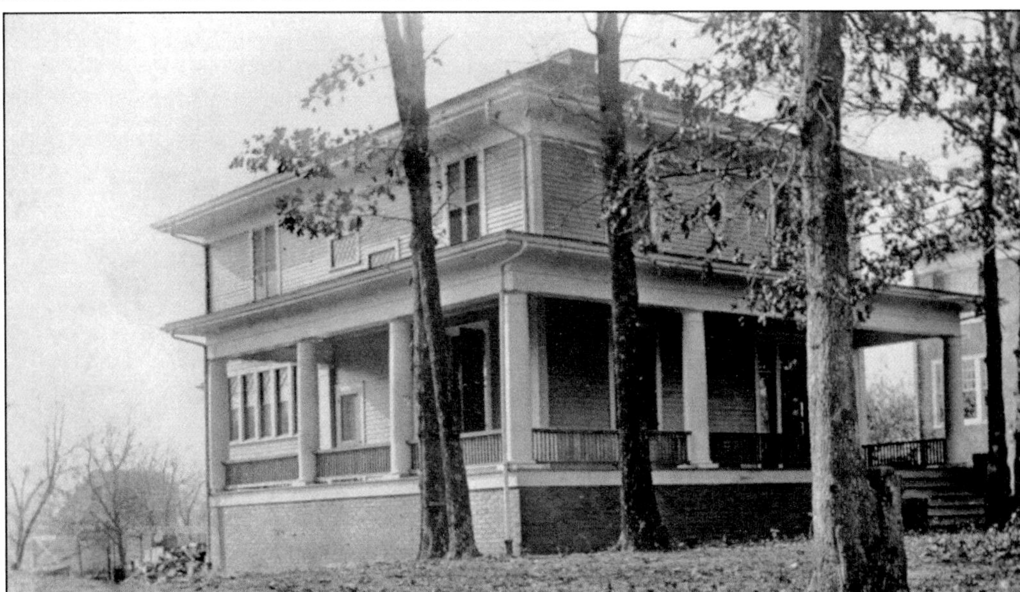

This home on the southeast corner of Hudgins and Walker Streets in the proposed New Territory of Chase City was completed in 1910 for Edward and Lucy Hudgins. They lived here until 1929, when they moved across the street into their home on five acres. Edward Hudgins (January 17, 1882–June 29, 1958) was a Scout leader and was involved in the First Baptist Church. He was transferred to Chase City by his Richmond law firm in 1908 to establish a branch office and considered Chase City his home. (MMMG.)

Lucy Morton Hudgins is pictured with baby Edward Morton Hudgins and her husband, Edward Wren Hudgins, in 1911. Lucy and Edward were married in Chase City in 1910. During World War I, Edward served in the YMCA for two years. He served in the Virginia House of Delegates for 11 years, was circuit court judge of Mecklenburg County for four years, became an associate justice of the Virginia Supreme Court in 1930, and became chief justice in 1947. Attending his funeral in Chase City were the current and four former governors. (MMMG.)

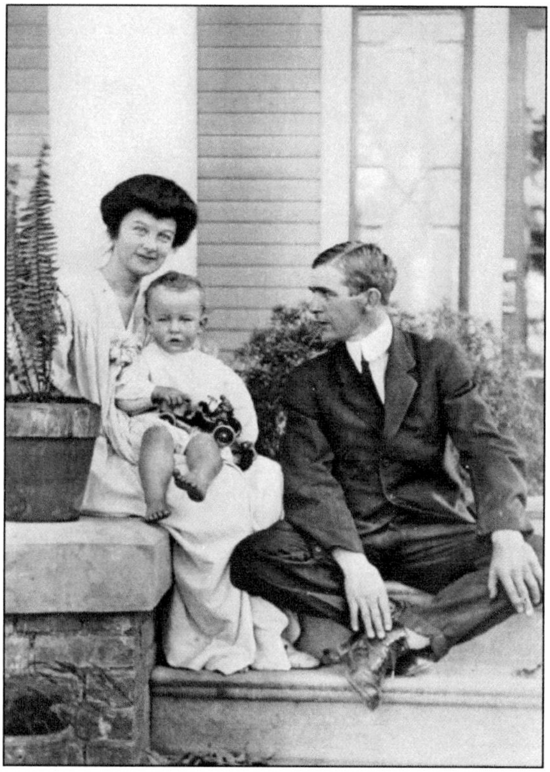

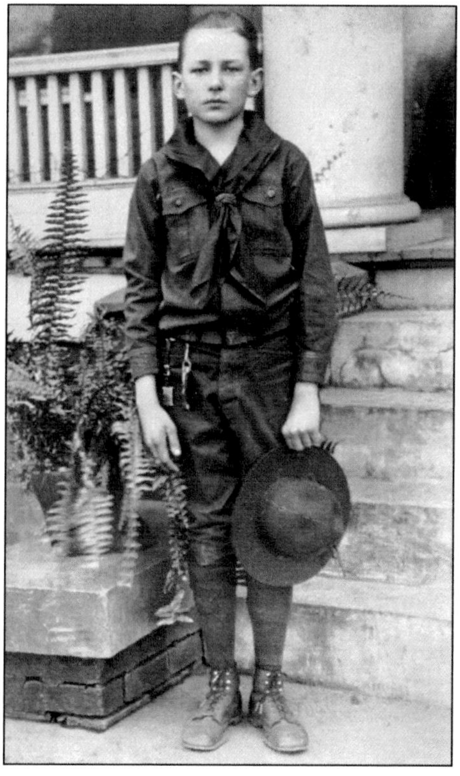

Pictured in 1922 in his Scout uniform, Edward Morton Hudgins went to University of Virginia and enlisted in the National Guard. He practiced law in Richmond. During World War II, he rose to the rank of brigadier general. He served as an aide to President Roosevelt, and at the end of the war, in the China-Burma-India theater, he stayed on as chief council of war criminals. After returning to America, he became vice president of the Chesapeake and Ohio Railroad and served six terms in the Virginia Assembly representing south Richmond. (MMMG.)

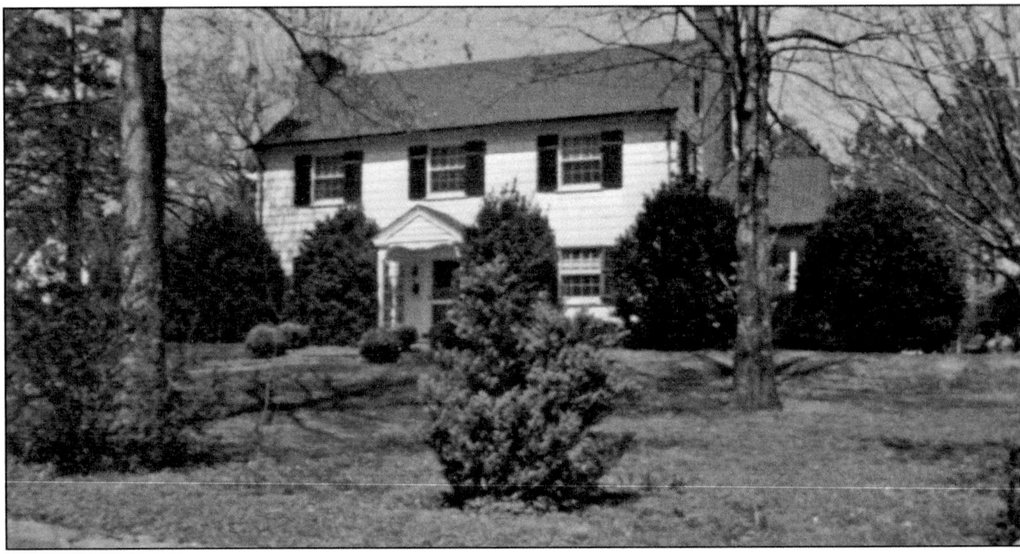

After the Hudginses moved into their new home in 1929, Lucy M. had a lot of free time, with her men traveling about the world, to develop her gardens in the back of her home. She is reported to have been the first town resident with a goldfish pond. Her second son, Adm. William Henry Hudgins, supported his mother's dream. As he traveled the world, he sent artifacts for her garden. This is now MacCallum More Museum and Gardens. (MMMG.)

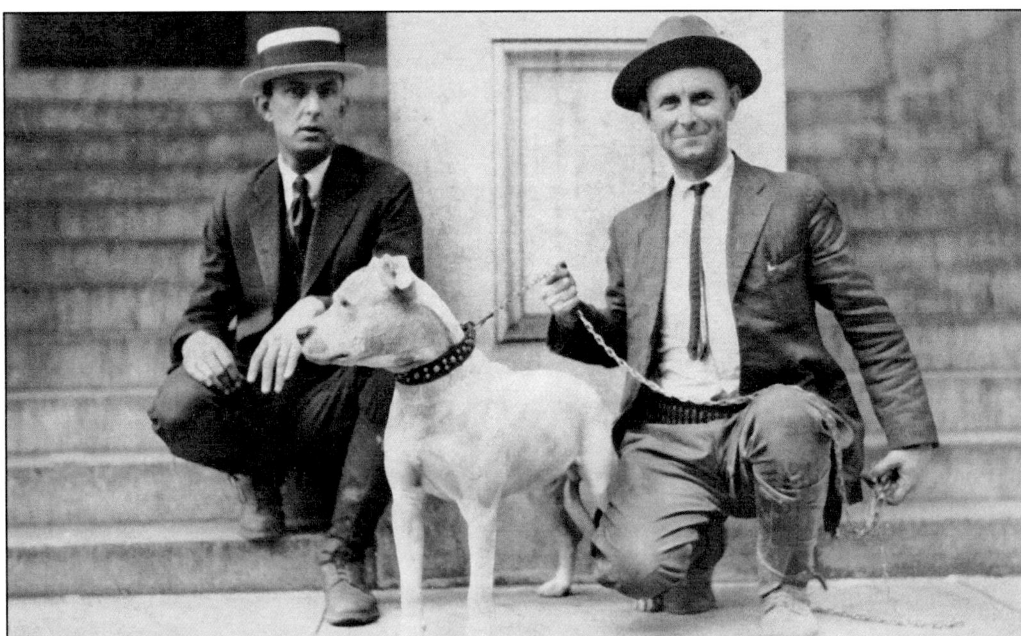

By 1915, Chase City had serious problems with robberies, drunkenness, and unlicensed dogs. On January 11, 1915, Walter Willis became the town's first night police officer. Having already served for eight years as a special events officer, he was well qualified. His first order was to shoot all unlicensed dogs. On April 3, 1916, he became the town sergeant, but he resigned on June 3, 1918, as most of his time was spent overseeing the town power plant. On March 3, 1919, he became the fire chief. (Charles Willis Jr.)

Just beyond Chase City's town line, Robert Jeffreys and his sons began to organize and develop a large new manufacturing company in 1910. This company, Jeffreys-Spaulding Manufacturing Company, Inc., began manufacturing lumber and box shooks (large wooden crates for shipping vehicles and parts). At one point, they employed more than 200 people. (WCG.)

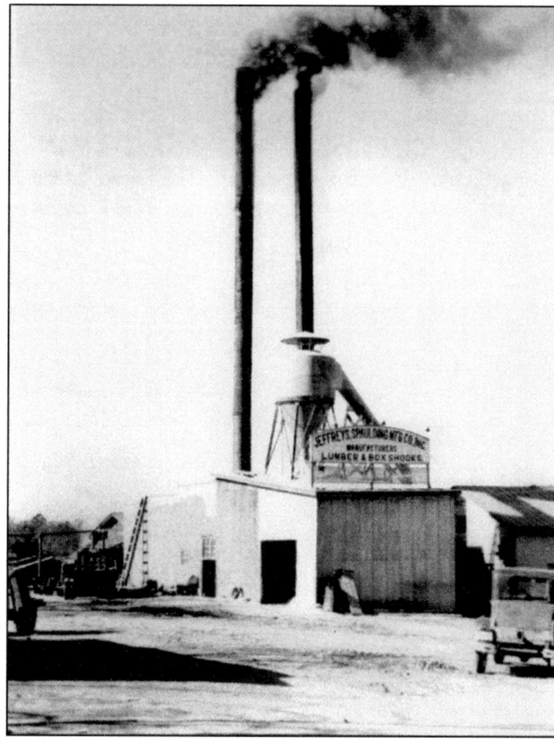

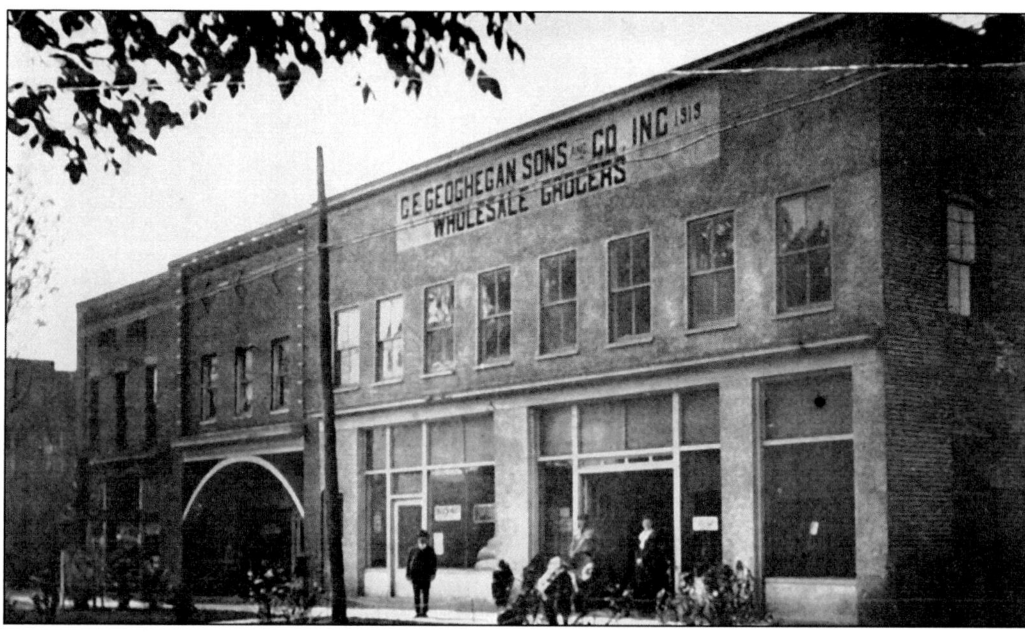

In 1919, North Main Street began to be developed near Fifth Street, primarily by C. E. Geoghegan. In 1919, C. E. Geoghegan and Sons Company began a wholesale grocery business. Formerly having sold coal, oil, and fuel, this was the company's first business on Main Street. In 1921, Geoghegan built the Cozy Theatre, which connected the wholesale store to Chase City Drug Store, founded in 1891. In 1924, the section of the drugstore next to the Cozy Theatre became Ellett Furniture store. (SVHP.)

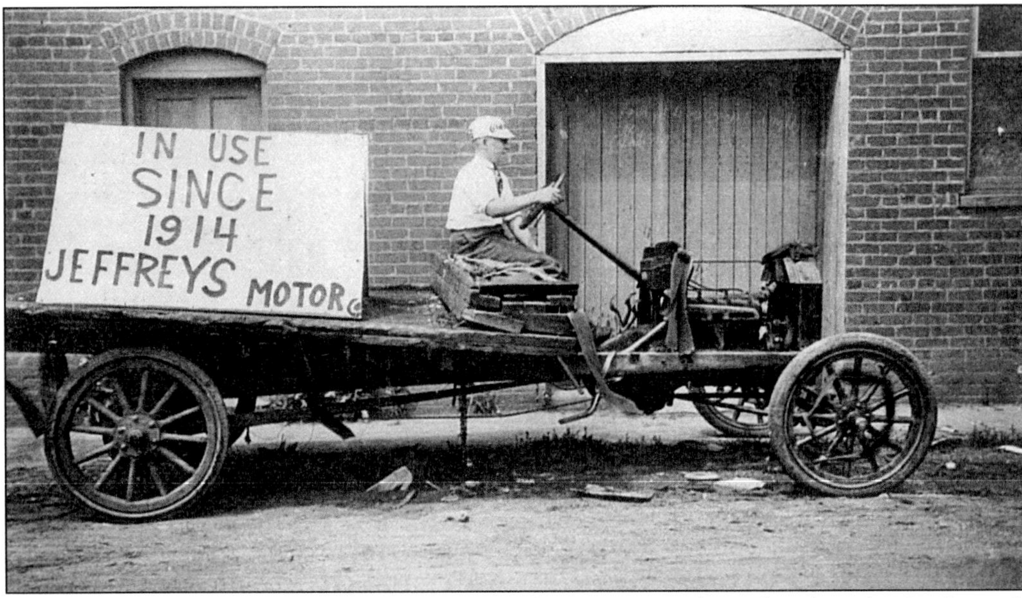

In 1914, Jeffreys Motor Company opened on Fifth Street near the railroad tracks. In the early 1920s, Robert and Willie Jeffreys moved to a building adjoining the Chase City Electric Auto Light Company, a Willys Light dealership. In 1922, Jeffreys hired Fred Ward in sales. The Auto Light Company was purchased after the Depression by a South Hill auto dealer and renamed Chase City Motor Company. This is one of the first trucks Jeffreys Motor sold, and they were still parading it in the 1940s. (WCG.)

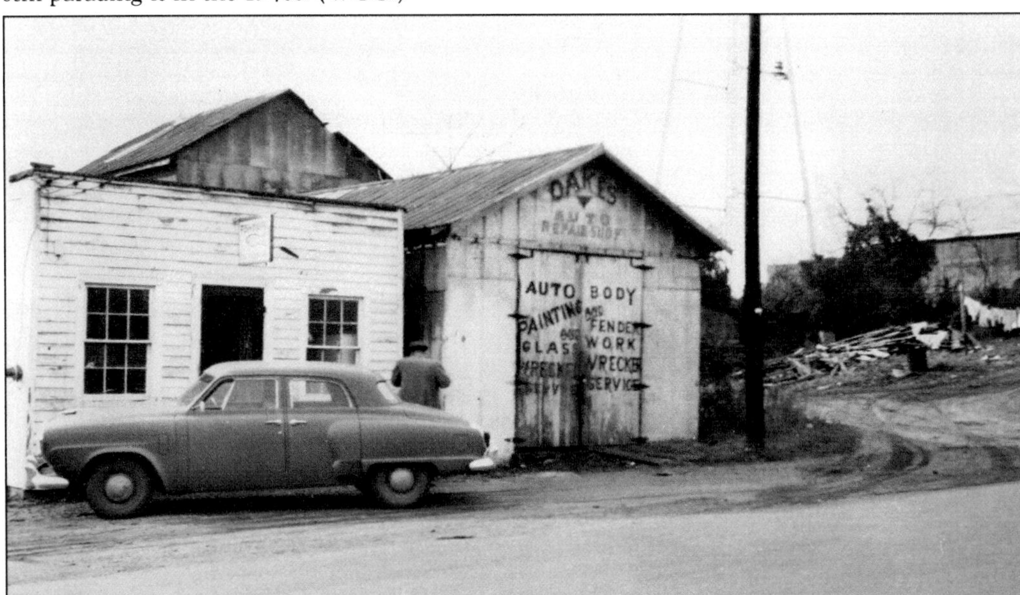

On Boyd Street between Third and Fourth Streets was one of the first private garages in town. The R. C. Oakes garage offered body, welding, and interior work in the 1930s. By the 1940s, Oakes offered a glass shop, and in 1946, a 24-hour wrecker service was added. Next door was the Boyd Street fresh meat market, open from around 1915 to 1929. These two buildings became the additional offices for Southside Supply Company around 1950. (LLE.)

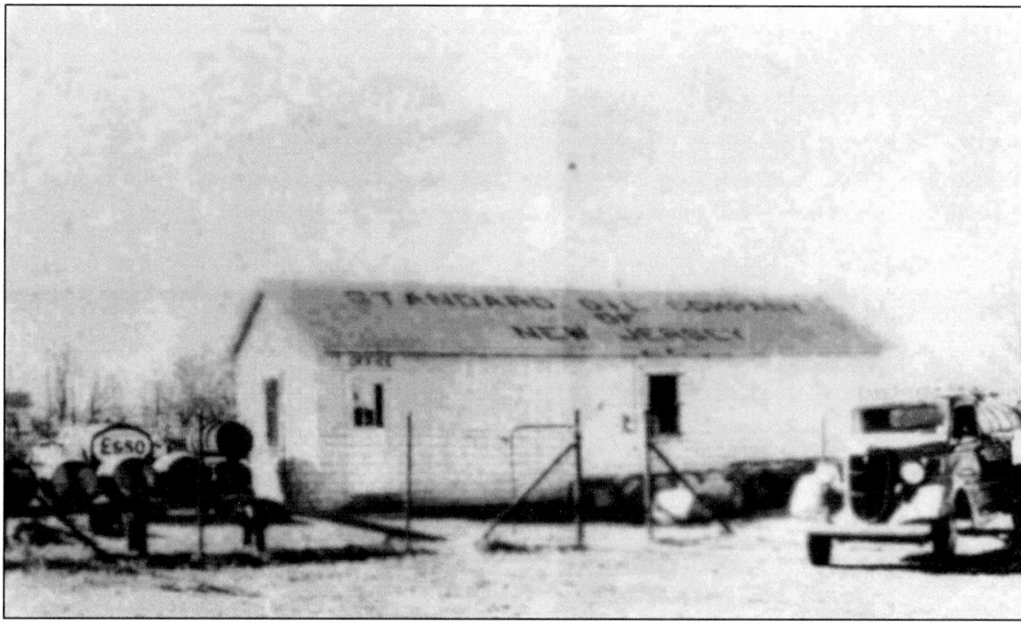

On June 11, 1911, Standard Oil of New Jersey was granted a permit to install oil and gasoline storage tanks on the Sudley lot at the northwest corner of Fourth and Washington Streets and to run a pipeline from the railroad to the building. They also built a small office next door. (NP/SA.)

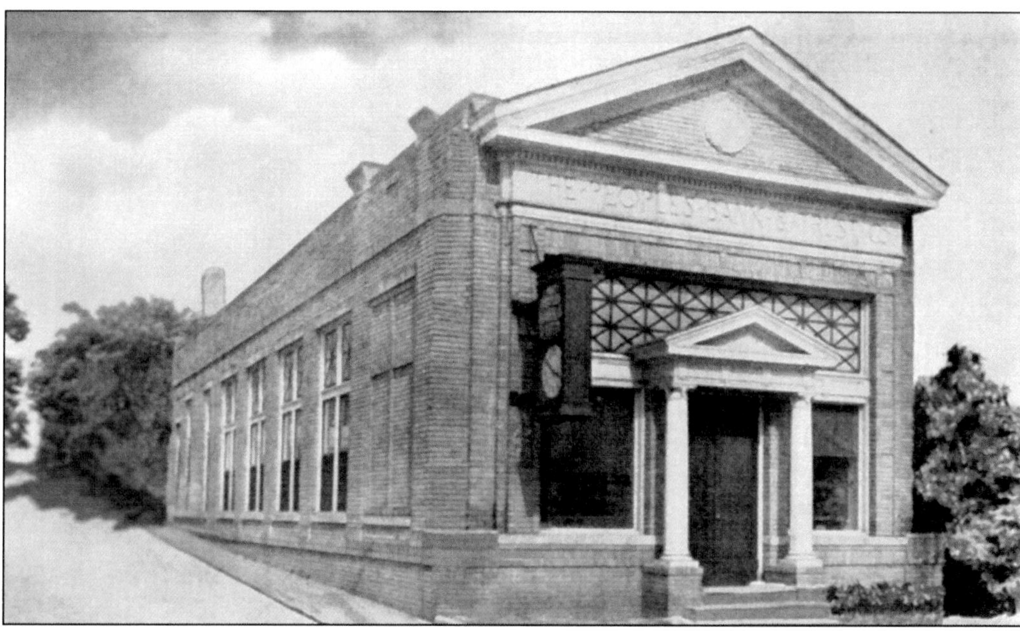

In 1915, Chase City's third bank began operation. The Peoples Bank and Trust Company was operated by Charles M. Boswell of Albemarle. He was assisted by Hugh and Tom Goode, who he brought in from another bank. This was the only bank in town to survive the Depression. Later it sold to Fidelity National, and the bank building is now town hall. (LLE.)

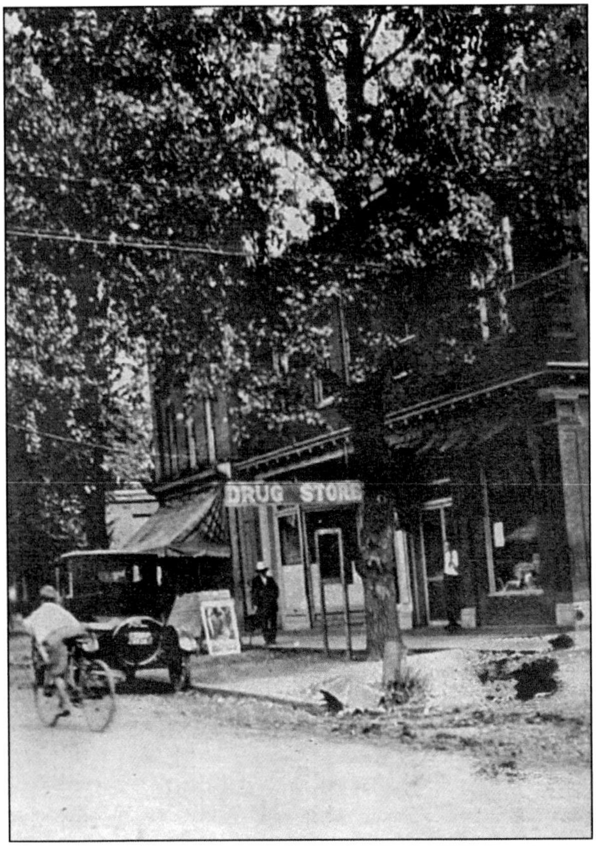

This 1920s photograph of the old town hall shows Dr. H. L. Burwell's Mecklenburg Drug Store with the post office still next door. The new building with the awnings, Modern Beauty Shop, later became Pauline's women's shop and fashion store. Bicycles and roller skates were new and very popular to people in town. Shortly after this photograph was taken, Dr. Burwell became seriously ill. In 1927, he and his wife moved to Roanoke, and he died in 1929. (WCG.)

Next door to the Chase City Department store was Chase City's fourth drugstore. The store was operated by P. H. Maddox from 1915 until 1945, when he suffered an untimely death. A year later, the store and contents were purchased by Hilda Lewter Love, and she moved her drugstore operation to the new location but continued the operation of the old store, which was being managed by a family member. (JG.)

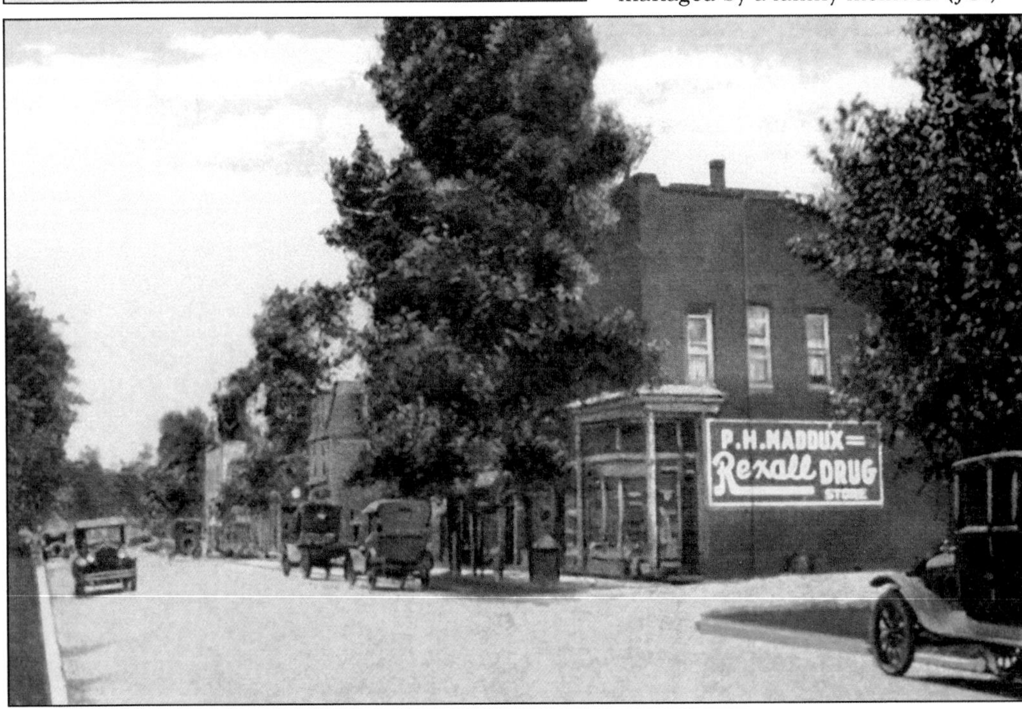

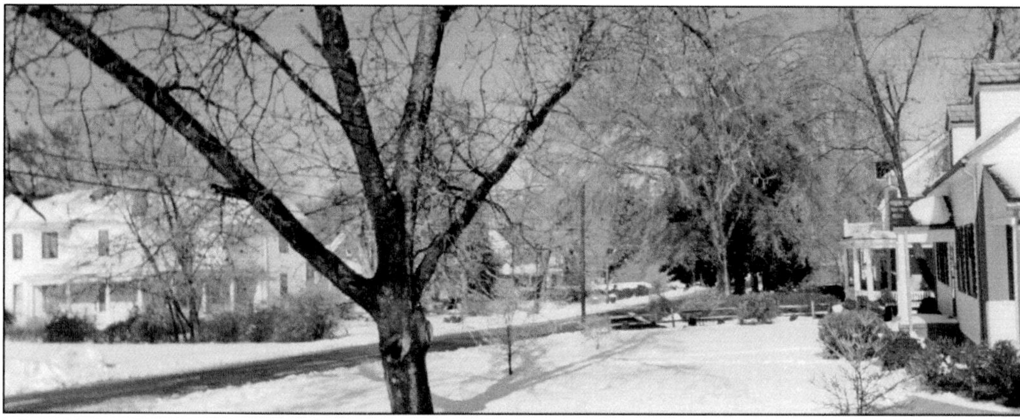

The Chase City Hospital (left) on Boyd Street was begun in June 1921 by Dr. Adam Finch. Dr. Finch's personal residence was next door. The small hospital served the community by delivering babies and performing surgery until Dr. Finch died on February 22, 1933. The hospital was converted to an apartment building and in the 1960s served as the Chase City Private School for two years during construction of the new school building. (CDS.)

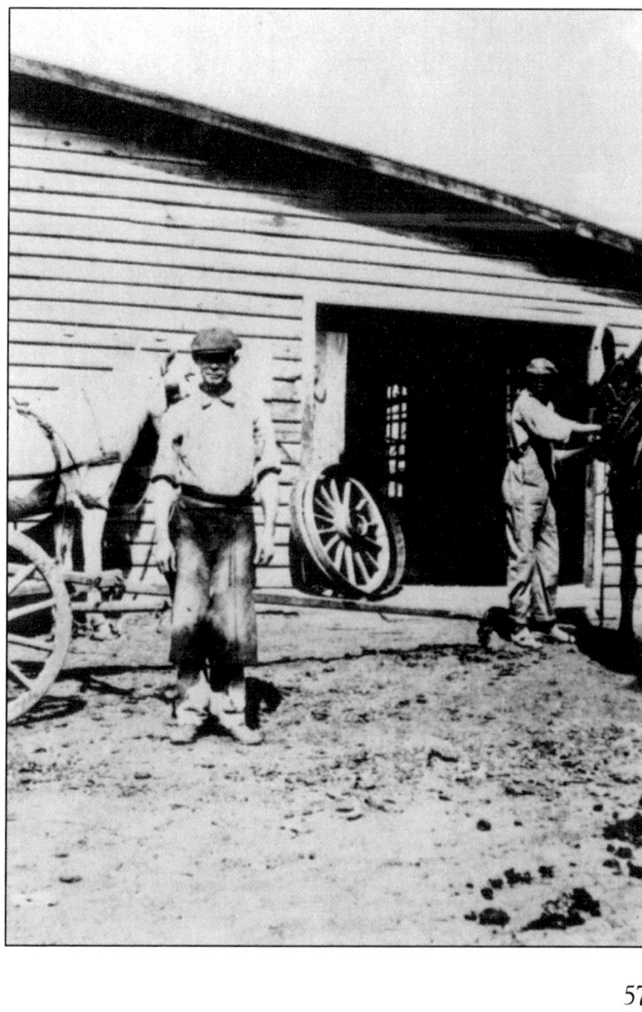

The Willis family was a dominant service-providing group in early Chase City, with Willis and Willis Livery and Blacksmith at Third and Boyd Streets, Willie and Willis Livery and Blacksmith shop on Second Street near Main Street, and J. B. Willis Blacksmith on North Main Street. They provided wagon repairs, tack repairs, and many other services to the town and its people. Here is William (Willie) Willis (January 8, 1887–November 24, 1953) at the blacksmith shop on Boyd Street after closing his shop on Second Street around 1940. (Jane Willis Morris.)

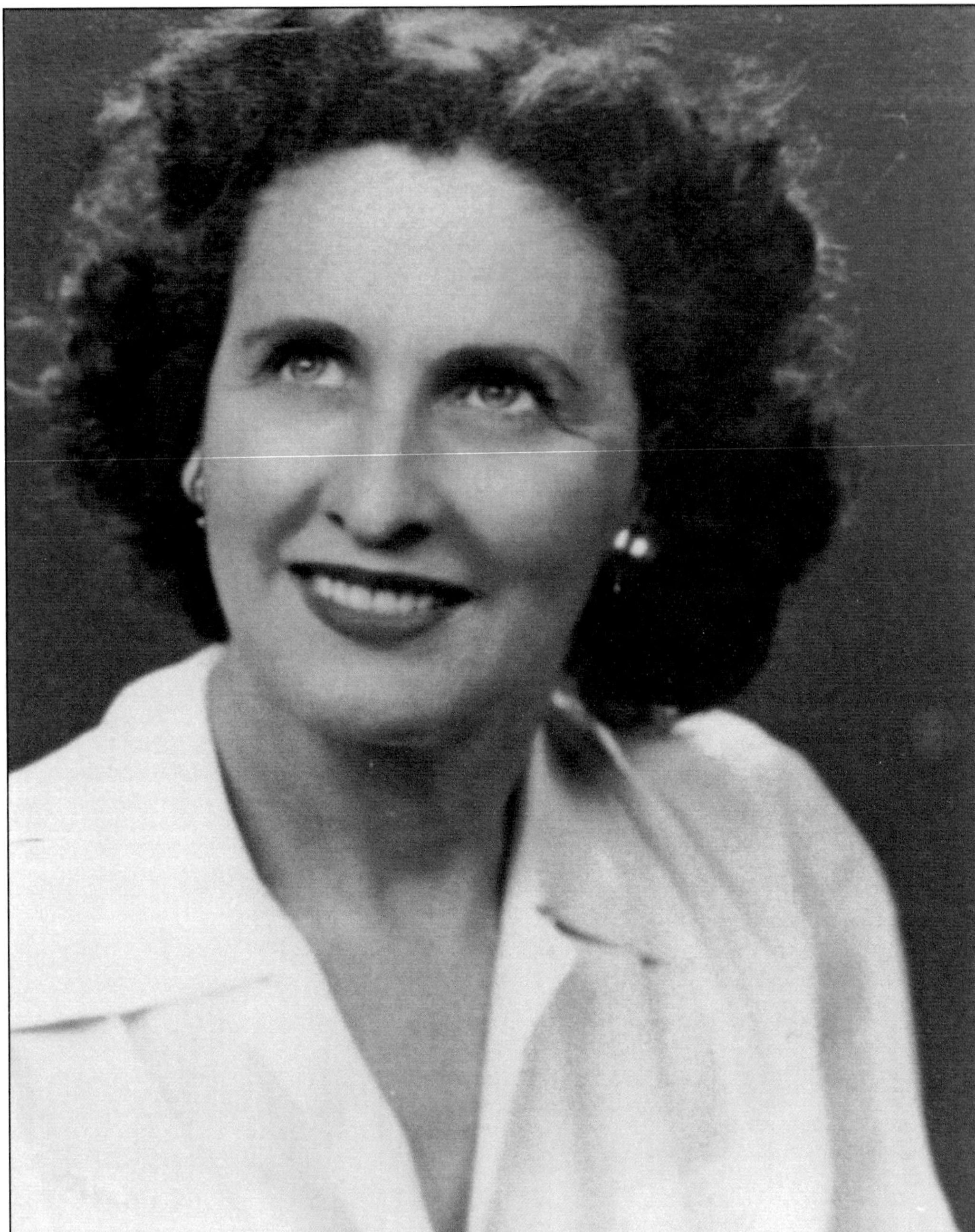

Another first for Chase City was Hilda Saunders Lewter, the daughter of William H. and Eunice Saunders of Blackstone. William sold the Saunders Drug Store and moved to Chase City. A trained accountant, he soon became justice of the peace in Chase City. William and Eunice had five children: Harold, Hilda, Mary, Della, and Ben. Hilda chose to go to the Medical College of Virginia's School of Pharmacy. In 1920, she was the first woman to graduate from the school. Returning to Chase City, she worked with her great-aunt until 1931, when she purchased her own business. Her husband, James Lewter Sr., was also a registered pharmacist. He went to work for Dr. Burwell but died in 1927. (James Lewter Jr.)

Three

THE GOLD
BRIGHT LEAF TOBACCO AND SURVIVING THE DEPRESSION

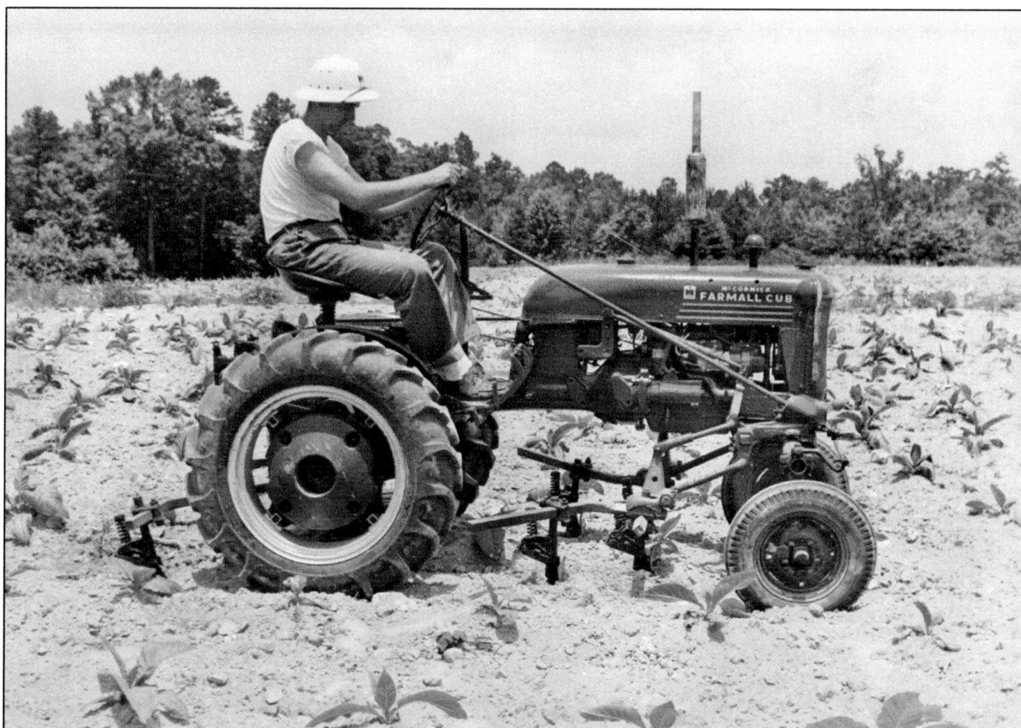

In the late 1940s, the Cub Cadet tractor revolutionized tobacco farming from an intensive, hands-on labor to a more mechanized operation that many farmers could afford. The tractor could do the work a lot faster, neater, and without the aggravation or concern over the endurance of the animal or farmer. From 1935 through 2005, the U.S. government controlled acreage (later poundage) of tobacco that a farmer could grow. This system carried a guaranteed government price support system, so farmers knew what to expect at market. It wasn't always this clear. The earliest cash crop in Virginia was dark and burley tobacco. In the 1880s, bright leaf tobacco took over. Many small farmers worked parcels ranging from 3 to 30 acres for a percentage of the gross sales. Sharecropping laws enabled many to produce an income without a capital outlay. By 1890, Chase City had four tobacco warehouses, and a fifth was begun in the late 1920s. (Robert Tucker.)

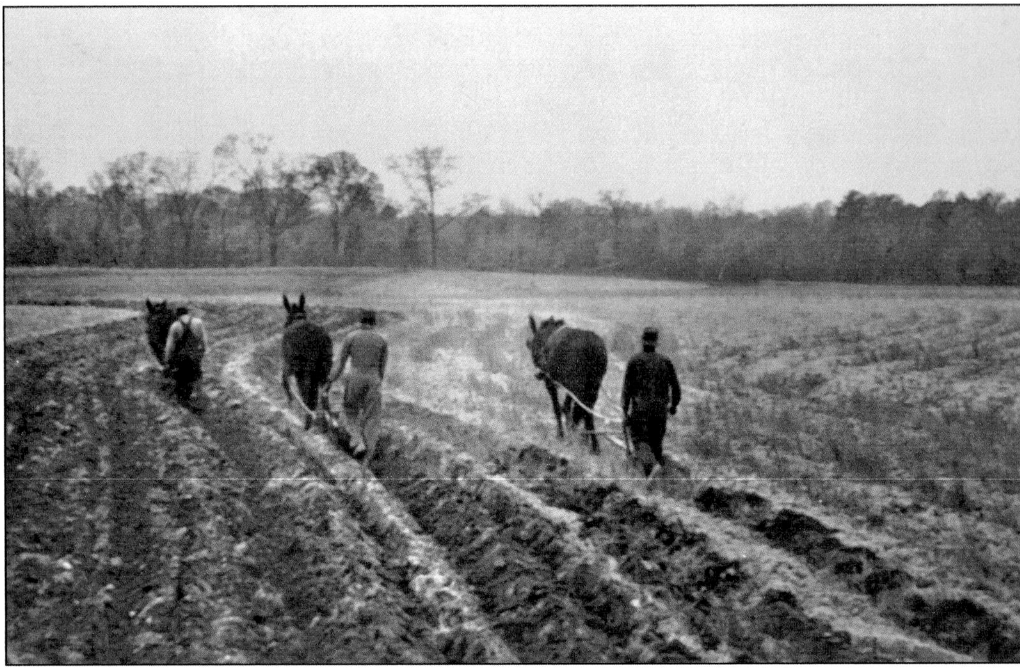

Fields had to be plowed, cultivated, and furrowed, developing mounded, straight rows for planting. Tobacco was grown in essentially this fashion since 1635 and has been the staple cash export crop since. The Southside region is the largest tobacco growing area in Virginia. (EM.)

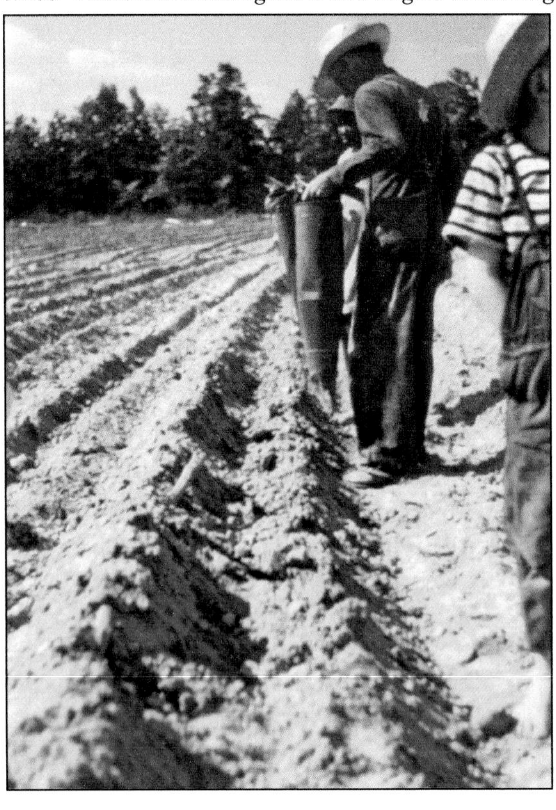

The planting took place by burrowing a hole in the top of the mound with a peg. The tobacco was planted in the hole with a little water. Around 1920, an effective hand planter was invented. With a canister that holds sufficient water for 10 to 14 plants, it was simple to insert the end of the canister into the mound, drop a plant down one side, squeeze the handle, and the plant with water would be in the hole. This saved many backbreaking bends and was faster. (EM.)

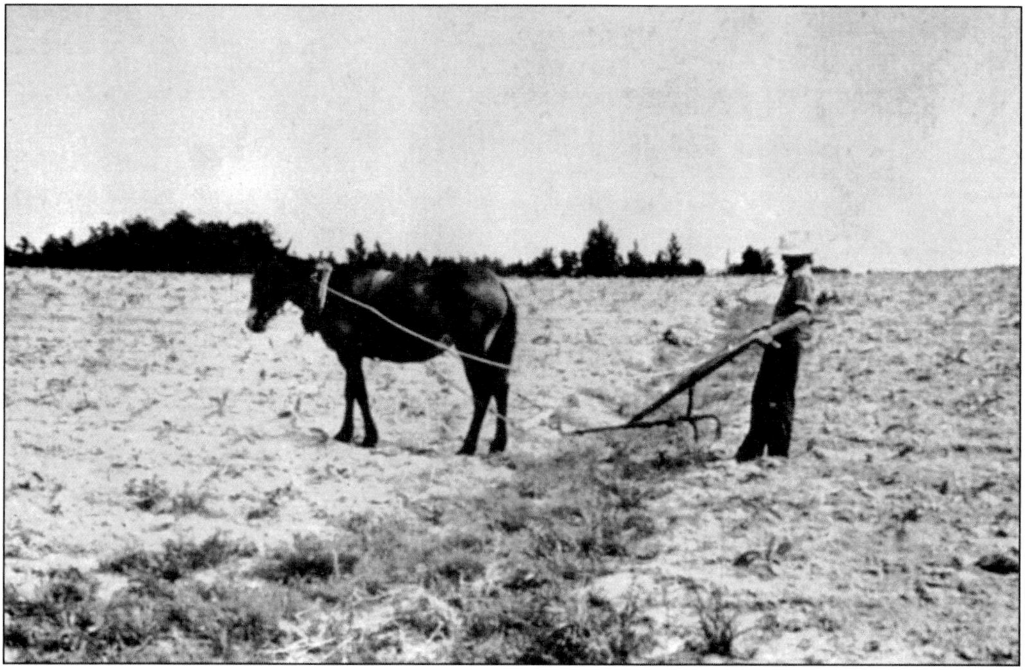

The farmer had to cultivate several times to prevent weeds and grasses from robbing nutrients from the tobacco plants. If necessary, the farmer may also have to water the plants. Cultivating helped to aerate the soil to hold the maximum amount of rainwater. Planting usually starts in May, after the threat of frost is over. The plants are begun in special covered hothouse-style plant beds in March. When the fields are ready, the plants are transferred to the newly formed rows. (EM.)

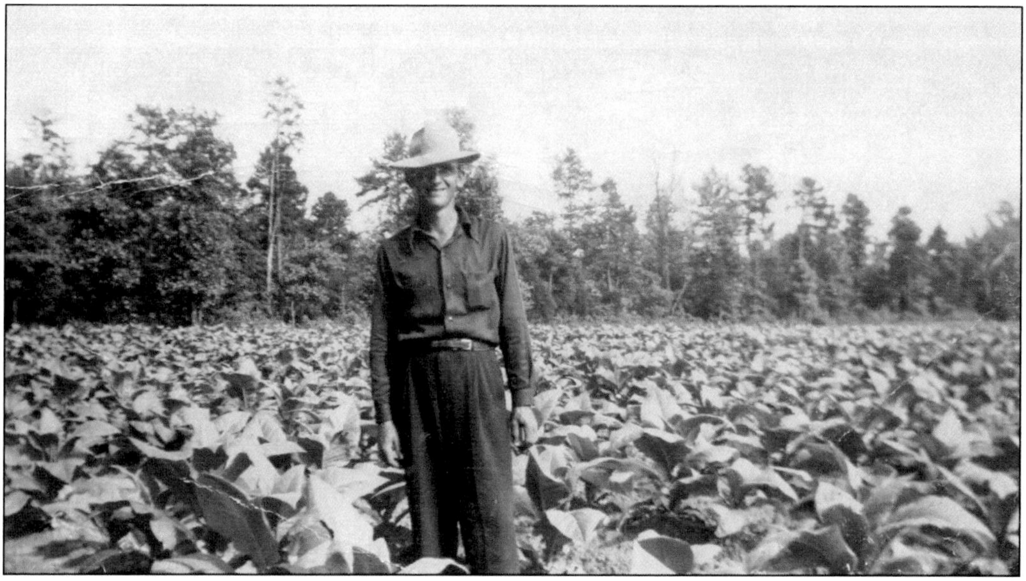

A sharecropper from the mountains of North Carolina, Arthur Fay McKinney, inspects his month-old tobacco fields. There must be constant vigilance, guarding the plants from pests and diseases. A good stand of tobacco reaches five feet, and once the plant blooms, the top is broken out, leaving 18 or 19 leaves on each plant. Once the top is removed, the wound is sprayed with oil to help it heal and to prevent sucker growth. (Betty McKinney Caknipe.)

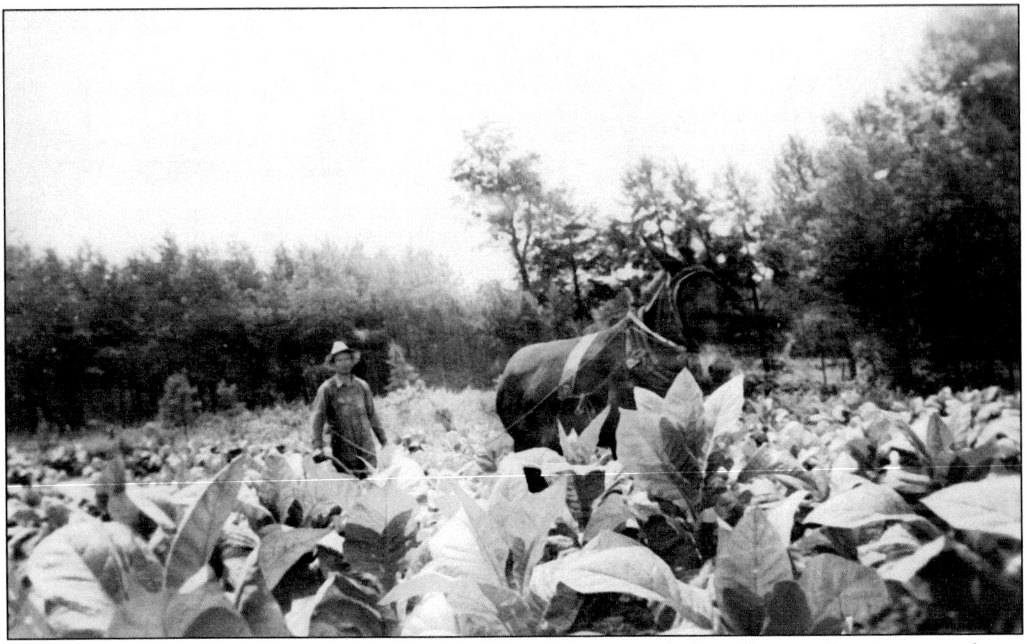

Cultivation is important throughout the growing stages, until the tobacco plants are too large for mule and plow to pass through without injuring the leaves. Once topped, the farmer must inspect the plants for sucker growth. A sucker, or new plant, may emerge between a leaf and the stalk to start a second growth. The suckers must be removed to maximize leaf growth and quality. (EM.)

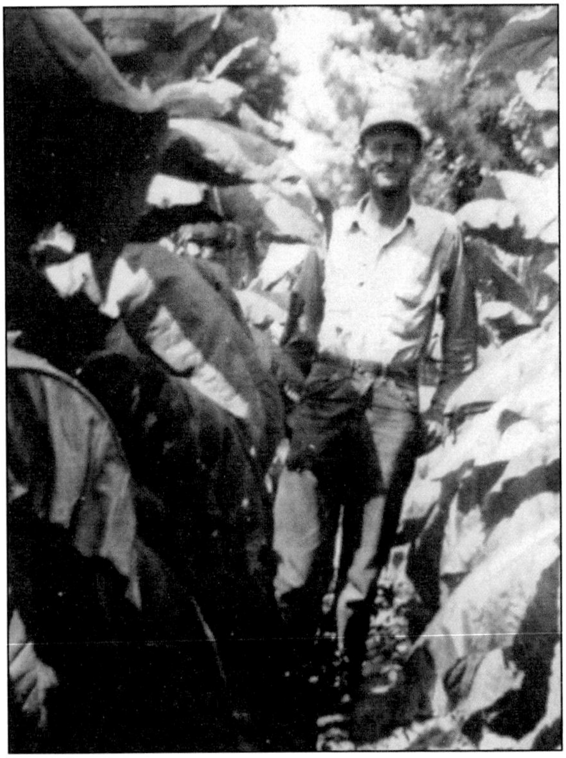

It is an extremely good year when the tobacco plants reach more than six feet. This provides for large, heavy leaves that can exceed 30 inches in length. Properly processed, they will bring a premium price at market. Here Fred Carnes, a North Carolina sharecropper, stands in his exceptional tobacco field. His expression tells how pleased he is. (Fred Carnes.)

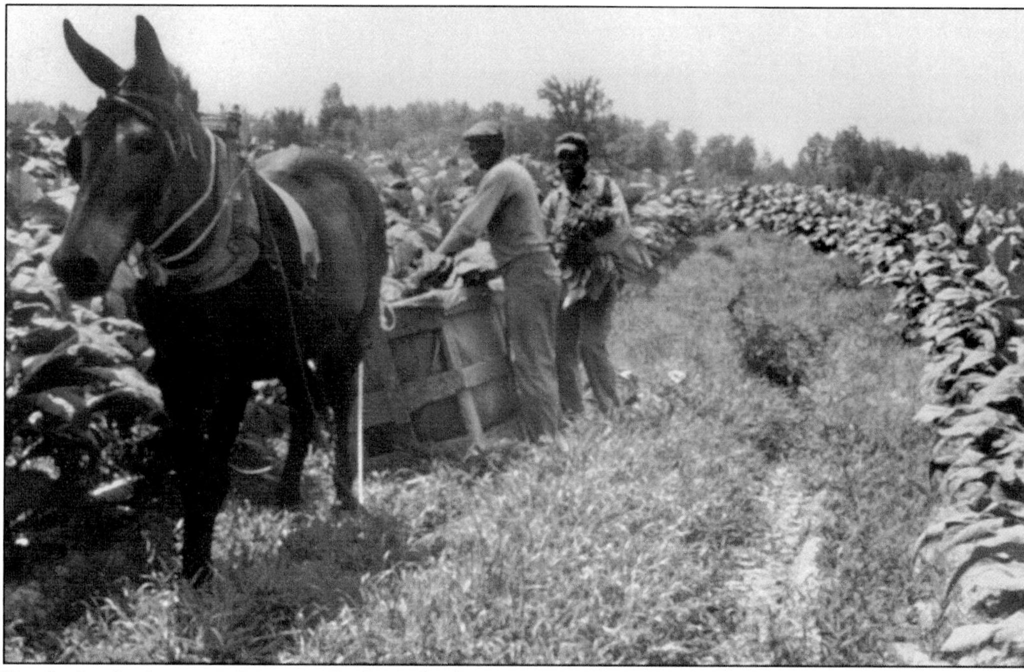

Bright leaf tobacco is harvested when the leaves ripen to a near yellow color. The puller starts at the bottom of the plant, taking three leaves with each harvest, and this process usually begins in late August. The pulled leaves are placed in a slide, pulled to the barn, and placed on a table. With Chase City's history as part of the "Virginia Black Belt"—45 percent of the population being black—farming, especially sharecropping, seems to have bridged some of the racial gap. (EM.)

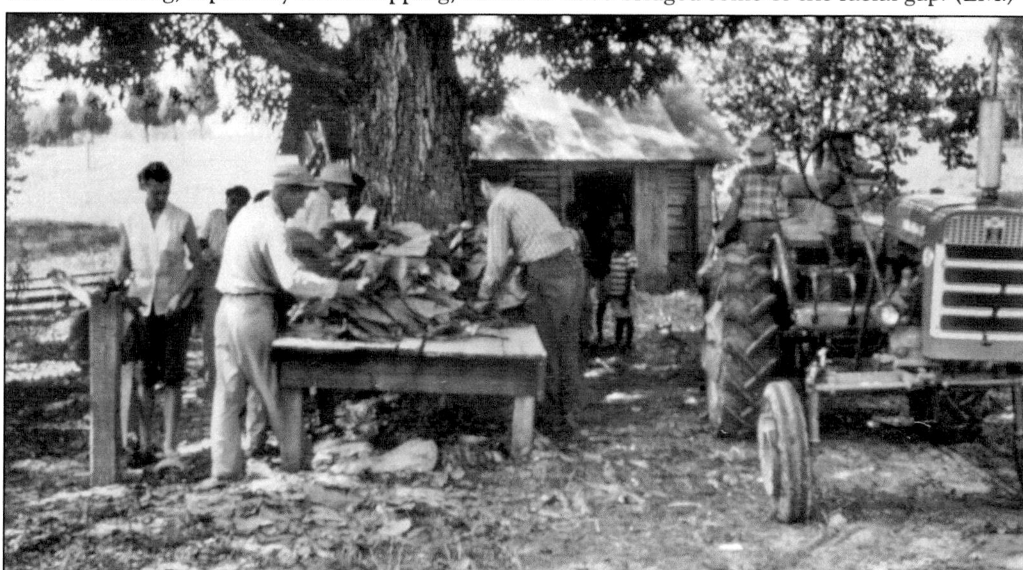

Once on the table in the barn area, a hander takes an average of three leaves and evens the stems into a bundle, then hands them to a stringer. The stringer wraps the bundle by the top to a stick, alternating sides until there are 26 to 30 bundles on each stick. The sticks are hoisted into the barns and hung from drying poles. A fire is built and the tobacco is flue-cured by heat for three to six days to a golden yellow. (EM.)

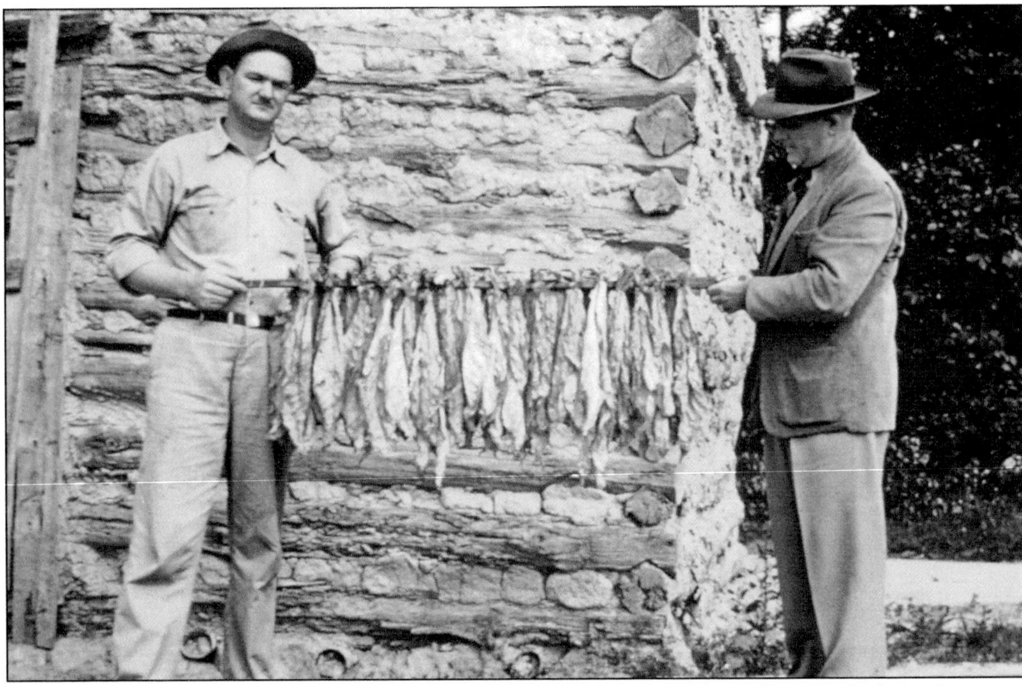

The flue-cured tobacco is taken from the barn to an ordering room, usually a dug hole under a strip room. Once the tobacco is supple and doesn't pulverize, it is ready for the next step. Flue-cured tobacco is the staple tobacco for the primary filler in cigarettes. Here Richard Ferrell (left) and "Andy" Oscar Dodd Ferrell are standing in front of their "yellow gold." (Norman Ferrell family.)

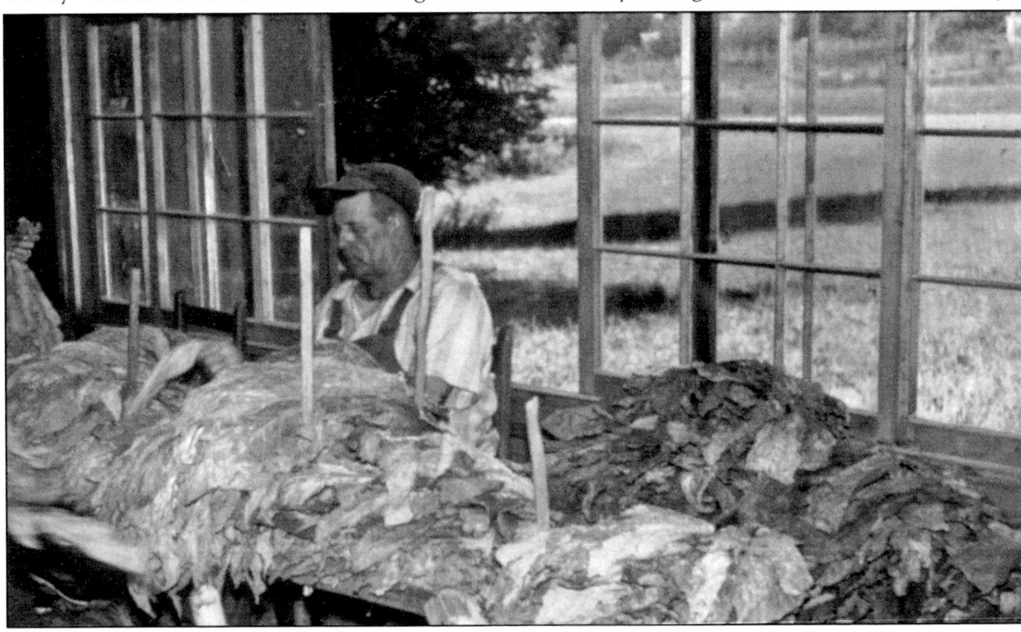

Once it is "in order" (moist enough), the tobacco is removed from the sticks and laid out on a table. A grader sorts through, leaf by leaf, for color and clarity and arranges the tobacco into areas for bundling. The grades range from premium yellow to dark brown and green. The brighter the yellow, the better the price, and the darker the color, the lower the price. (EM.)

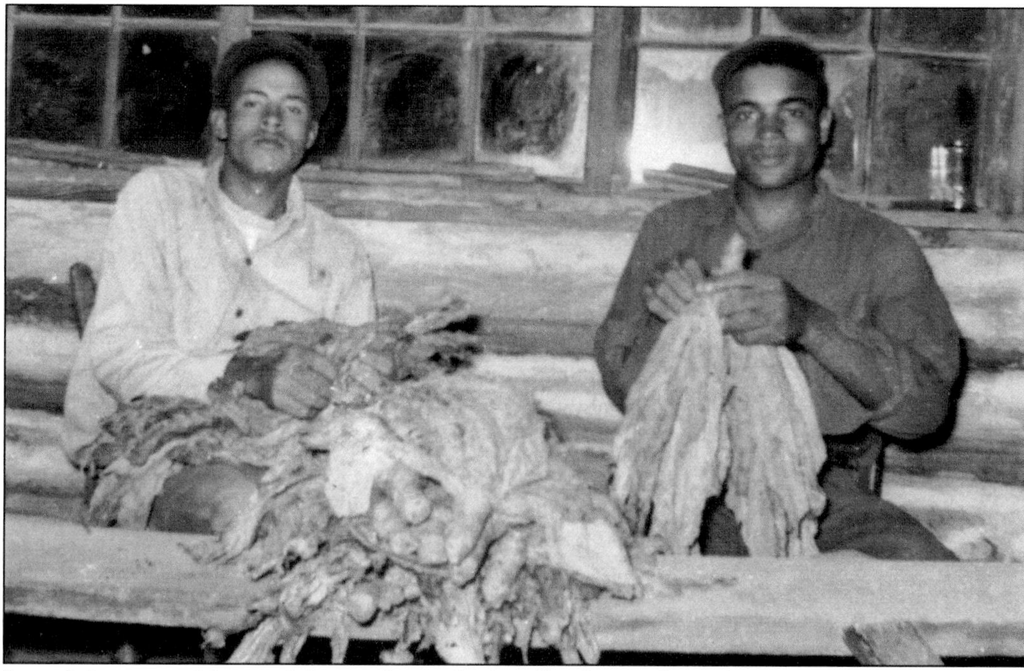

Leon Johnson and Junius Johnson Jr. tie the bundles for market. The bundles are a quarter-size handful of tobacco wrapped about the top with a folded leaf of the same grade. The remaining stem from the folded leaf is pushed through the bundle under the wrap to secure it. The bundles are arranged evenly on a tobacco basket in layers. When the basket is stacked two to three feet high, it is ready to be loaded and taken to market. (KW.)

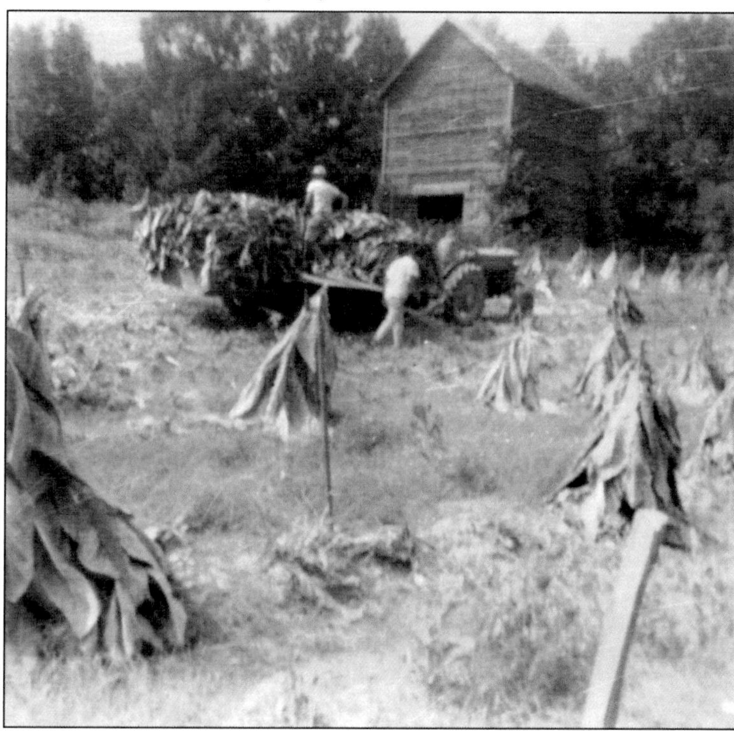

Burley tobacco, the first tobacco grown in Virginia, is dark and is used in cigarettes as it burns more evenly and faster. Dark tobaccos are allowed to grow until near the end of season (late September to early October). They are air-dried rather than flue-cured and are used in the making of chewing tobacco and cigars. There were 50 plantations within six miles surrounding Chase City, which was reported to be the wealthiest area in Virginia in 1850 because of the dark-tobacco boom. (HL.)

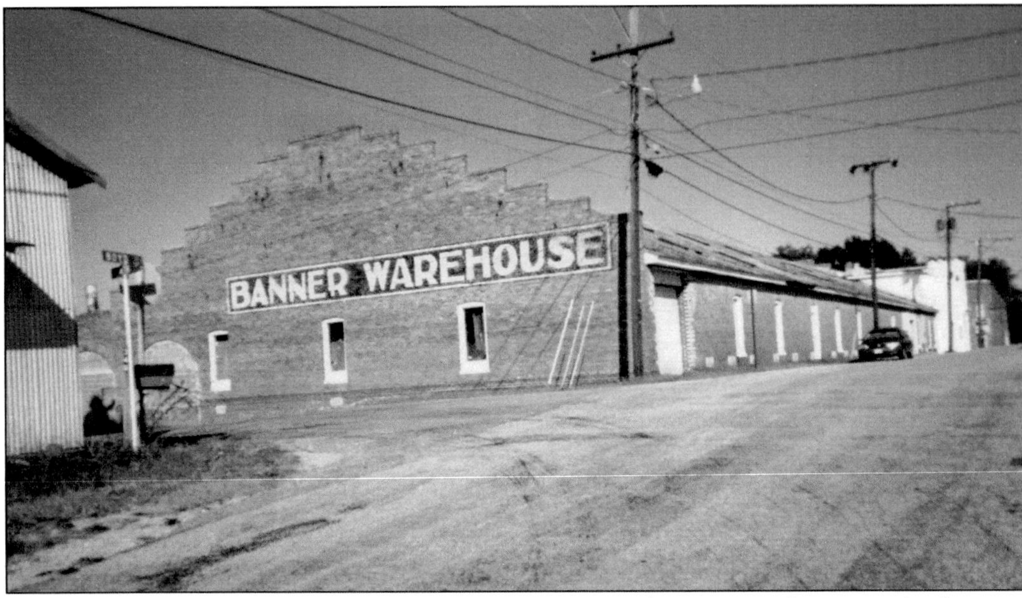

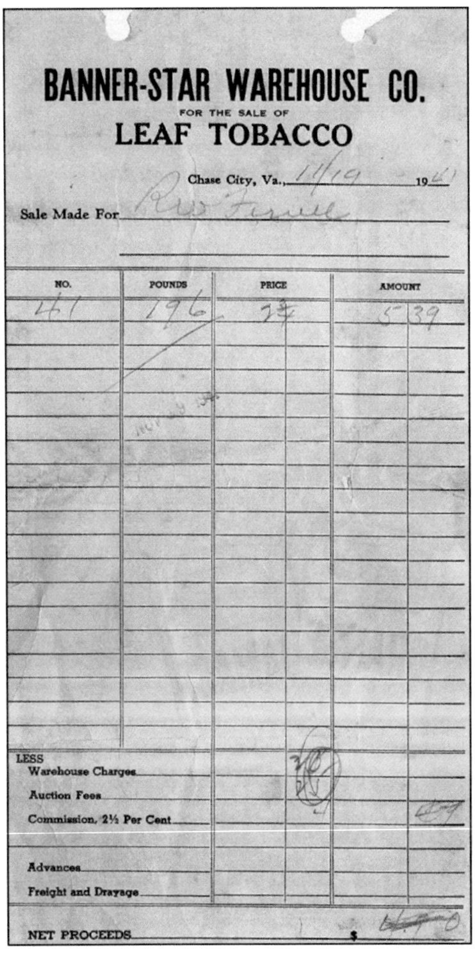
BANNER-STAR WAREHOUSE CO.
FOR THE SALE OF
LEAF TOBACCO

Chase City, Va., 11/19 1941

Sale Made For R W Ferrell

NO.	POUNDS	PRICE	AMOUNT
41	196	2¾	5 39

LESS
Warehouse Charges
Auction Fees
Commission, 2½ Per Cent
Advances
Freight and Drayage
NET PROCEEDS $

Banner Warehouse opened in 1888, the first brick warehouse "with the best and most lighting" and the largest scales near the depot. Originally owned and operated by C. B. Elam, W. H. Smith, and H. E. Edmonds, it was the most popular warehouse, drawing farmers from 30 to 40 miles away. In the off-season, it served as a roller rink and an activities house. In 1941, when the Star warehouse became a parachute factory, the two merged. (JC.)

This sales ticket from November 19, 1941, shows the merged warehouse name. This ticket shows the sale of R. W. Ferrell's crop as spot No. 41—196 pounds of tobacco at 2.75¢ per pound (a very bad price for very poor tobacco). As this was done on November 19, it was probably the final sale of leftovers by Ferrell. In this era, average prices were around 40¢ per pound. (Norman Ferrell family.)

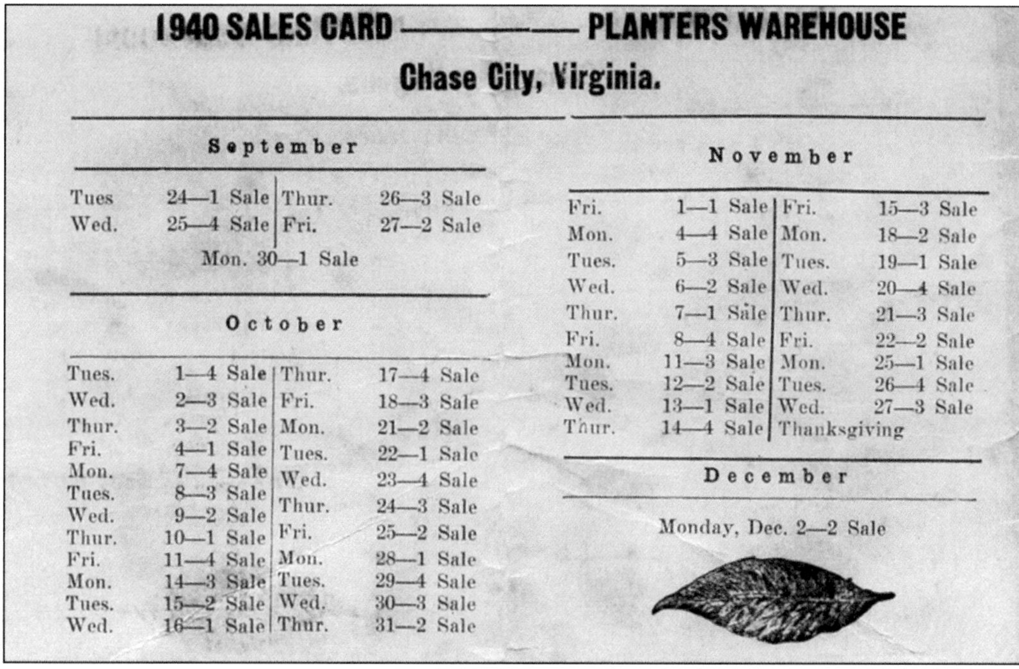

1940 SALES CARD ——————— PLANTERS WAREHOUSE

Chase City, Virginia.

September

Tues	24—1 Sale	Thur.	26—3 Sale
Wed.	25—4 Sale	Fri.	27—2 Sale

Mon. 30—1 Sale

October

Tues.	1—4 Sale	Thur.	17—4 Sale
Wed.	2—3 Sale	Fri.	18—3 Sale
Thur.	3—2 Sale	Mon.	21—2 Sale
Fri.	4—1 Sale	Tues.	22—1 Sale
Mon.	7—4 Sale	Wed.	23—4 Sale
Tues.	8—3 Sale	Thur.	24—3 Sale
Wed.	9—2 Sale	Fri.	25—2 Sale
Thur.	10—1 Sale	Mon.	28—1 Sale
Fri.	11—4 Sale	Tues.	29—4 Sale
Mon.	14—3 Sale	Wed.	30—3 Sale
Tues.	15—2 Sale	Thur.	31—2 Sale
Wed.	16—1 Sale		

November

Fri.	1—1 Sale	Fri.	15—3 Sale
Mon.	4—4 Sale	Mon.	18—2 Sale
Tues.	5—3 Sale	Tues.	19—1 Sale
Wed.	6—2 Sale	Wed.	20—4 Sale
Thur.	7—1 Sale	Thur.	21—3 Sale
Fri.	8—4 Sale	Fri.	22—2 Sale
Mon.	11—3 Sale	Mon.	25—1 Sale
Tues.	12—2 Sale	Tues.	26—4 Sale
Wed.	13—1 Sale	Wed.	27—3 Sale
Thur.	14—4 Sale	Thanksgiving	

December

Monday, Dec. 2—2 Sale

The first warehouse in Chase City was the Centre Warehouse, but it burned in the tragic fire of 1903. The Planters Warehouse, in front of the Methodist church, opened before 1900 and was much smaller than its competition. This is a sales card from the Planters for 1940. The warehouse was operated by J. G. Adams, E. S. Vassar, and J. I. Woodyard. (Norman Ferrell family.)

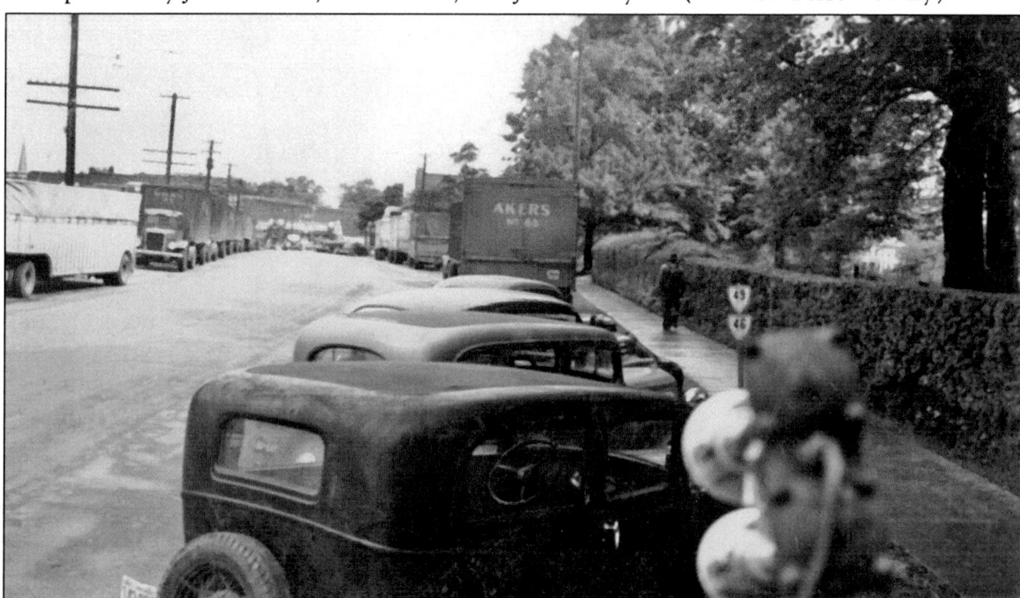

This is what Main Street looked like on tobacco sale day at the Advance Warehouse and the others. This 1939 photograph, taken in front of Shadow Lawn looking north, is of a typical sale day. The farmers would arrive early in the morning, unload their tobacco, have it weighed and placed on a numbered spot, receive an auction ticket, then wait for the results—often coming late that night. (GLG.)

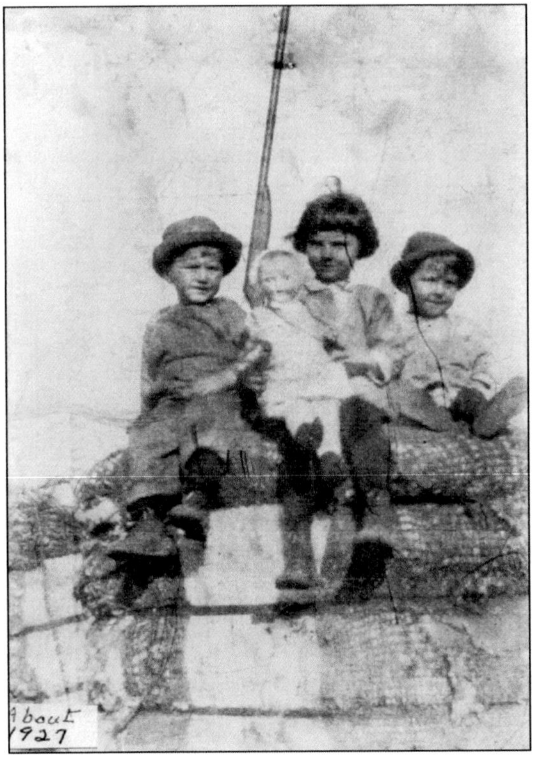

This 1927 photograph of Irene Morgan Brooks (left), W. T. Morgan (center), and Kramer Morgan shows the Morgan cotton harvest for that year. Bales of cotton are ready for the gin. When the cotton is ready to be picked, the pod containing the seed and cotton ball opens and becomes very dry. This dry hull casing is like four knife blades pointed at the picker, and often the pickers have bloodied hands early into the harvest. (IMB.)

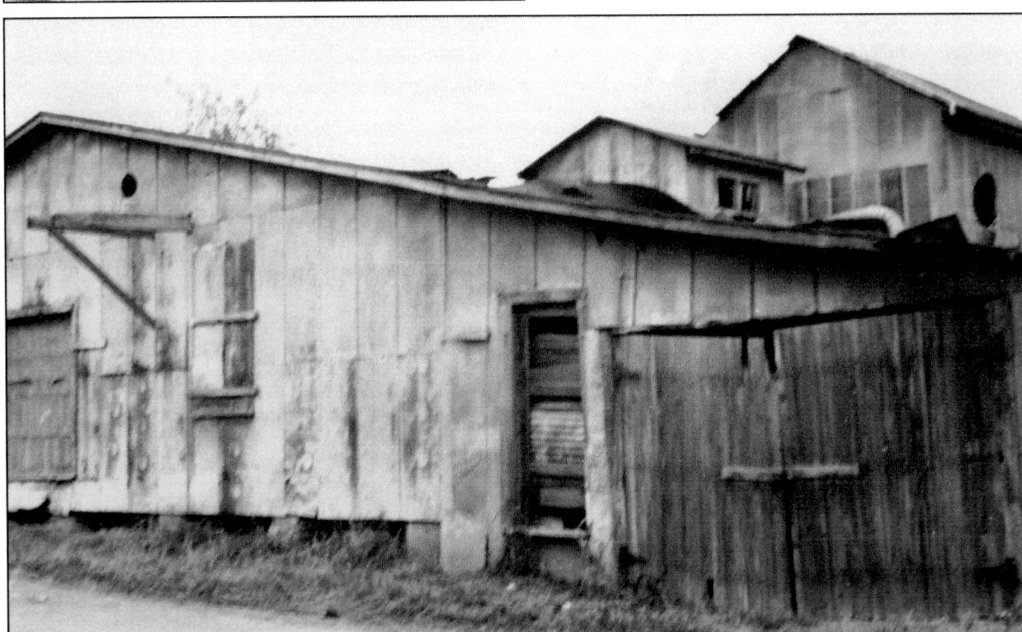

Southside Supply Company operated the only cotton gin in town, which opened in 1912. The gin removes the seed so the cotton can be processed into thread. On February 1, 1924, the company announced a new, state-of-the-art gin. This new gin had the capacity to process 40 bales of cotton per day. It operated at 309 Randolph Street until the troops left for World War II in 1941. Closing the gin closed the chapter on cotton farming in the Chase City area. (LLE.)

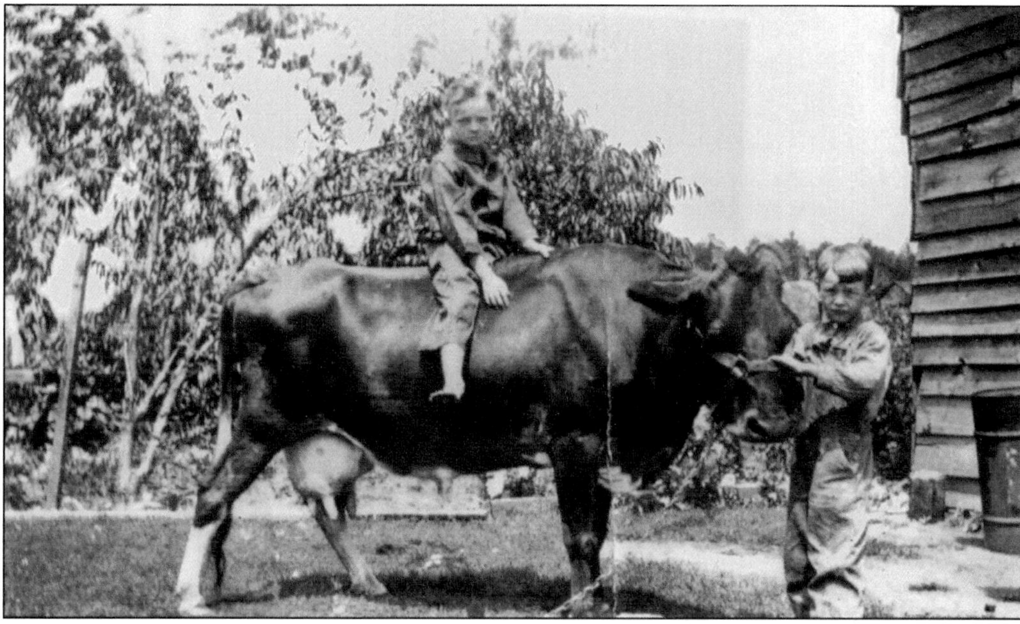

This is a 1926 photograph of Fred Carnes (riding) and his younger brother, Neal, taking the family cow to be milked. Mae Carnes was noted for her excellent butter by several stores in Chase City. She sold all she could produce, with constant orders for more. Dairy farming became big business in Chase City from the late 19th century until the 1970s. With so many federal regulations, many dairies began to close, especially the small ones. (Fred Carnes.)

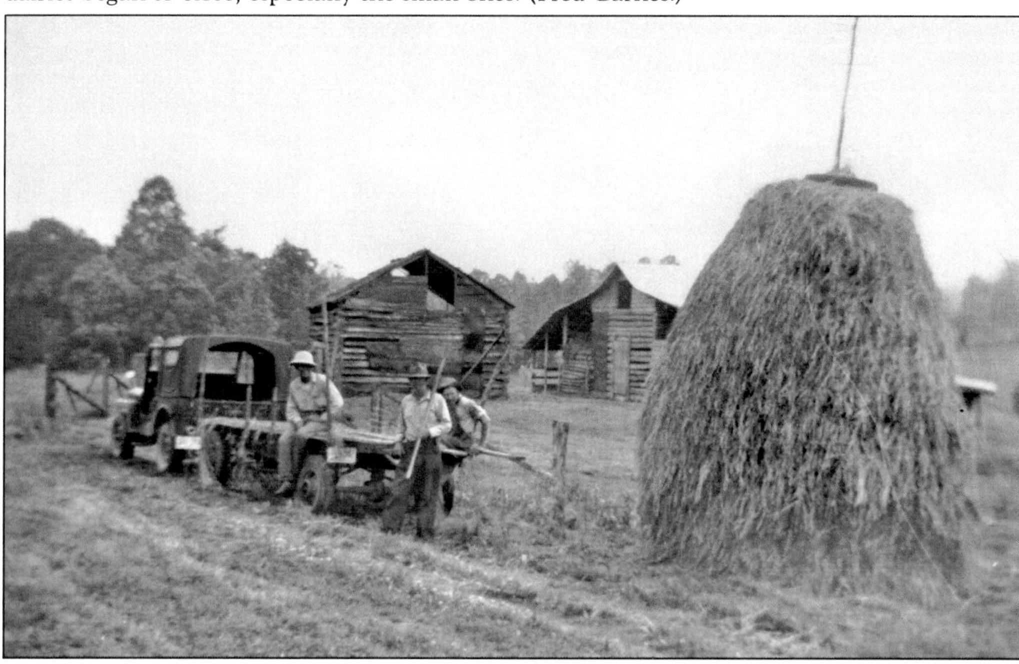

This late-1940s photograph shows an unidentified farmer (left), Buster Brooks (center), and Will Morgan using a jeep and a wagon to gather up their hay. Pitchforks and labor intensity were still the same, but instead of a hay barn, the hay was stacked around a pole with a weight on top (generally an old tire) to hold it in place until time to use it in the winter months. (IMB.)

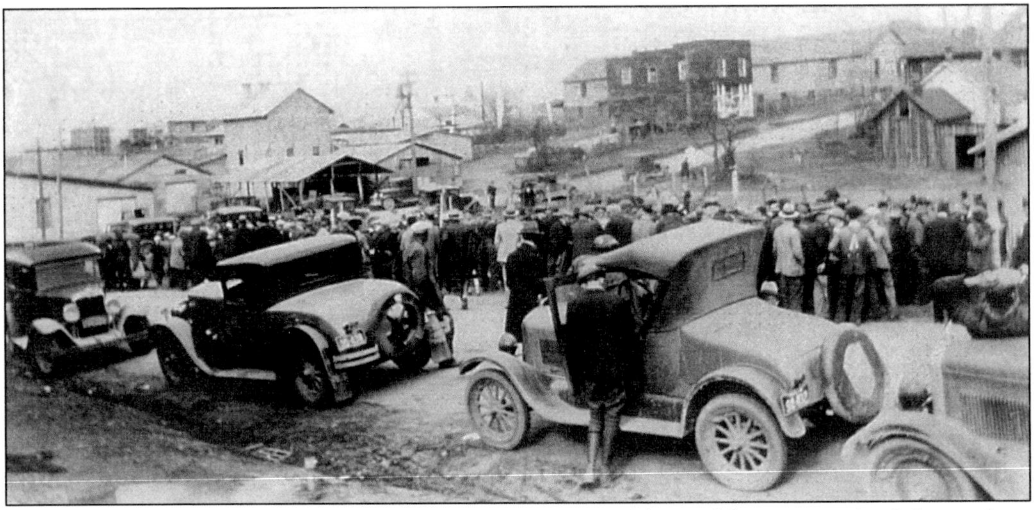

G. L. Garnett's sales and stables and Waverly Owens's stables and livery were both located on Boyd Street between Third and Fourth Streets. This February 25, 1933, photograph shows that area on auction day. Two to three times per year, local horse traders would travel to Kentucky and Tennessee, purchase mules and horses, and bring them back to Chase City. This would be a full day of sales, trading, and auctioning. (WCG.)

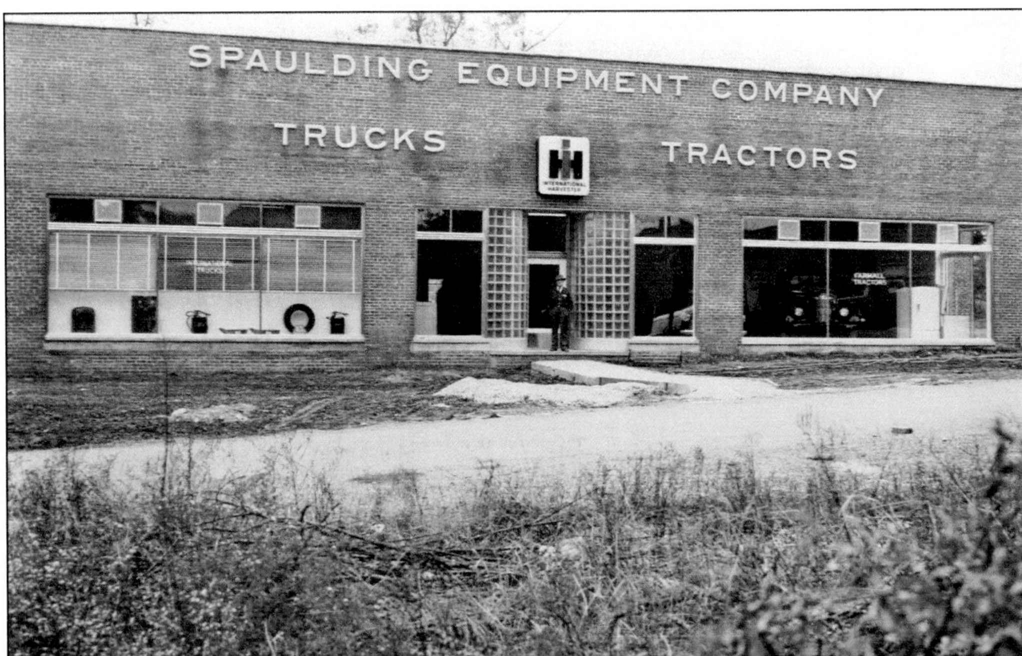

With the closing and sale of the Mecklenburg Mineral Springs Company, Spaulding Equipment Company located on the same property on the new Mecklenburg Street. This began a new era in farming of all types in Chase City. The business opened in 1949 and offered tractors, farming equipment and implements, parts, and service. It grew very rapidly and expanded to a larger parcel of land on the west side of Chase City. (Ann Wagstaff Dembrowski.)

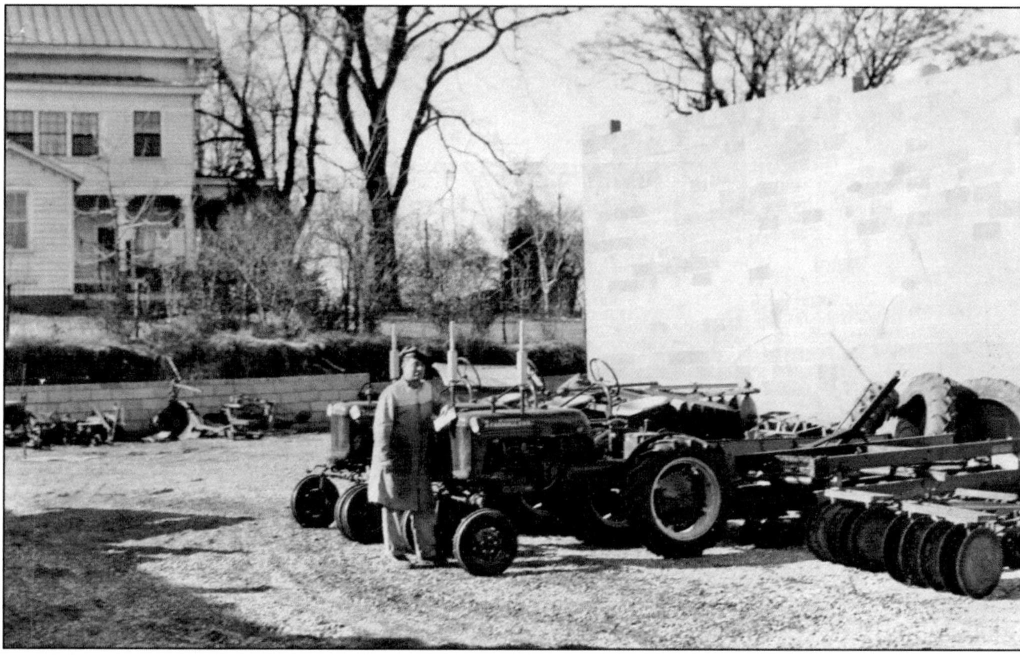

Spaulding Equipment Company extended to abut the backyard of Shadow Lawn. Lee Emory stands in the sales yard with a meager inventory, but soon the yard, street, and all around the business was filled with inventory. The tractors were brought to town and paraded down Main Street to the lot, a spectacular show and another parade. Spaulding became the largest equipment seller in the area and opened a new showroom in nearby South Boston, Virginia. (Robert Tucker.)

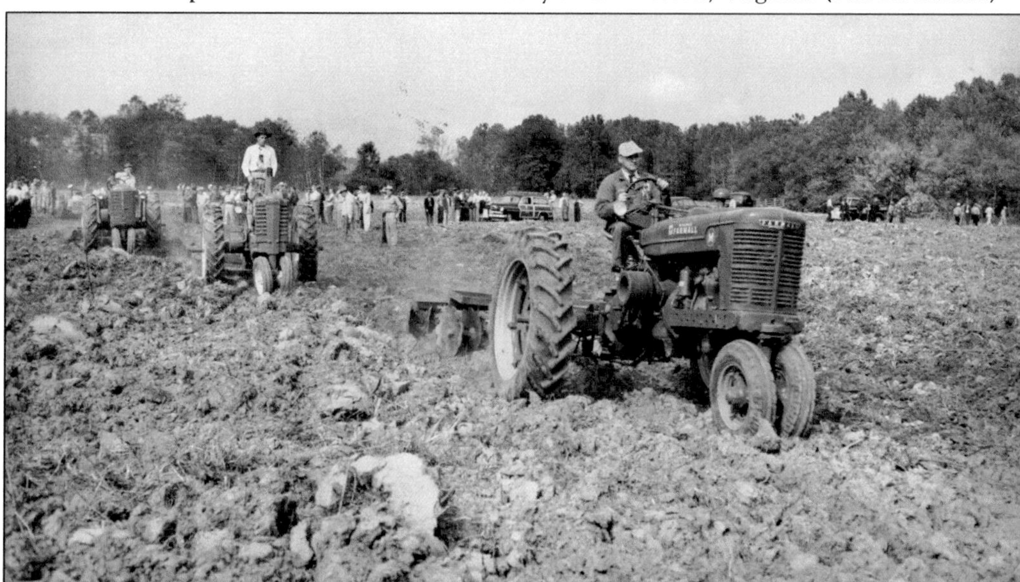

The 1940s closed with manufacturing representatives and county and state agricultural officials converging on Chase City to educate farmers about modern, affordable machinery. This is a photograph of one of many demonstration projects conducted by Farmall Tractor representatives and staff of Spaulding Equipment showing how quickly a field could be plowed, cultivated, and made ready for planting. (Robert Tucker.)

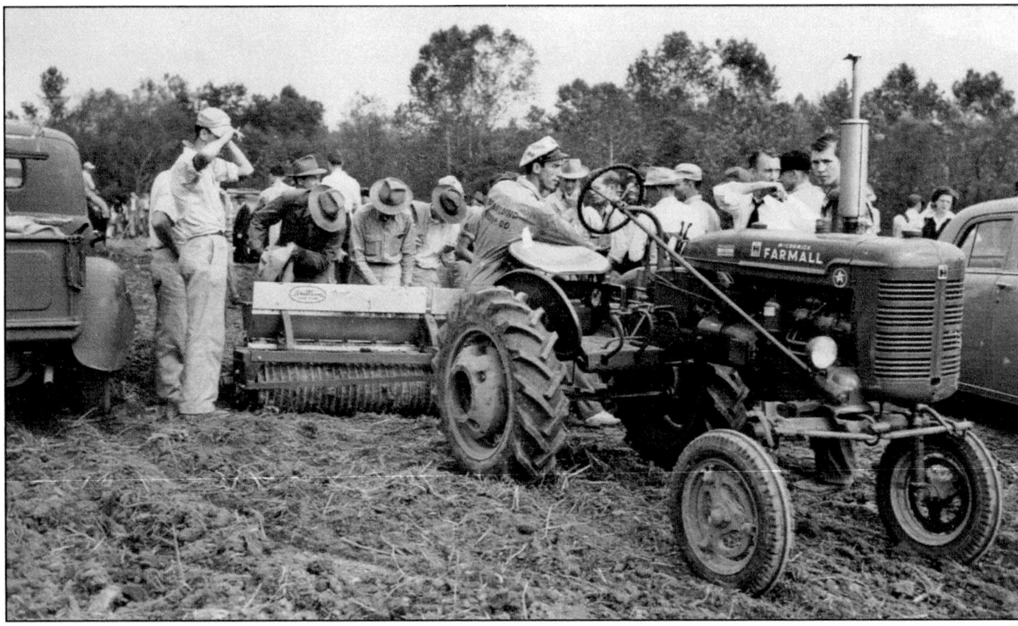

With a Super A Farmall and a Brillion seeder, the field was done in hours versus days. All this equipment brought with it new farming practices to combat land erosion, drainage, and runoff, maximize nutrients in the soil, rotate and space crops, and control weeds and pests. (Ann Wagstaff Dembrowski.)

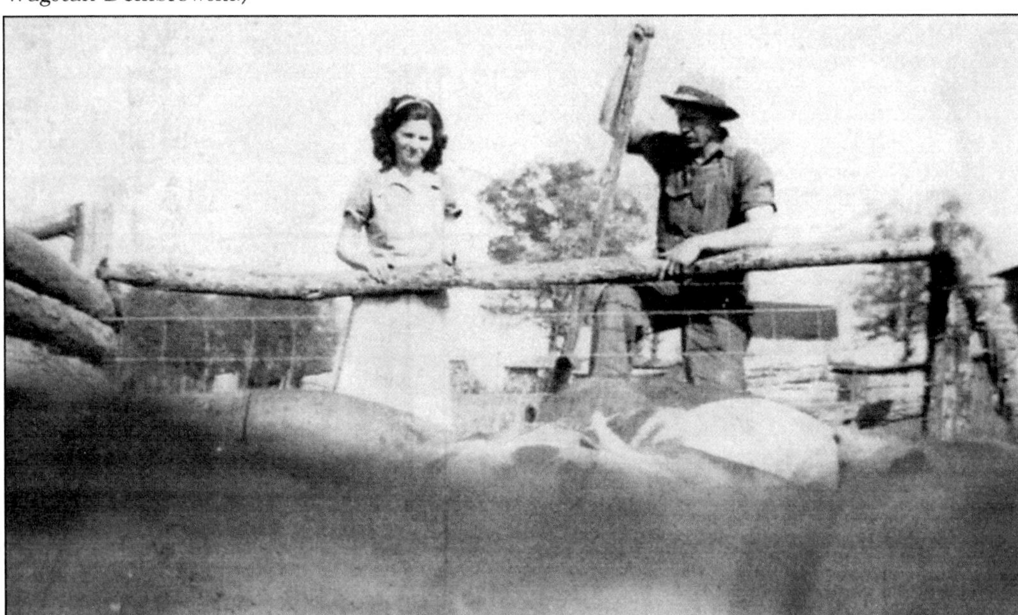

This 1940s photograph of Irene Morgan Brooks and Buster Brooks tending the hog pen illustrates one of the most controversial farming practices in Chase City. From 1893 until 1930, numerous hog-farming ordinances were passed and rescinded. There was also major controversy over hog farming in the old town versus the annexed New Territory from 1913 until 1930, when hog farming was banned within city limits. With many strict government regulations in the 1970s, hog farming for small farmers was over. (IMB.)

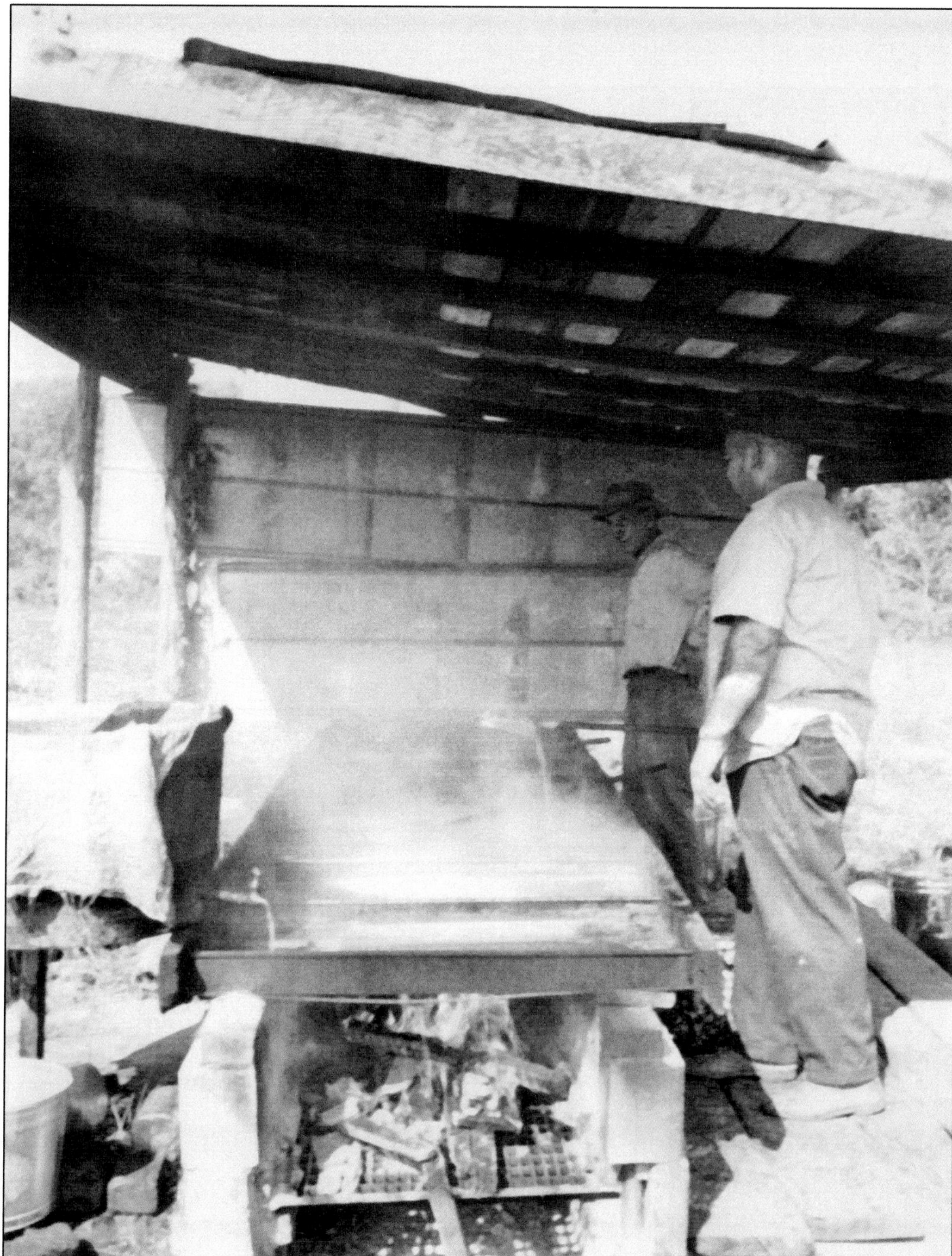

This 1960s photograph shows the production of sorghum molasses. Lathan Edwards (right) and Howard Driggs cook a batch of sorghum cane syrup to thicken it. When ripe, the field of sorghum cane is burned to rid the stalks of chaff and leaves. The stalks are cut and placed into a press, where the syrup is extracted. This used to be done by a mule attaching to a pole walking in circles around the press, pressing the cane as the farmer fed the hopper. The syrup is cooked to a thick base. (Madeline Ashworth Edwards.)

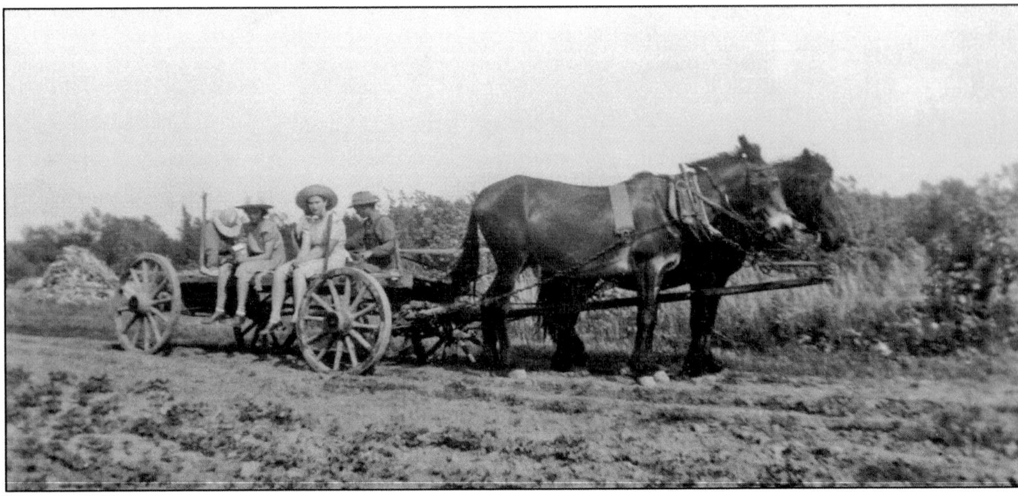

Farming did have its moments of leisure. Just going for a ride and enjoying the farm life, even with the muddy trails in this 1943 photograph, was a nice break from the daily work schedule. From left to right, Grace Morgan Lail, Dorothy Morgan Stump, an unidentified male, and Sam and Kate the mules are out for an afternoon stroll. Today hayrides like this are popular at Halloween and other gatherings. (IMB.)

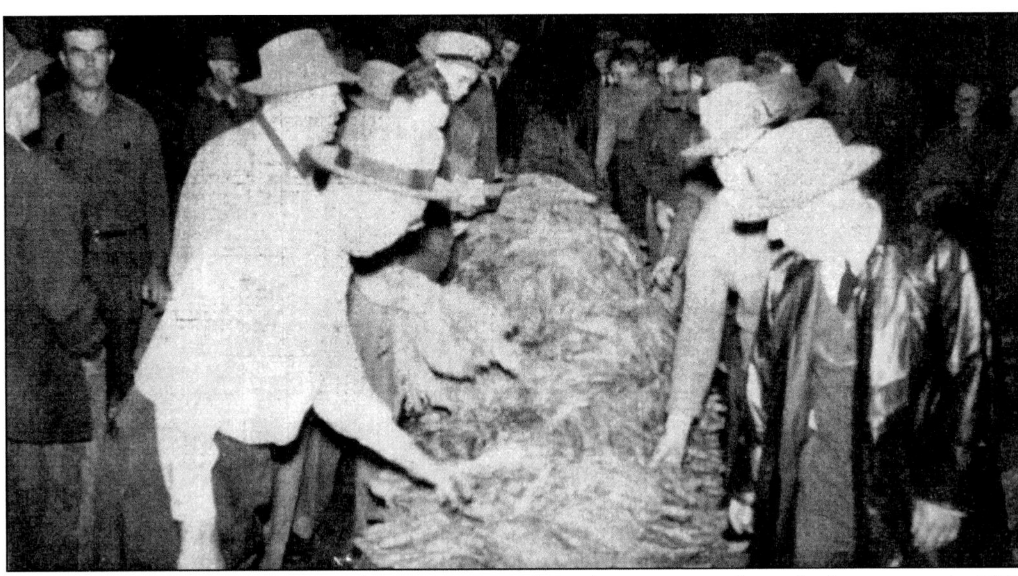

This is a photograph of a 1940s tobacco auction, done the same way from the beginning in 1873. The auctioneer walks up and down the rows of baskets of tobacco, followed on both sides of the rows by buyers. He points to a basket and begins to auction it. The buyers respond, and the highest bidder is recorded on a sales sheet. The recorder usually walked just ahead of the auctioneer to maintain a clear view. (WCG.)

Four

Depression Then War
Prosperity Following Each

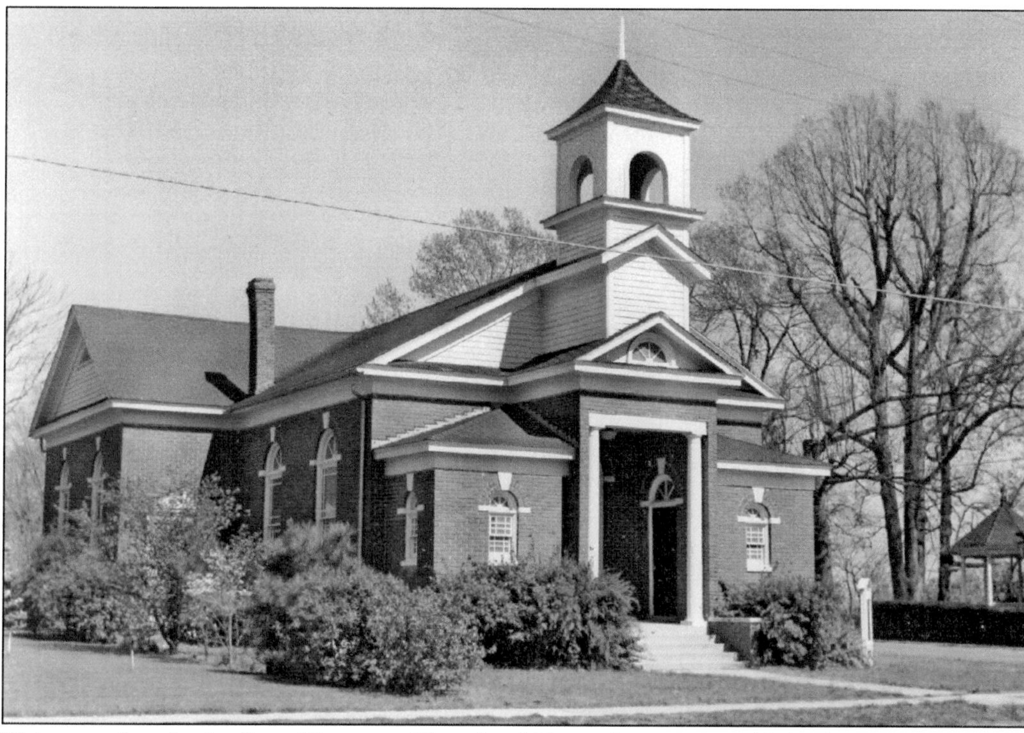

This new church, the First Christian Church of Chase City, was established in 1929 in part by the local YMCA. It began services just as the Depression was announced. Citizens in Chase City pulled together, and farming, family, and friends protected the community from the turbulent and devastating era from 1929 through 1935. In some instances, Chase City actually grew during this period. The little church is located at the northeast corner of Walker and Marshall Streets. All of the churches pictured in this book continue operation today, and several more denominations have come to Chase City and continue to flourish. (Bryan Queensberry.)

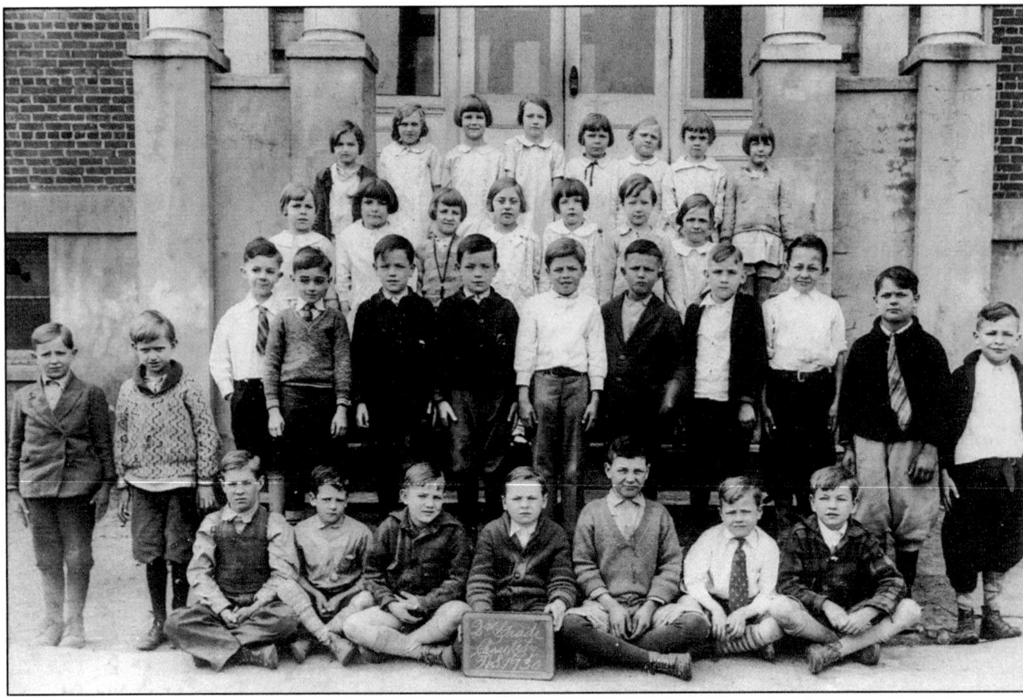

The second-grade class of Winnie Williams poses for its picture in front of Chase City Elementary School on Endly Street in 1930. This was the last class to finish in this building, as the elementary school was moved. The new Robert E. Lee Elementary School began classes in September 1930. (Karen N. Pennington.)

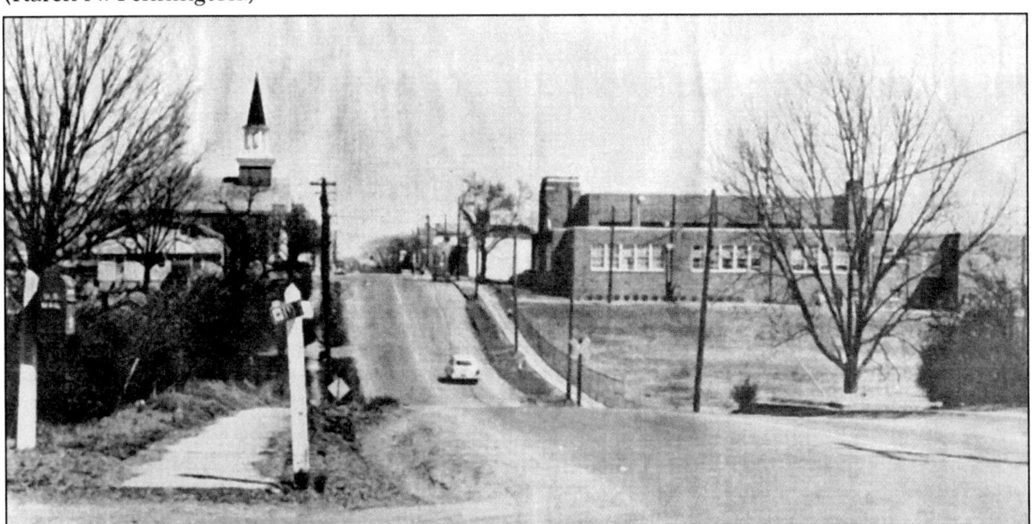

The school is located on Second Street where Boyd Street ends (right), across from the original elementary school in the Holloway house (left). In front of the Holloway house is the newly remodeled First Baptist Church. This unique photograph was taken atop the hill at Second and Endly Streets. There is now a bridge over the railroad tracks and Church Creek, which runs parallel to the tracks the entire length of Chase City. From where this photograph was taken, one can no longer see downtown. (RS.)

In 1938, Chase City High School published an annual, reportedly the only one until after the war. This is the faculty page from the 1938 *Mirror*. The 1946 annual continued with the name of *Mirror* and this name continued through 1956, when the school was closed. Mecklenburg County Consolidated Schools took over the Chase City Schools that year, and high school students were bused to a new high school centrally located for the western half of the county residents. (LLE.)

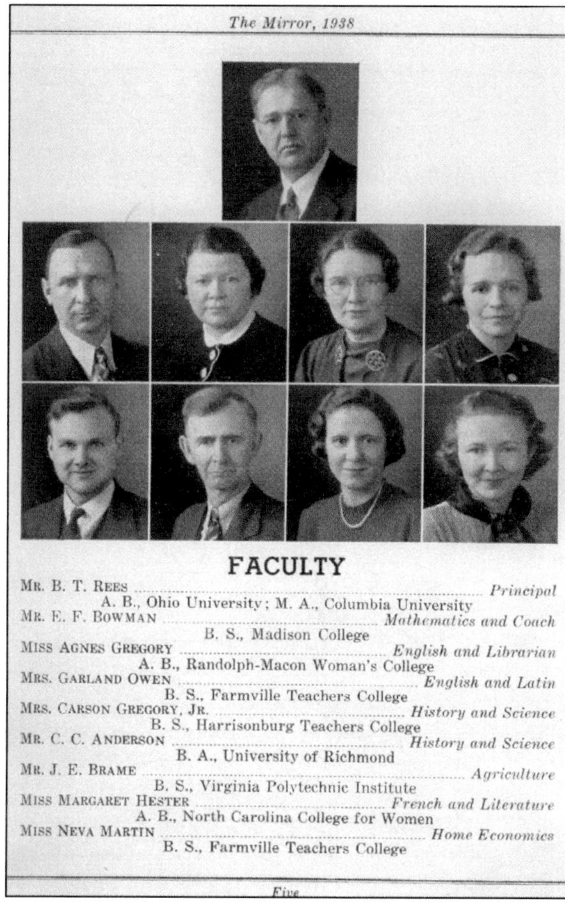

The Mirror, 1938

FACULTY

Mr. B. T. Rees .... *Principal*
A. B., Ohio University; M. A., Columbia University

Mr. E. F. Bowman .... *Mathematics and Coach*
B. S., Madison College

Miss Agnes Gregory .... *English and Librarian*
A. B., Randolph-Macon Woman's College

Mrs. Garland Owen .... *English and Latin*
B. S., Farmville Teachers College

Mrs. Carson Gregory, Jr. .... *History and Science*
B. S., Harrisonburg Teachers College

Mr. C. C. Anderson .... *History and Science*
B. A., University of Richmond

Mr. J. E. Brame .... *Agriculture*
B. S., Virginia Polytechnic Institute

Miss Margaret Hester .... *French and Literature*
A. B., North Carolina College for Women

Miss Neva Martin .... *Home Economics*
B. S., Farmville Teachers College

Five

The J. W. Davis Café opened on Fifth Street in the early 1930s. Even in the 1960s, it was considered to have the best hamburgers and hot dogs in town. Across the street, the Standard Overall Factory came to town in 1935. Next door to the café was a barbershop, but it closed in 1949. That year, Davis's café became known as the Red Door, and in the barbershop, Davis's cousin opened a second café. (KW.)

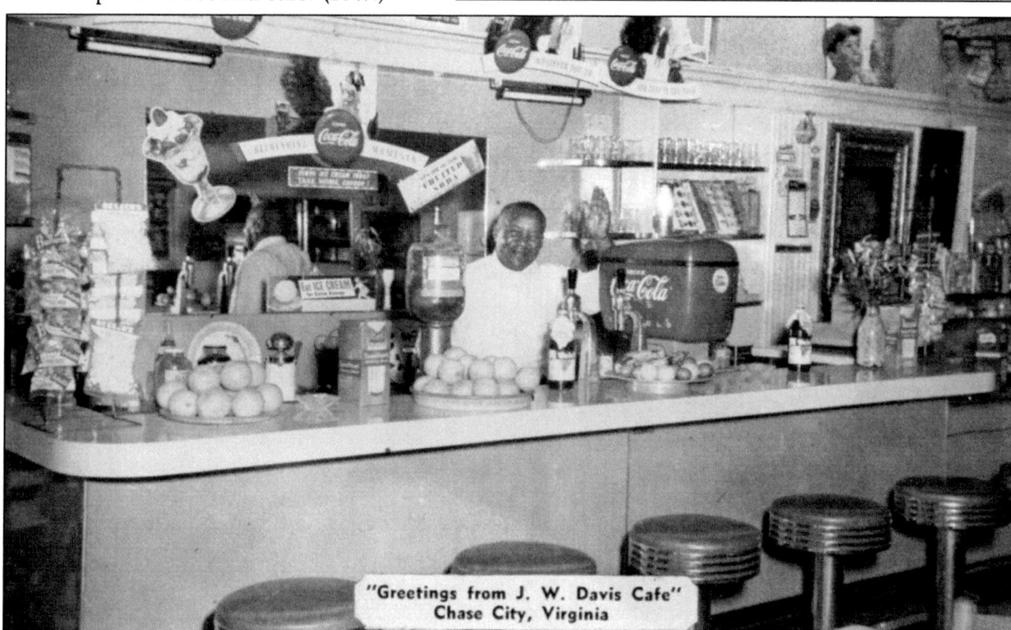

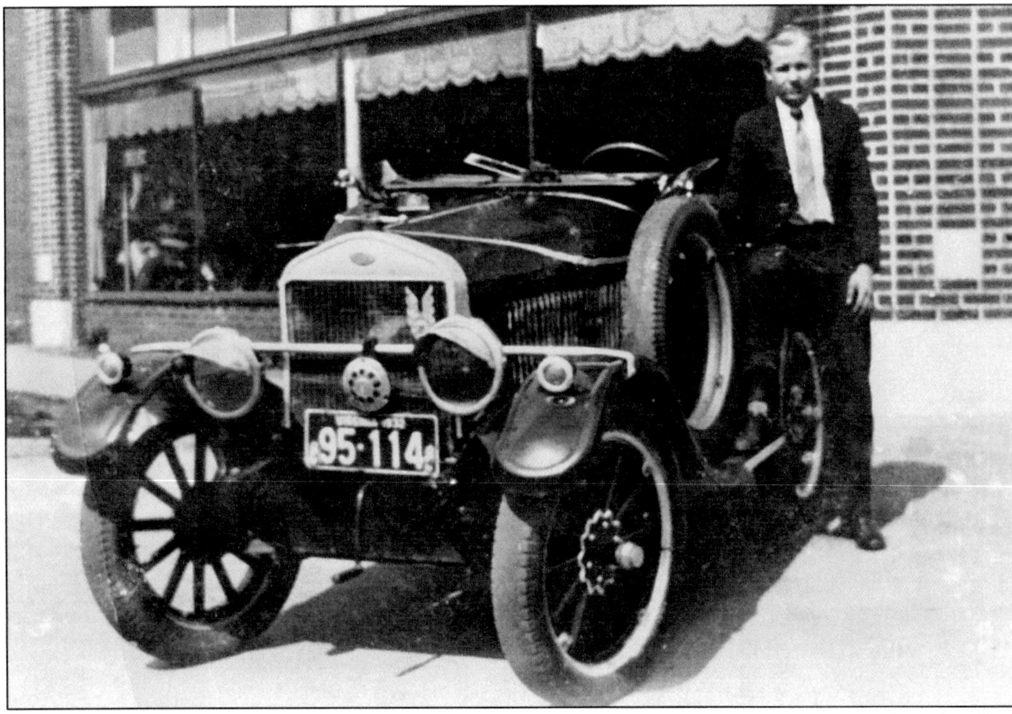

During the Depression, many individuals in Chase City exercised creativity. One such individual, Emile Mull, formerly from the mountains of North Carolina, had come to town and opened Emile's Electronics and Supply Maytag store in the old Gallion (or Gallyon) Pool Hall building on the southeast corner of Main and Second Streets. Pictured here in 1932 is Emile with the second car he built from accumulated parts from several different makes and models of vehicles in town. (Jo Anne Wortman Andrews.)

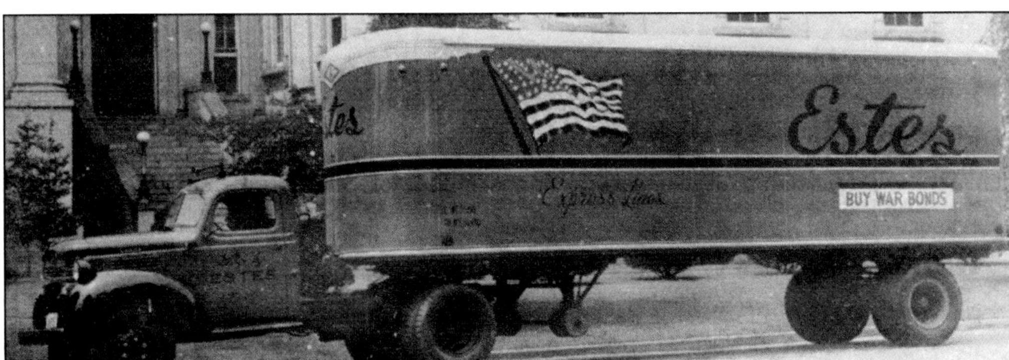

From humble beginnings, Web W. Estes developed a broad Mid-Atlantic trucking industry, even with new interstate trucking regulations in the late 1930s. Many family members and extended family continue to work in the business, but all are expected to begin at the bottom. Robey W. Estes Sr. (son of Web), who was wounded in World War II, began as a driver in 1946. Becoming president and chairman of the board of the company in 1971, Robey expanded the business internationally. (*News Progress*, Charles Queensberry.)

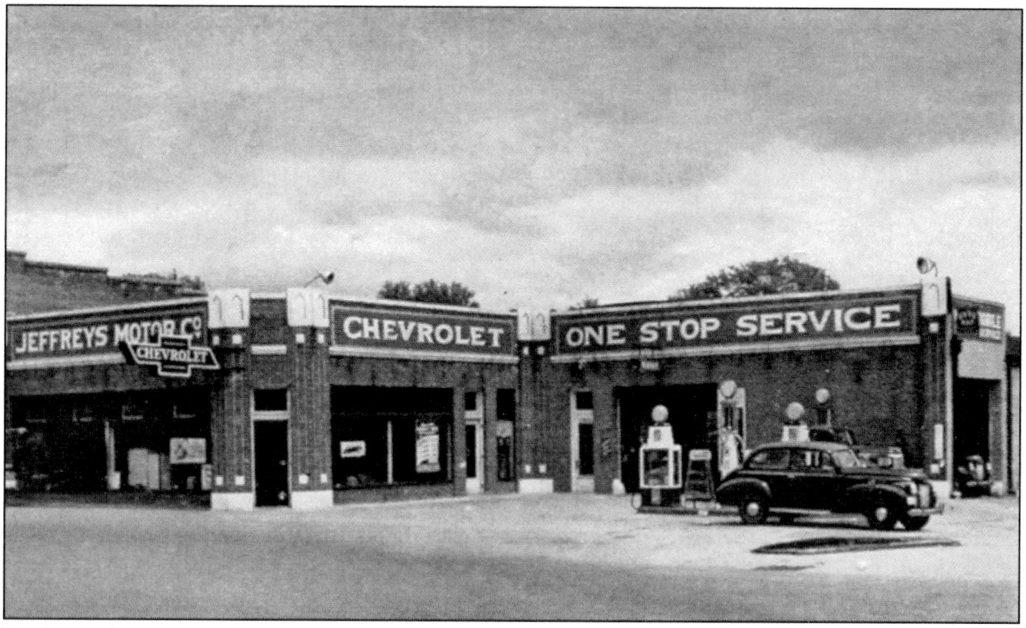

In the early 1940s, Jeffreys Motor Company moved its dealership to their showroom location at Second and Main Streets, the site of the former Little Mecklenburg Hotel. The company offered new car sales and service along with an attended gas pump station. In 1973, Jeffreys became Jackson Motor Company and opened a used car lot on the former site of the First National Bank building. Chase City was changing and growing weekly. (Rose Wallace Tucker.)

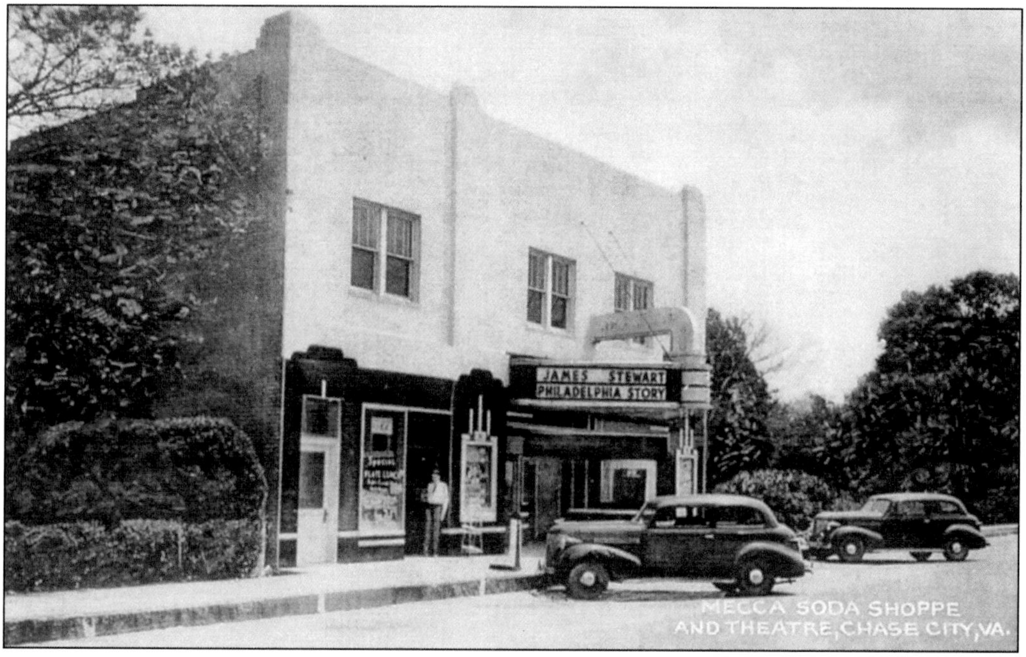

In 1936, Ridley Green, the nephew of the owner of the Cozy Theatre, built the Mecca Soda Shoppe and Theatre in the 100 block of Main Street. In 1947, the theater caught fire. Movies were shown under a tent in the parking lot across the street until repairs were completed in 1948. In addition to the repairs, new seats, curtains, and a new marquee were installed. (WCG.)

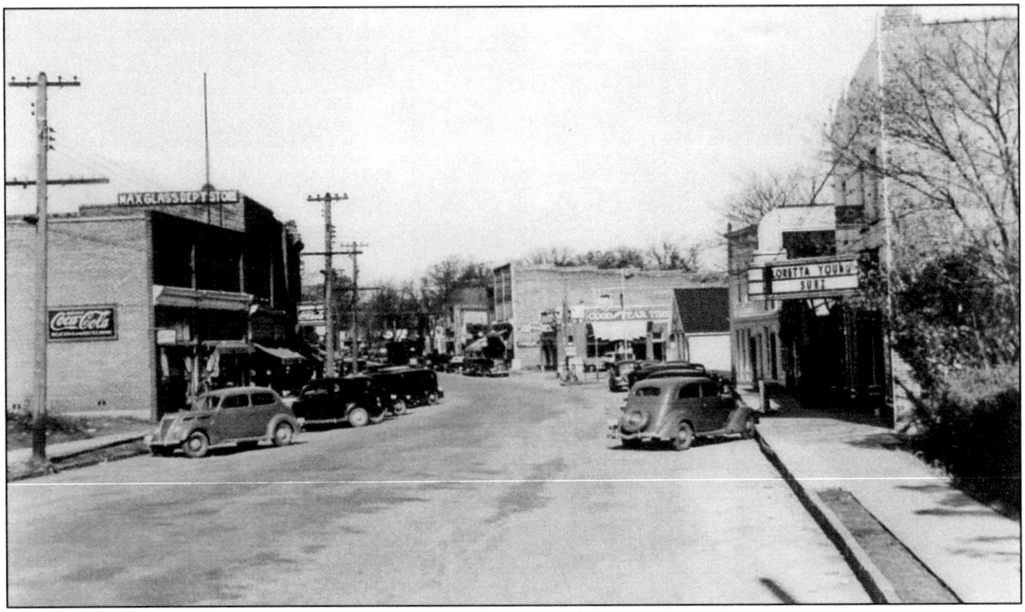

Across the street, the Mecca was joined in 1938 by Max Glass Department Store. Garret and Company opened in 1932 as a pharmacy, soda shop, wholesale distribution, and the Greyhound station. The building was formerly Gregory's Music Company from 1924 until 1931. There was a continued presence of the Hardy and Williams stores. Beside the Mecca were Dr. W. H. Saunders's drugstore and Emile's Electronics. Between the electronics store and Jeffreys Motor Company was Second Street (Highway 47), which connected Chase City to nearby South Hill in 1937. (WCG.)

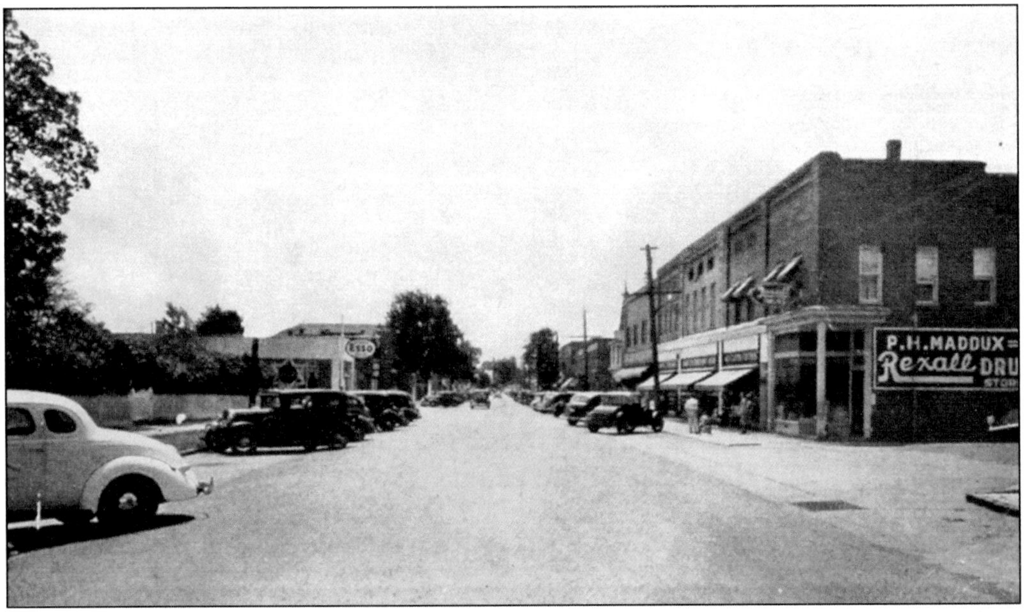

By 1940, the 300 block of North Main Street was almost completely developed. P. H. Maddox's drugstore with doctors' offices in the rear and the Chase City Department Store occupy the next three doors. Craddock-Terry Shoe Company, which opened in 1938, is located behind the next two doors. Across the street on the left is the Esso service station and garage of B. A. Garner. (Wyatt Garrett.)

On the southeast corner of Third and Main Streets is the Republic Service Station and Garage, which opened in 1937 and offered prepared, packaged foods, beverages, and an attended gas pumping station. (Karen N. Pennington.)

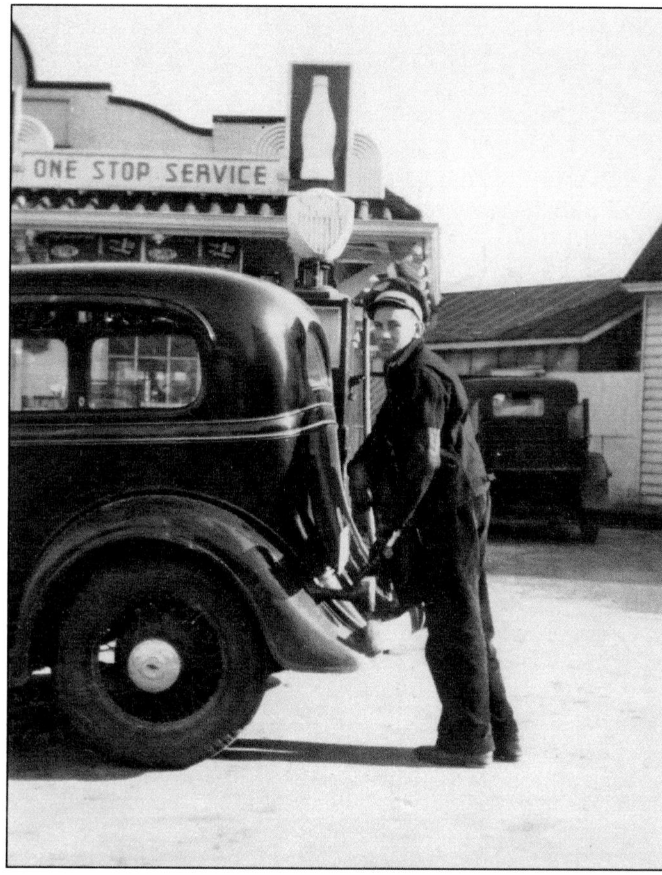

The quality of the shirts from the Standard Overall Company of Baltimore (later renamed Hampco) was considered excellent, and they manufactured many name-brand shirts that were shipped to major distributors all over the country. Few people realized the company, commonly called the Chase City Shirt Factory, manufactured 500 of the same shirt with 10 to 50 different labels sewn in. This is a late-1940s photograph of the sewing room inside the old factory. Note the antiquated sewing machines, lighting, and ventilation systems. (DT.)

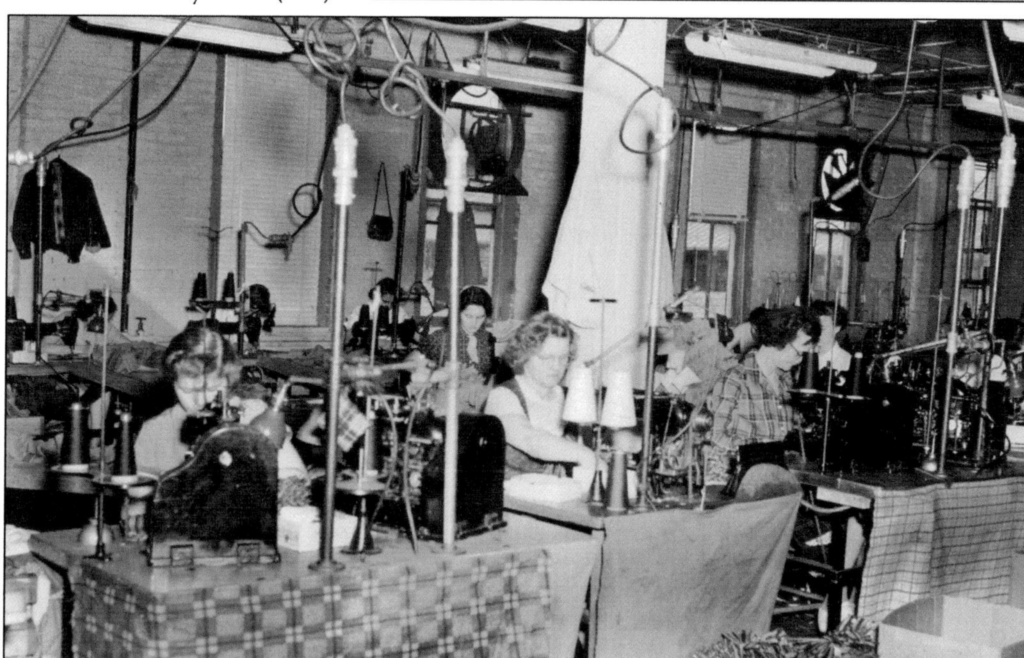

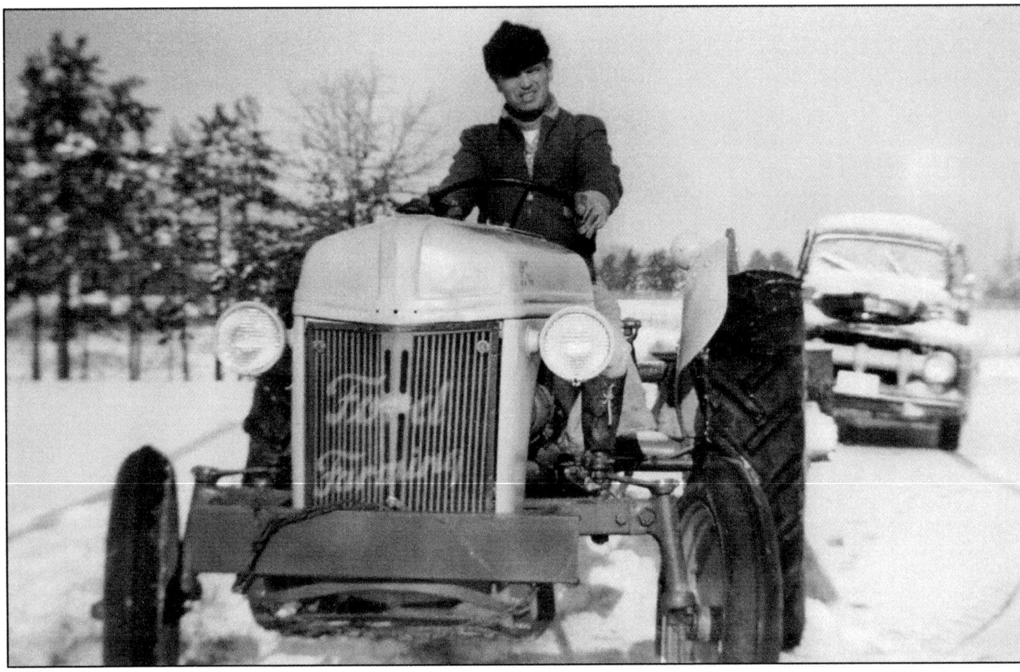

The snowstorm of 1940 paralyzed Chase City. It was the worst in recorded history for this area, bringing in excess of 20 inches. A pedestrian path was cleared in the center of Main Street, but it was nearly a week before traffic could resume. Tractors became important to townspeople once the storm passed. Many had been stranded and had to abandon their automobiles and walk home. (Susan Guill.)

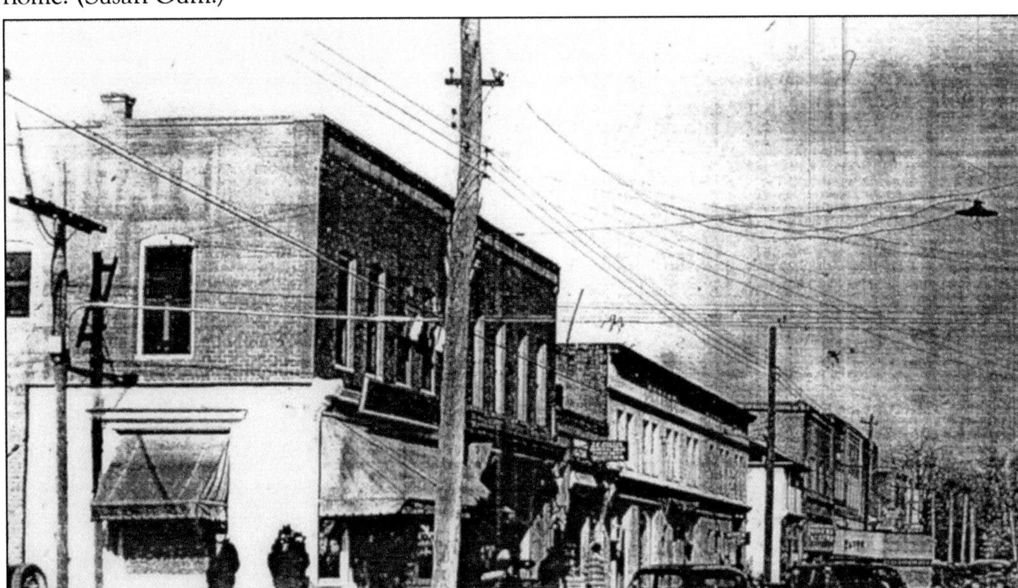

This 1941 photograph of the west side of the 300 block of North Main Street shows that State Bank is now White Front Grocery, the Bigger store is now J. C. Collis grocery, and next door are the Craddock and Terry Shoe Company and the Gregory Hotel, with an Estes truck in front. At the end of the street in the distance is the Jackson Hotel. (Carol Hupp Adams Roark.)

In 1938, Craddock and Terry Shoe Company was located between the Gregory Hotel and the Chase City Department Store. In 1949, the shoes were displayed in New Jersey during World Trade Week, and sales skyrocketed. The company hired more employees and doubled its operation over the next four years. Hiring as many as 200 people to prepare the tanned leather and cut, manufacture, and assemble the shoes, it soon had to move to larger quarters. This photograph also shows the Bandbox Cleaners at left in 1945. (Janette Hutchins Collins.)

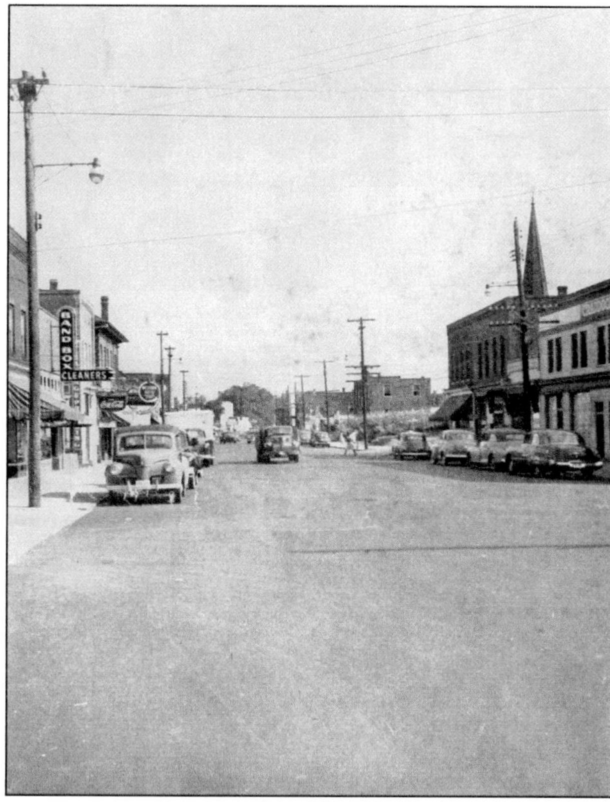

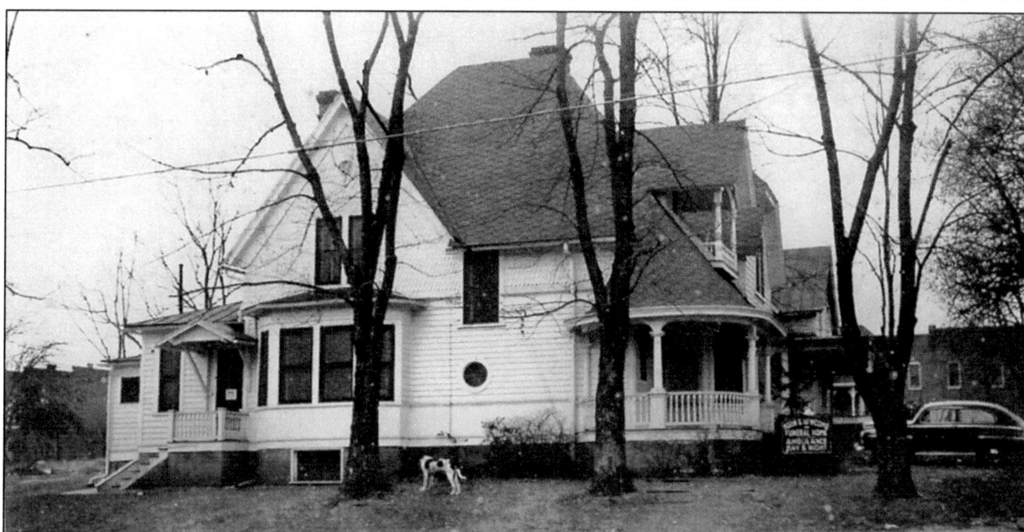

In 1941, the Moon-Newcomb Funeral Home came to Chase City (reportedly the first funeral home in the county). Having previously begun a funeral home in Keysville, Virginia, in 1939, they relocated to the southwest corner of Fifth and Main Streets across from the new Newman and Bevell Motor Company. Newcomb and his family moved next door to the funeral home. Many state and federal laws now oversee funeral homes, unlike the old days of the undertakers. (Charles Magann.)

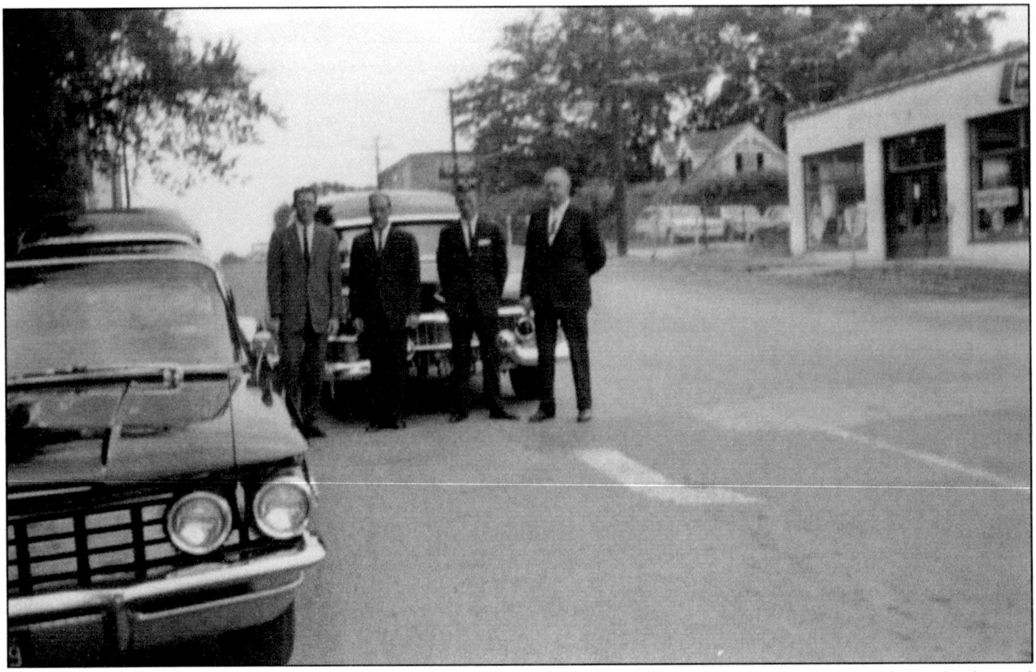

Pictured here from left to right in 1959 are Edward C. Moon, Otis Philbeck, unidentified, and Garland Newcomb Sr. with their new hearse. To the right are Tucker-Bevell Motor Company and garage, the Bragg home, and the former L. W. Biting store, which is now Joe's Pool Hall. (Newcomb and Allgood Funeral Home.)

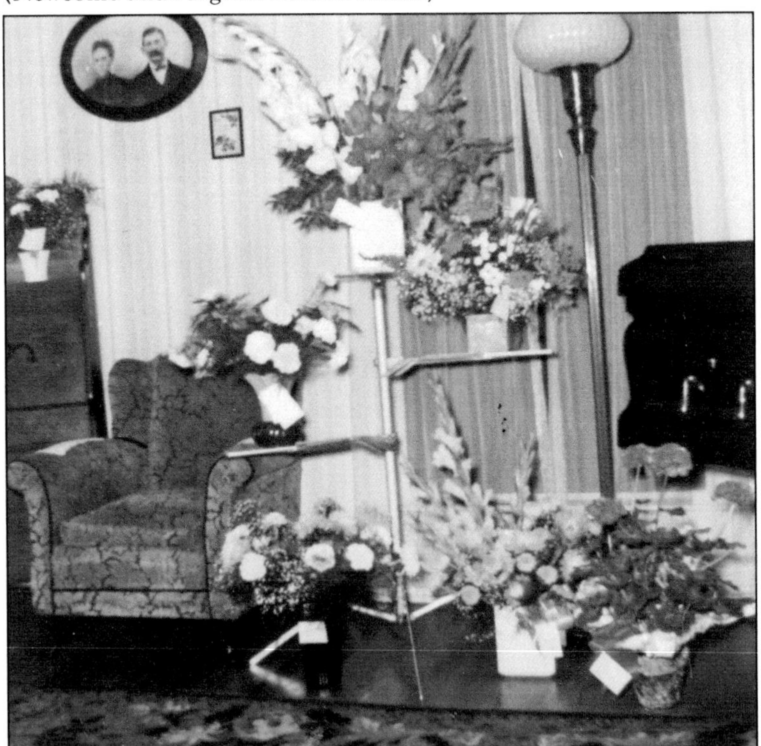

This is one of the parlors of the funeral home. Moon-Newcomb was the only white funeral home in the area for many years, as this was relatively a new concept. Previously stores such as Pruden and Hutchinson in Chase City sold caskets from their basement and employed an embalmer. Once embalmed, the body in a casket would be returned to the home, with an undertaker watching over it until burial the next day. (Newcomb and Allgood Funeral Home.)

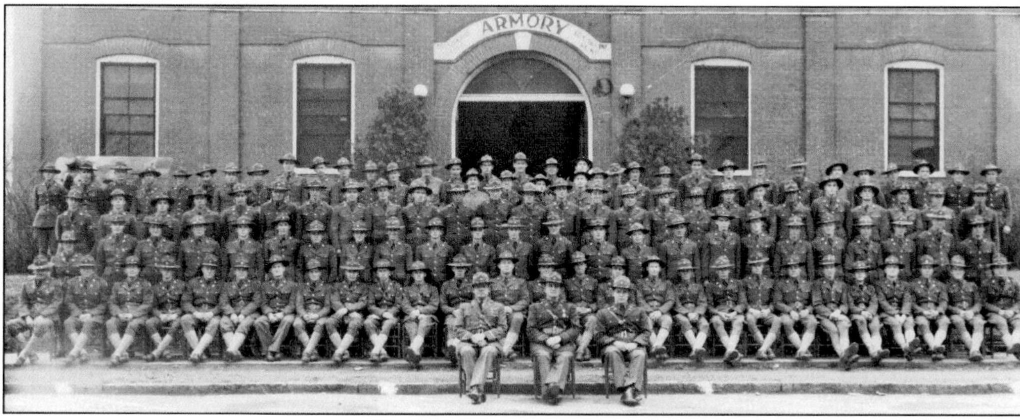

Chase City's growth slowed in 1941. Company E, 116th Infantry of the Virginia National Guard, was called to active duty. Commanded by Capt Edward Wilmouth, Lt. Garland Owen, and Lt. Sam Hubbard, the company formed in front of the Chase City Armory to ready for departure to Fort Meade, Maryland, for training. (BML/HJ.)

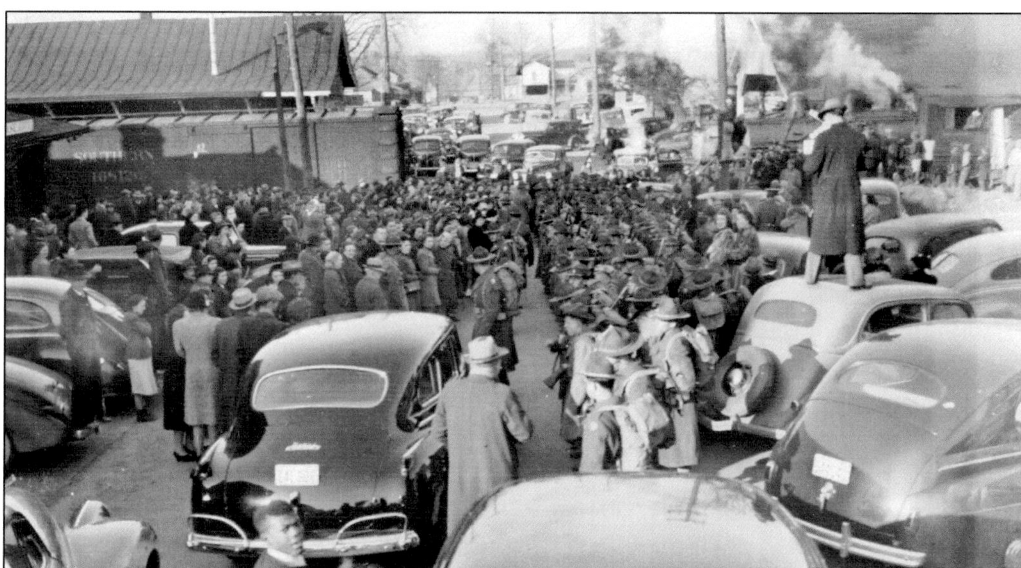

This February 25, 1941, photograph shows Company E members with family at the Chase City train depot on Fifth Street. They are sending their farewells and boarding the train for their departure to Fort Meade. The company did not return to Chase City until after the war, in late 1945 or early 1946. In the distance is the Davis Hotel for African Americans. Next to the steam engine is a vacant lot where the furniture store and auction house were located. (Mark W. Colgate.)

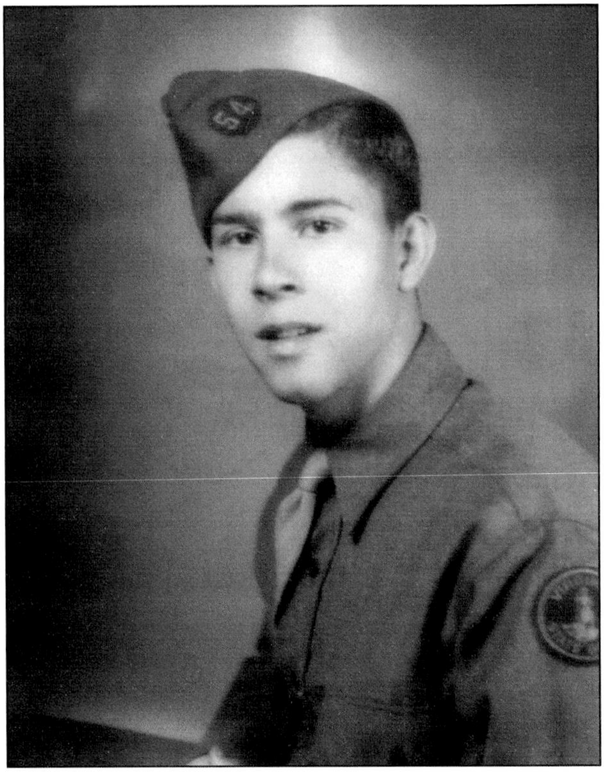

After the departure of Company E, Chase City formed a home guard under the Virginia Protection Force. Residents were eager to join, but many were turned away because of age—recruits had to be at least 17. One young man uniquely persuaded the guard to allow him to enlist at the age of 15. W. Gordon Willis enlisted in the home guard in 1943 as its first company bugler. (Charles Willis Jr.)

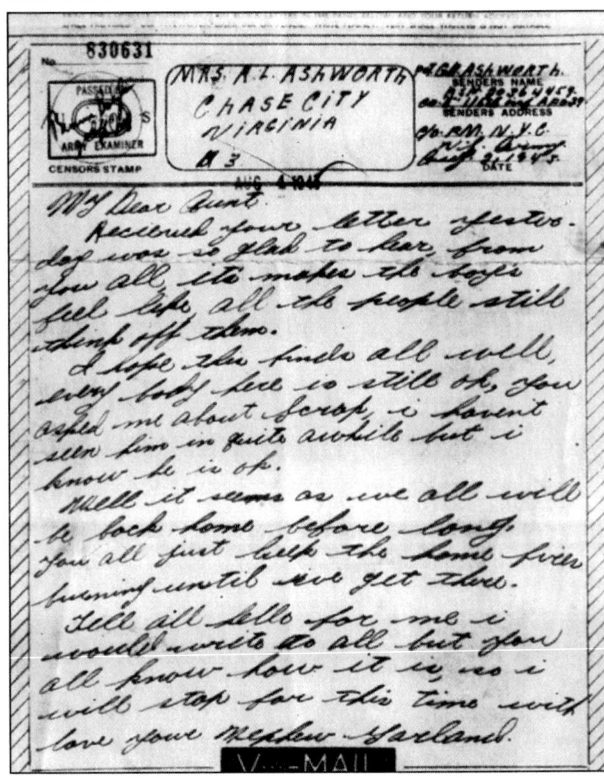

No. 830631

PASSED BY ARMY EXAMINER

CENSOR'S STAMP

MRS. A. L. ASHWORTH
CHASE CITY
VIRGINIA

SENDERS NAME

SENDERS ADDRESS

DATE

My Dear Aunt.
Received your letter yesterday was so glad to hear from you all, its makes the boys feel like all the people still think off them.
I hope this finds all well, every body here is still ok, you asked me about Scrap, i havent seen him in quite awhile but i know he is ok.
Well it seems as we all will be back home before long. You all just keep the home fires burning until we get there.
Tell all hello for me i would write to all but you all know how it is, so i will stop for this time with love your nephew Garland.

V—MAIL

Correspondence during the war was sporadic and often had to be brief. The military created V-Mail for the soldiers. This is a V-Mail from PFC Garland Ashworth to his aunt in Chase City dated August 2, 1945. Soldiers simply filled in the blanks, and the military forwarded the letters along. (Madeline Ashworth Edwards.)

Little did anyone know that shortly after this V-Mail, PFC Garland B. Ashworth of Company E, 116th Infantry, would be seriously wounded during an invasion. Before he could be evacuated to a stateside hospital, he died. Ten members of Company E from Chase City died during World War II. Nine were killed in action. (Madeline Ashworth Edwards.)

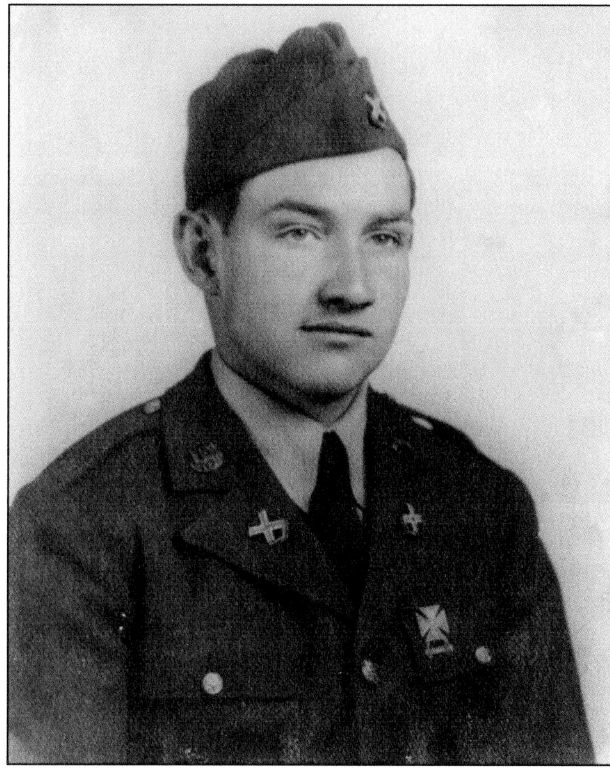

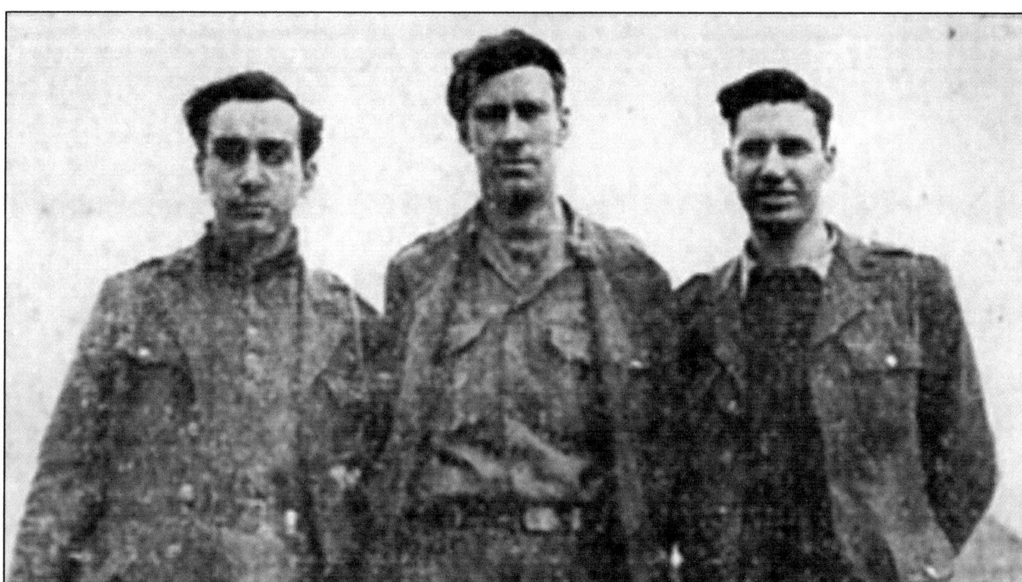

This *Chase City Progress* photograph is unique. It was reportedly sent to the paper by the American Red Cross. The three prisoners of war released include Sam Lendi (left), PFC H. Thomas Hupp (center), and Vernon Thurman of Chase City. The family had been told that Hupp was killed, and this photograph appeared in the paper before the War Department notified the family that he was a POW and had been released. Tom Hupp married Margaret Estes, went to work for Estes Express, and became first vice president before retiring. (*Chase City Progress*, Carol Hupp Adams Roark.)

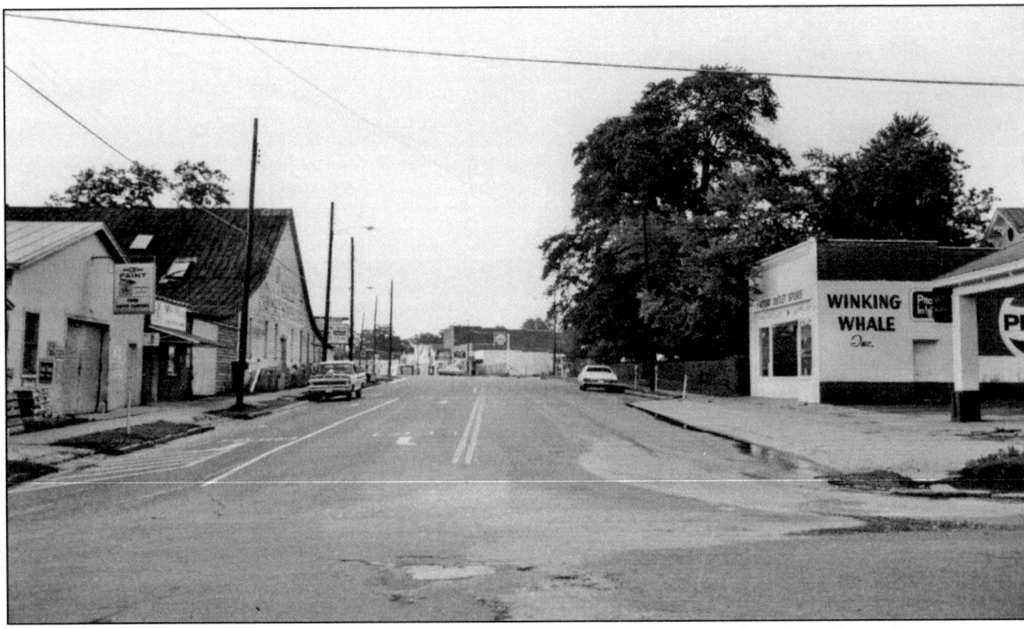

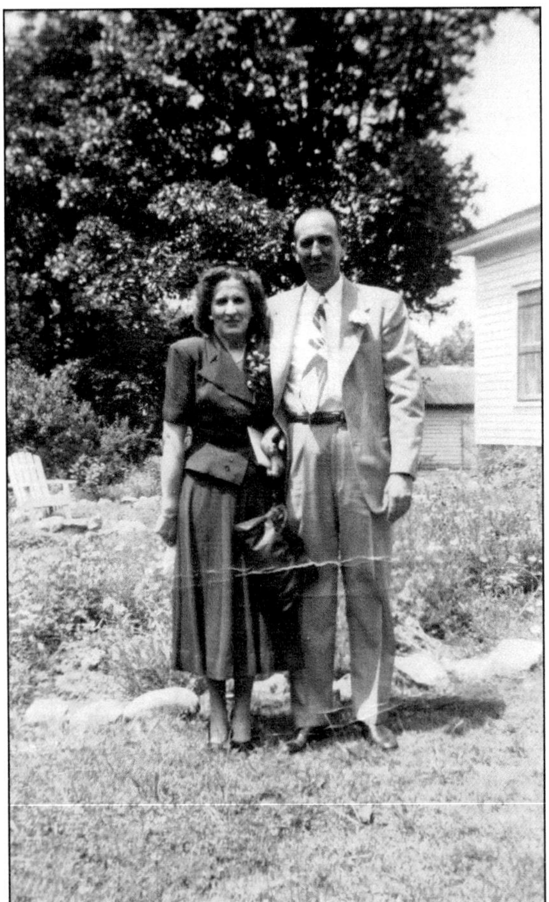

This photograph taken from Sycamore Street looking north up Main Street shows the roof of the Gulf station and Piedmont Motor Company (far right), formerly Boswell Tire Service, which began operation in 1924. Next is Winking Whale Produce outlet in the former bowling alley, the rooftop and treed lawn of Shadow Lawn, the Esso service station (formerly Sinclair Oil), and the C&R Confection Café, currently the home of Ladybug Junction gift shop. On the left are Alfred Owen's building materials and supply company and Advance Warehouse. (CC.)

Hilda Lewter and R. W. "Doc" Love were married prior to World War II. In 1945, Doc began Love Associates Construction Company above Dr. J. P. Price's drugstore. This company floundered for several years, then closed. (Ray DeJarnette.)

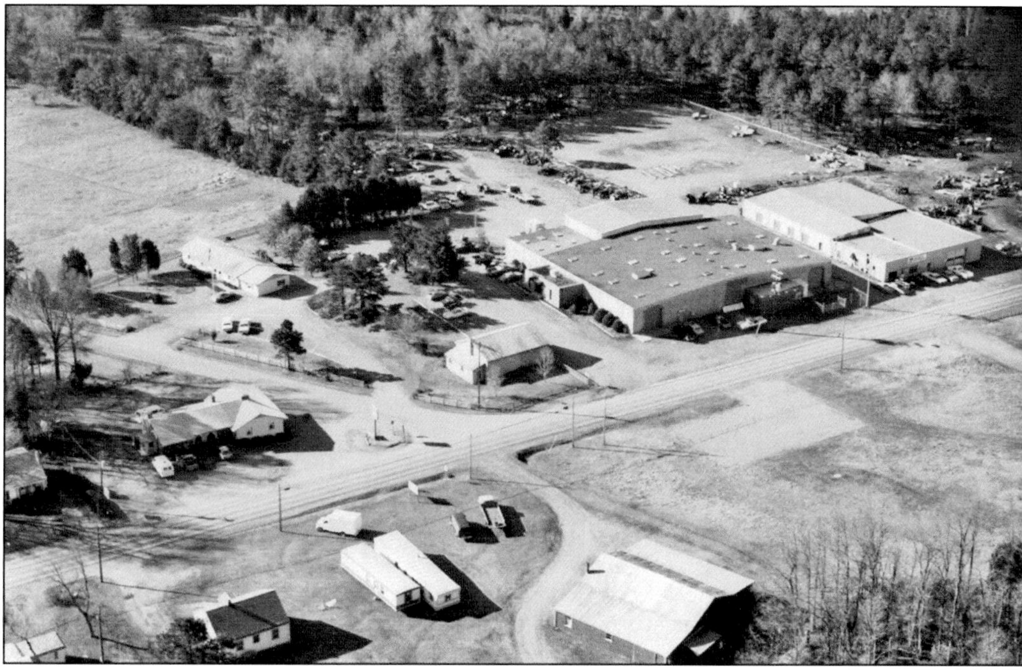

In 1946, Doc began Love Associates, a power line clearing company. Securing a contract to clear rights-of-way in Virginia and North Carolina for power lines to be installed from the developing John H. Kerr Dam project, this company grew into a multimillion-dollar corporation over the next 35 years before it was purchased by Monroe tree service, later Lewis tree service. To the left in the fork of the two roads is Hugh's Barbeque, formerly Hugh's Sandwich Shop, across from the livestock auction house. (Johnny Newcomb.)

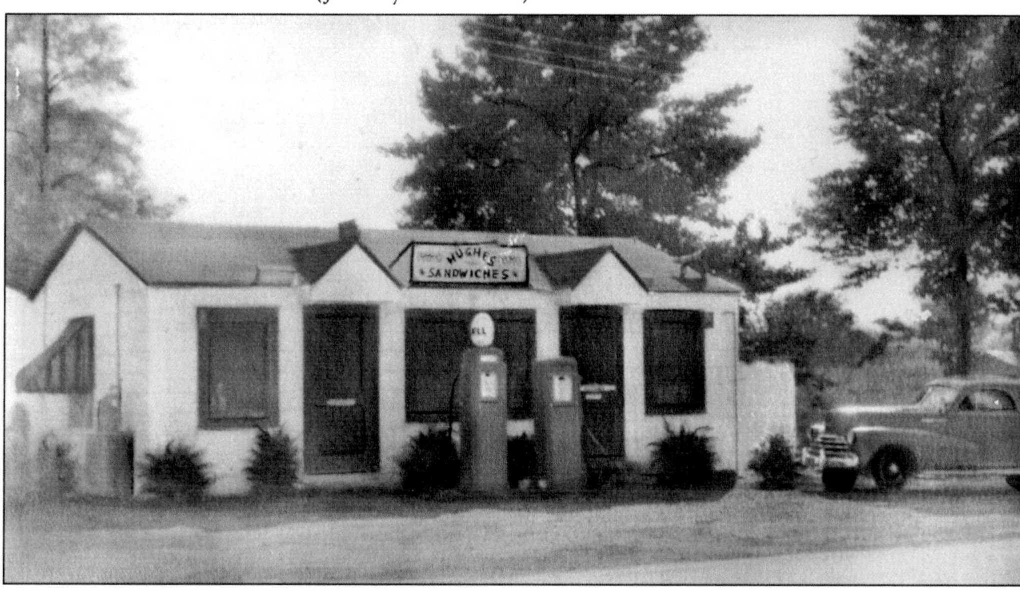

This photograph shows Hugh's Sandwich Shop, begun in 1946, to the east of Love Associates and across the street from the poultry and livestock auction house. Owned and operated by Hugh Lenhart, it became a favorite stop for most local residents. Experiencing a great deal of success in the late 1950s, he expanded and modernized his business. (Charles Magann.)

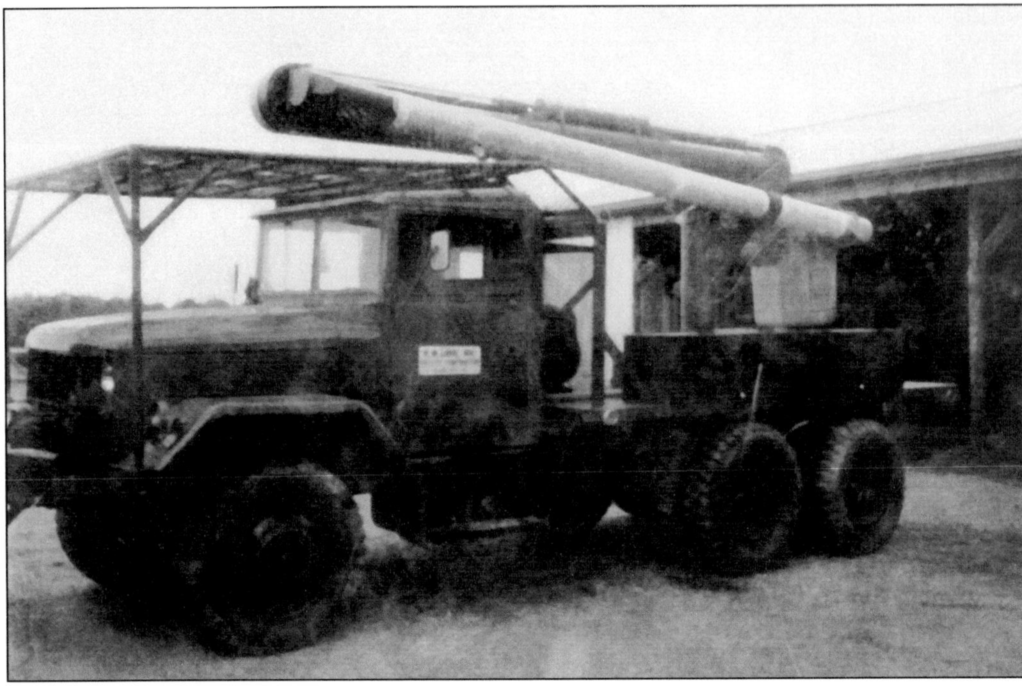

This 1948 photograph shows one of the first bucket trucks purchased by Love Associates. The background shows the garage, which employed four to six mechanics at all times to maintain the fleet of equipment necessary for clearing operations. (Ray DeJarnette.)

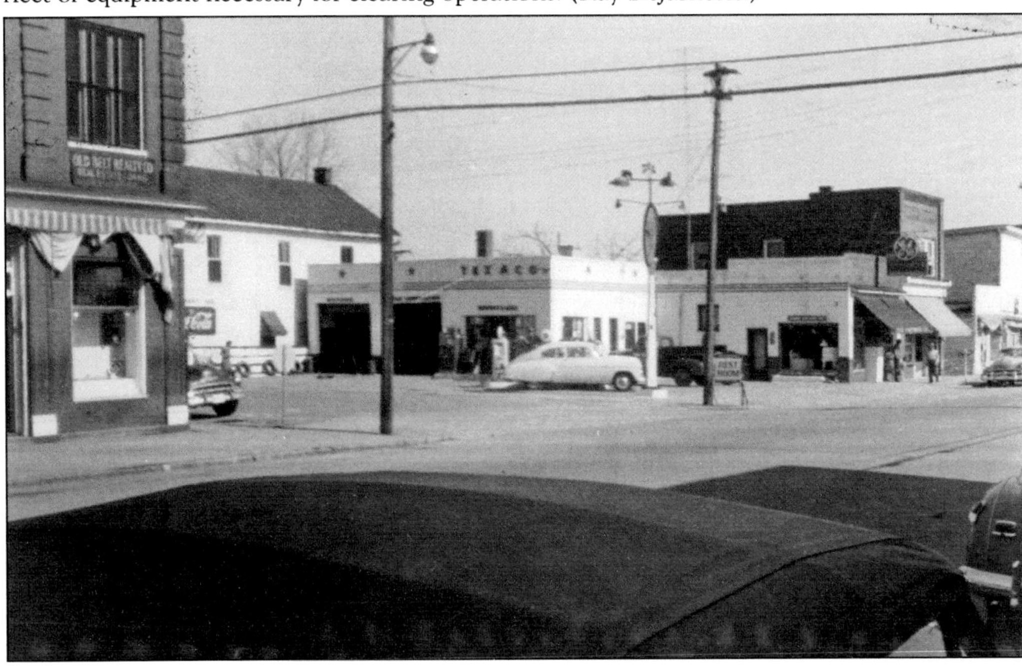

After the war, the old town hall building became Harvey's Floor Covering, with Dudley's Barber Shop next door and Old Belt Realty upstairs. Chase City Grocery was one on the few wooden buildings remaining in town, located on Third Street next to the Republic Texaco station. The first store on Main Street is the G. E. Appliance Store. (Charles Rockwell.)

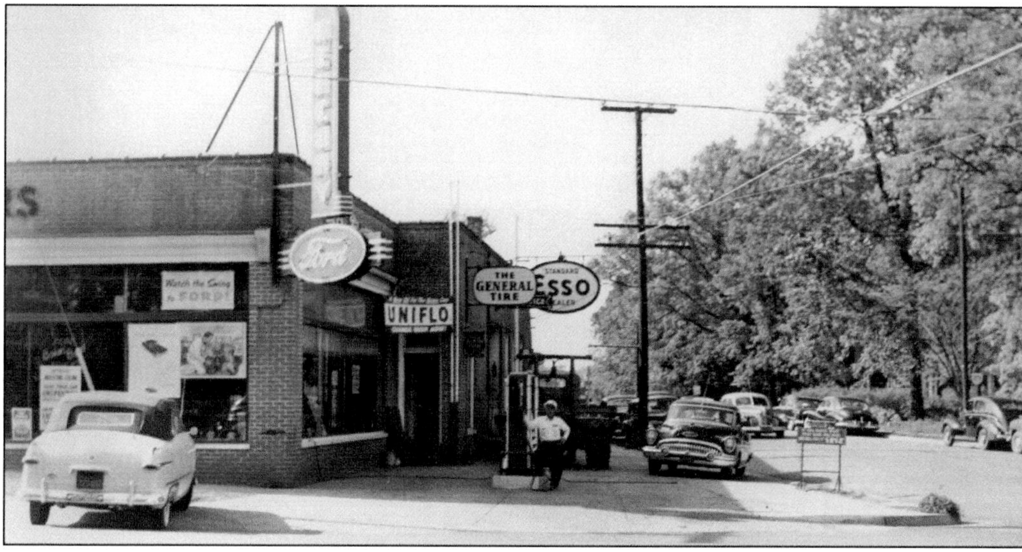

In the 1930s, the Chase City Motor Company sold to Bill Newman and Allen Bevell. The chief mechanic was Clarence Tucker. In 1941, Bill Newman, a member of Company E, sold his share of the business to Clarence Tucker. As soon as the war and rationing ended, the new Tucker-Bevell Motors grew in momentum, adding a line of tires, electronics, appliances, and an attended gas filling station, plus a full-service garage. (CDS.)

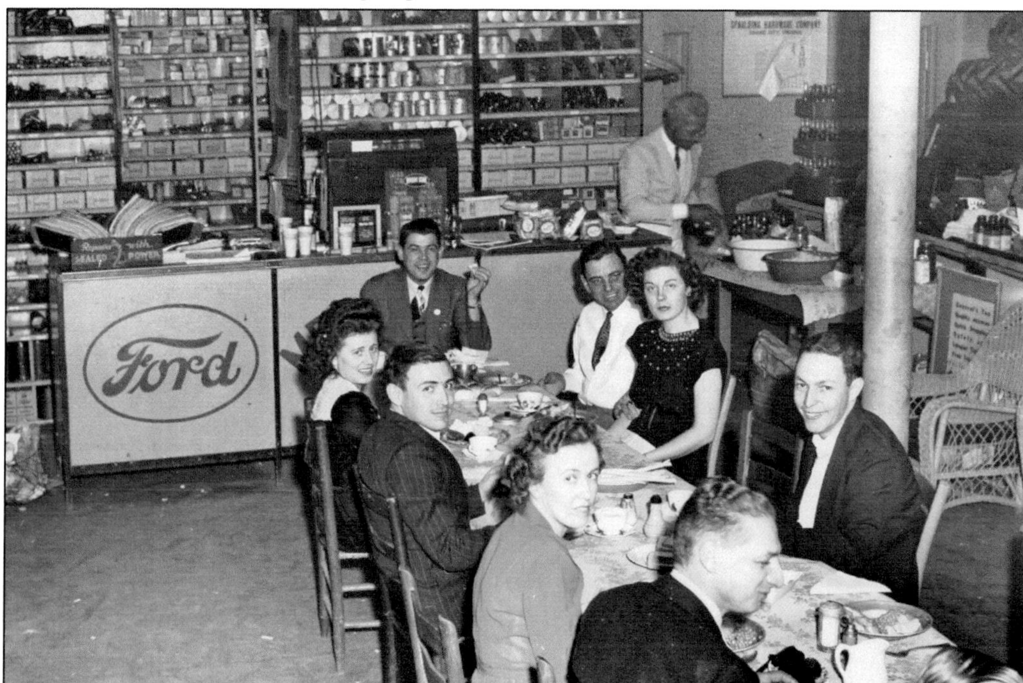

Purchasing the Chase City Wholesale Auto Parts store during the war, Tucker-Bevell began to grow. Inside the wholesale auto parts section was a staff luncheon. Clockwise from foreground are Allen Crump, Elva Crump, Hugh Lankford, unidentified, Clarence Tucker, Allen Bevell, Marion Young Holmes, and Jack Morgan. The man standing in the rear is believed to be Earl Davis from the Red Door. (CDS.)

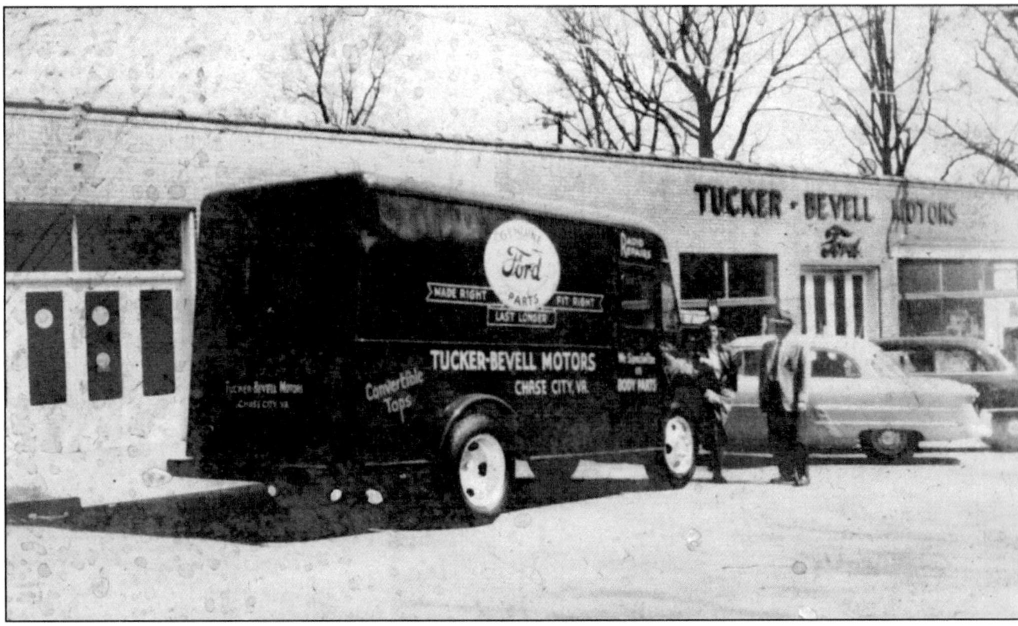

In 1947, the wholesale auto parts store began to provide parts to numerous garages in the surrounding communities. A sales staff included one route salesman with a van loaded to meet the needs of the customers in the region—not only their orders but also commonly needed items and tires. (CDS.)

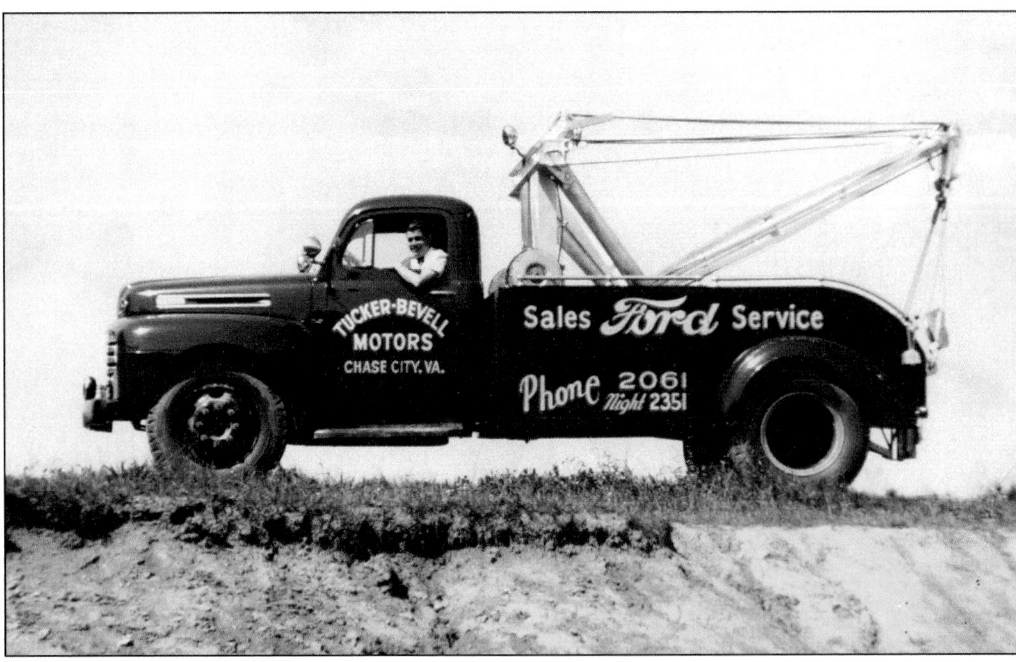

In 1947, a new wrecker service was offered by Tucker-Bevell Garage. Pictured here is Clarence Tucker with the new truck. Fitz Motor Company had purchased land and were building a showroom and vacating the adjacent building. This would become the new expanded garage service center. (CDS.)

On June 27, 1946, Fitz Motor Company opened on Fifth Street adjacent to Tucker-Bevell Motors in the old Jeffreys Motor Company building. The company needed a temporary location until it could build a new showroom. They sold Chrysler, Plymouth, and Dodge products and provided service for the same. (HL.)

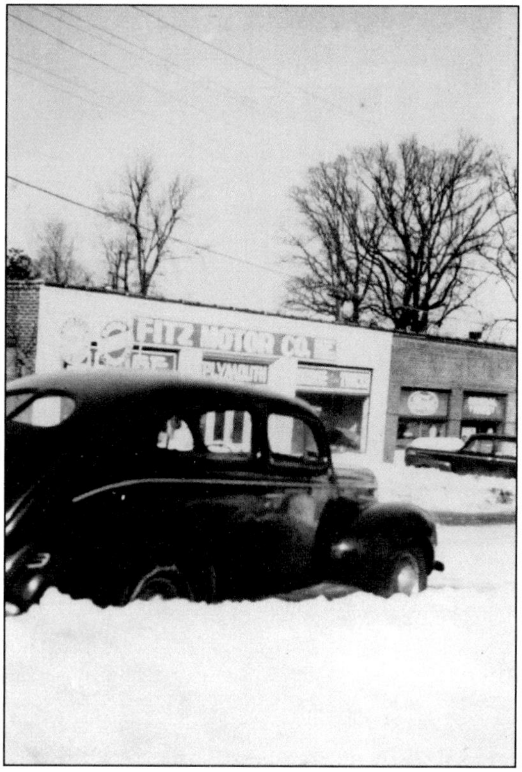

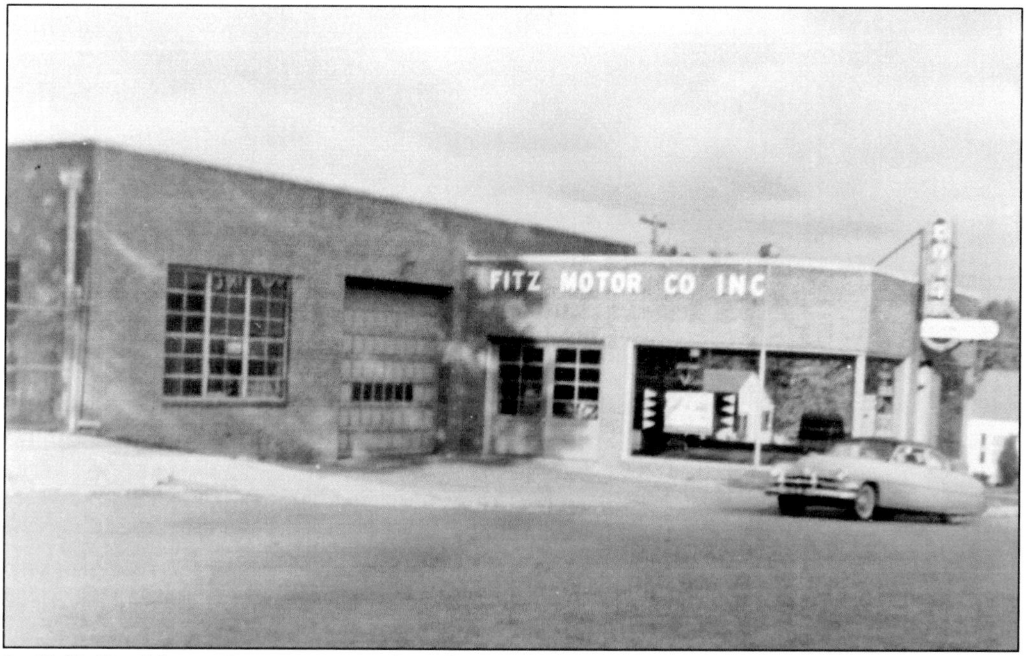

In 1948, Fitz Motor Company moved to their new showroom and garage on the newly created, dirt Mecklenburg Drive. Their building was situated on the fairway of the fourth hole of the old Mecklenburg Mineral Springs golf course, which was subdivided and the lots sold at auction in 1947. This was the first commercial building in the new subdivision. (HL.)

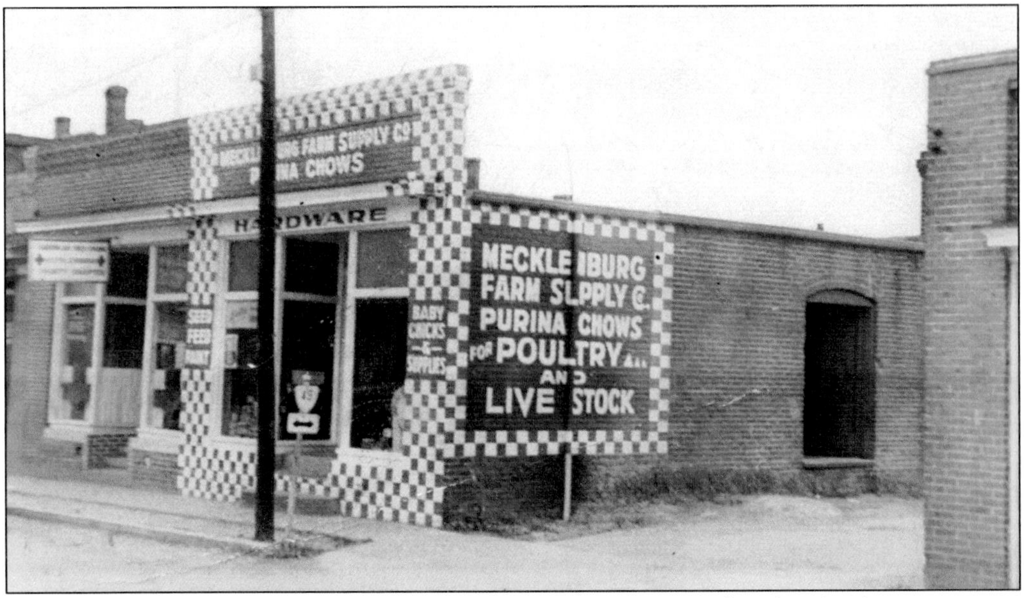

In 1945, the Mecklenburg Farm Supply and hardware store opened with a fertilizer store next door on Second Street behind the former Hardy and Company. This store was referred to as the "Checker Board" store and the slogan quickly took hold. The following year, owner Bill Pennington had a delivery van painted with the checkerboard pattern to be used for deliveries and parades. (Karen N. Pennington.)

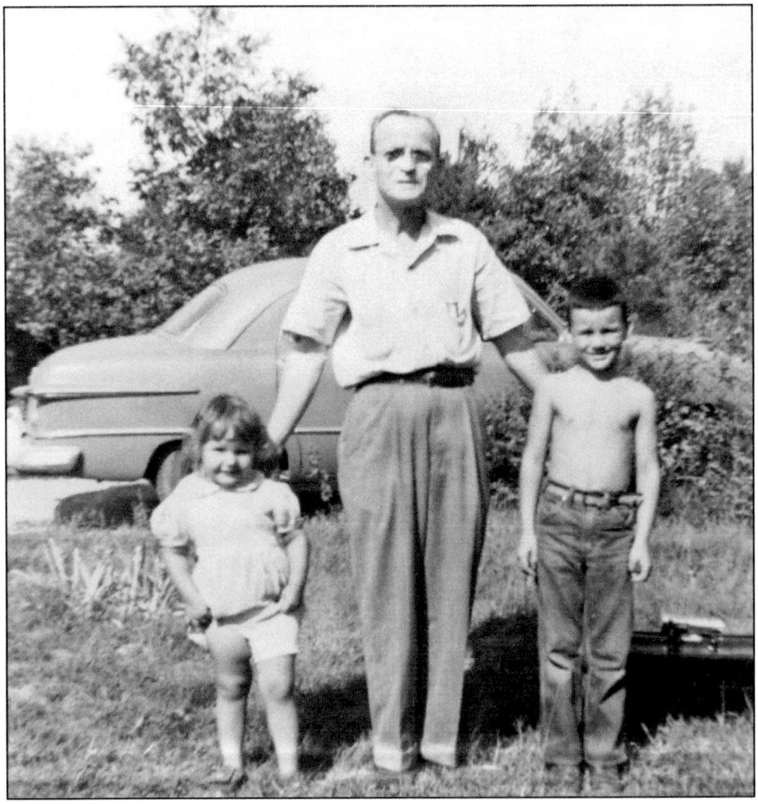

In 1948, a new physician came to town and located his office to the rear of the Lewter Drug store. Dr. John F. Phillips, a country doctor, spent most of his working hours on the road making house calls. He is pictured here with two of his patients in the 1950s, Ann and John Caknipe Jr. He always had a lollipop in his big black bag for the children. Having closed his practice in the early 1960s, he continued to see patients in his home until his death in 1969. (JC.)

In 1948, the first freestanding automatic laundry was built in Chase City. Augie's was located on an alley behind Colgate's Electronics Store on Main Street. The laundry was built by Rayford Rockwell, the owner of Oak Lawn, in his backyard. Pictured in the schoolyard of the Robert E. Lee Elementary School, near to the laundry, are Sonny Willis and Edith Coleman Willis. (Charles Willis Jr.)

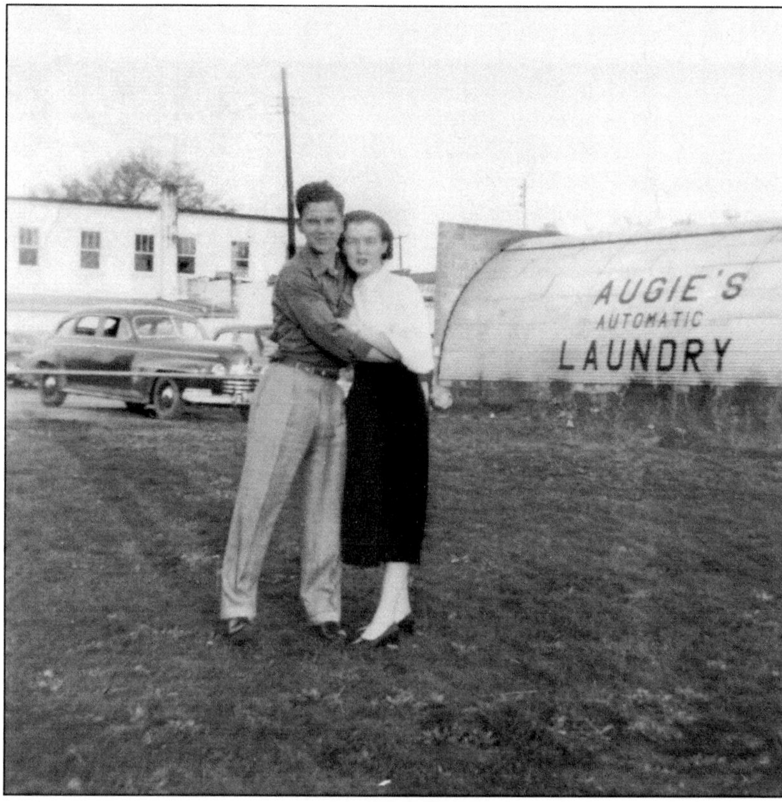

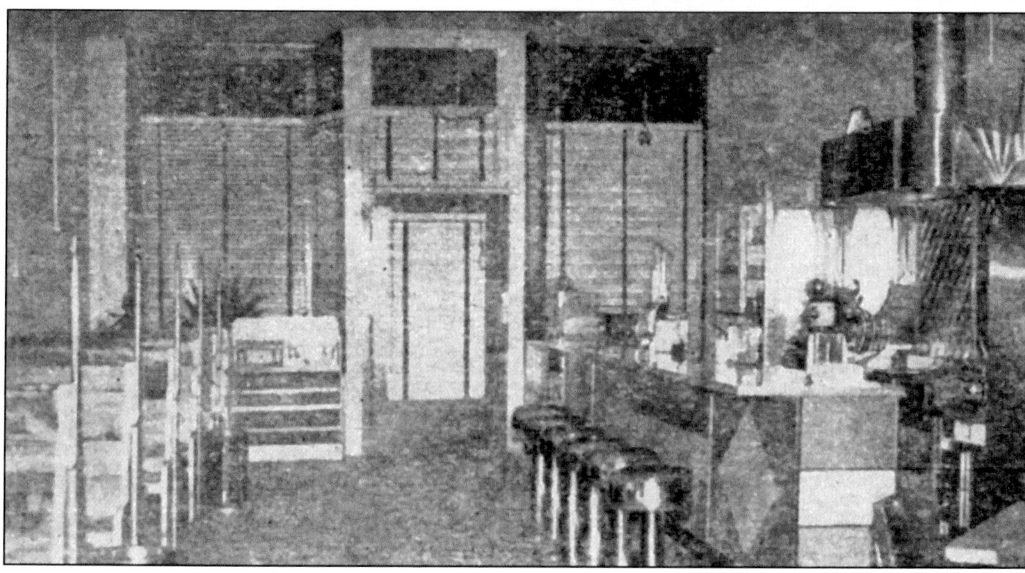

In 1949, the barbershop beside Davis's Café closed. Davis's cousin moved in and opened a second café. The new names for the two cafés were the Red Door (Davis) and the Green Door, both sharing the same building. The Red Door advertised "delicious old Virginia cooked foods, cigars, cigarettes, fountain drinks, sandwiches, magazines, Negro weekly newspapers, music while you dine (T-V) and curb service." The slogan for the café was "when your wife is in a fretful mood, come to The Red Door for your food." (KW.)

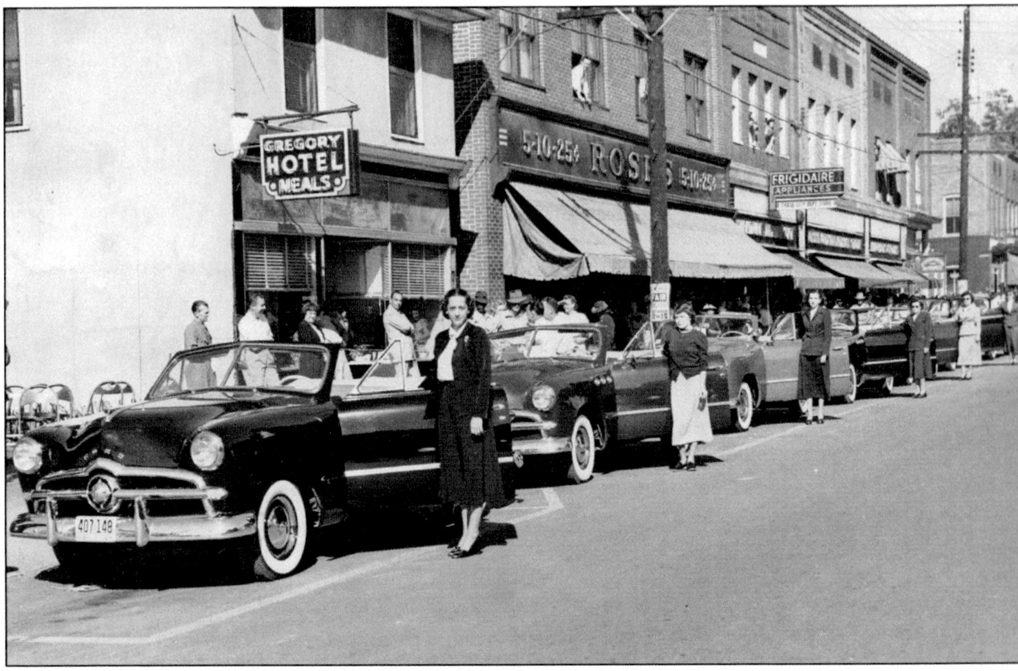

In December 1946, Rose's 5, 10, and 25¢ store opened next to Chase City Department Store on Main Street. Upstairs over the businesses were numerous service and sales businesses. Chase City Department had offices and showroom upstairs. Next to the electric pole is Lewter Drug store, with Dr. John F. Phillips's office in the rear. Next to that is Dr. J. P. Price's drugstore with Dr. H. H. Braxton's office in the rear. (CDS.)

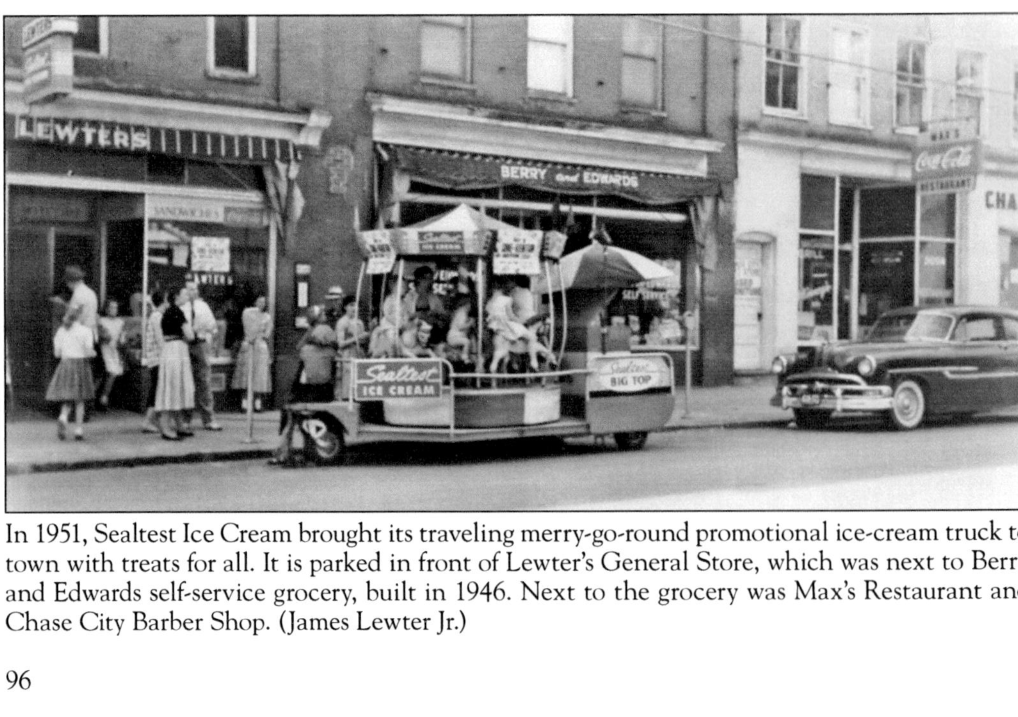

In 1951, Sealtest Ice Cream brought its traveling merry-go-round promotional ice-cream truck to town with treats for all. It is parked in front of Lewter's General Store, which was next to Berry and Edwards self-service grocery, built in 1946. Next to the grocery was Max's Restaurant and Chase City Barber Shop. (James Lewter Jr.)

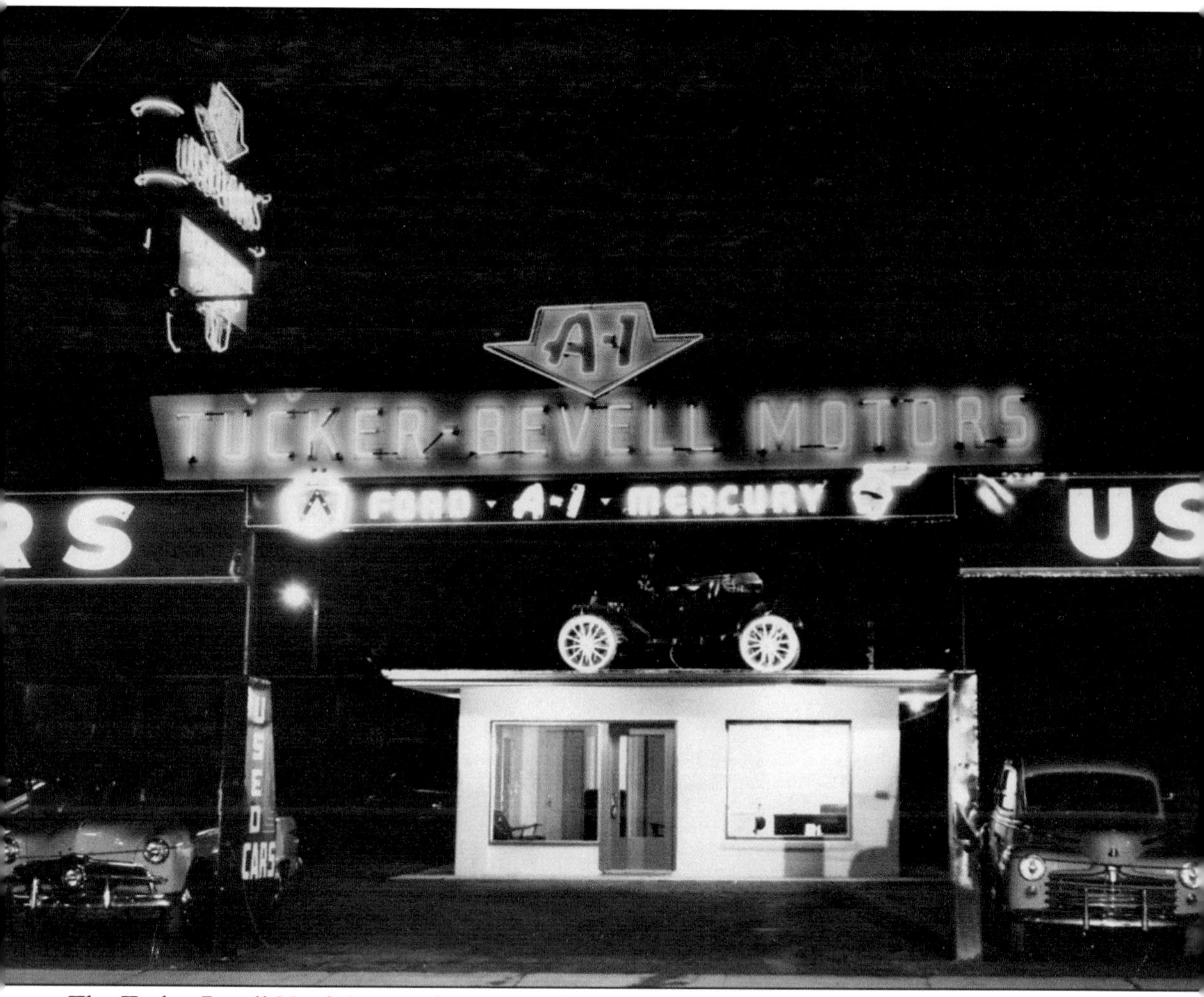

The Tucker-Bevell Used Car Lot has been a famous landmark for a number of years in Chase City. Built on the site of the former miniature golf course, the lot had to have over two feet of dirt removed to lower it to street level. Begun in 1949, the new lot opened in late 1950 with attention-getting neon lights and a Model A car atop the newly constructed sales office building. This is the present-day site of First Citizens Bank. (CDS.)

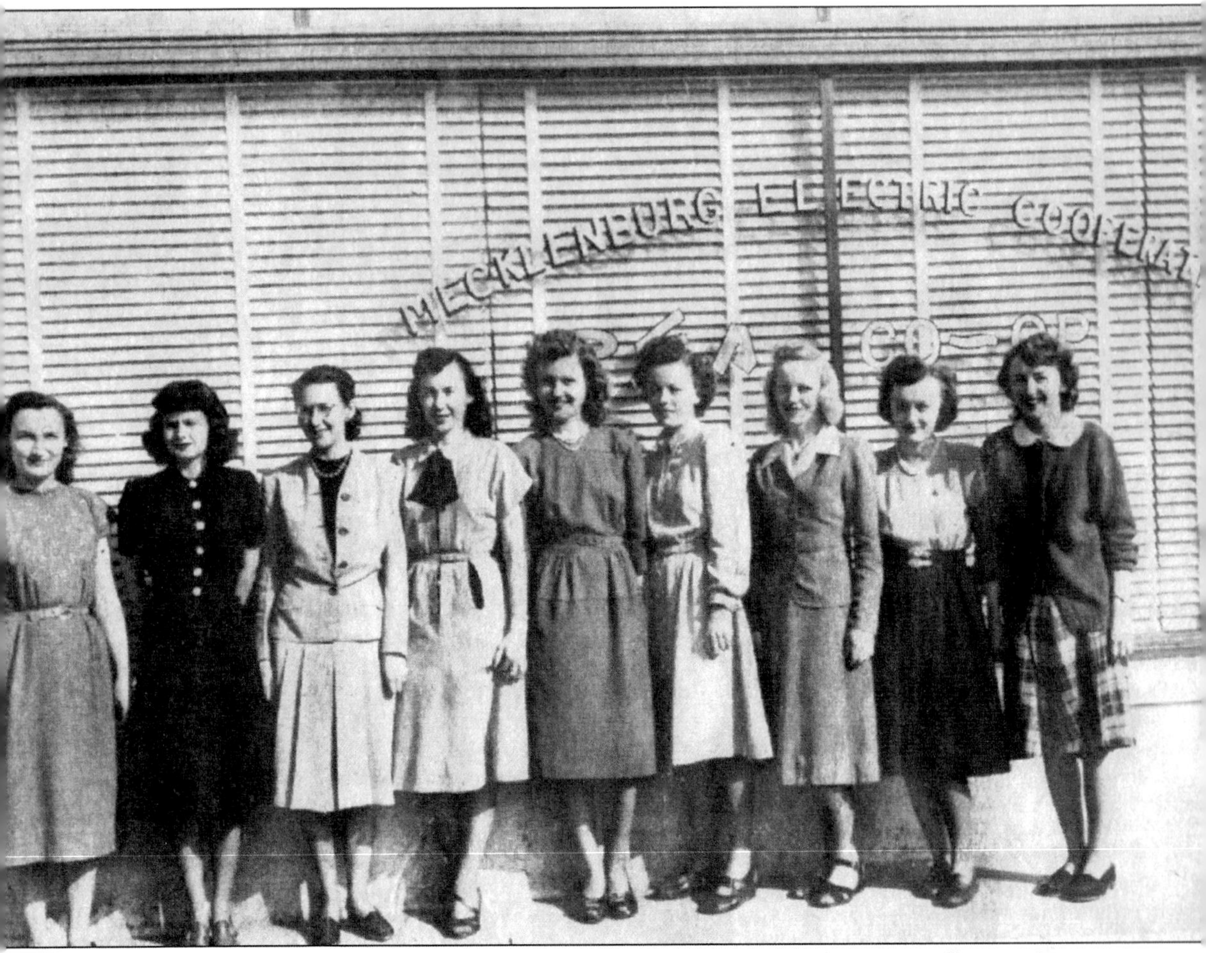

By 1948, the Mecklenburg Electric Cooperative had moved to their new office on Sycamore Street near Main Street (formerly the Piedmont Motor Company building). The co-op eagerly awaited the new John H. Kerr Dam, which would provide electricity to Chase City residents. Pictured here from left to right are Madge Wilson, Elizabeth Roberts, Gladys McKinney, Olean LaFeurne, Devora Towery, Helen Pennington, Pauline Carter, Peggy Brankley, and Julia Ann Gillispie. (*News Progress*, Lisa and Glen Gillispie.)

Five

Recreation, Sports, and Parades

Celebrations of Chase City

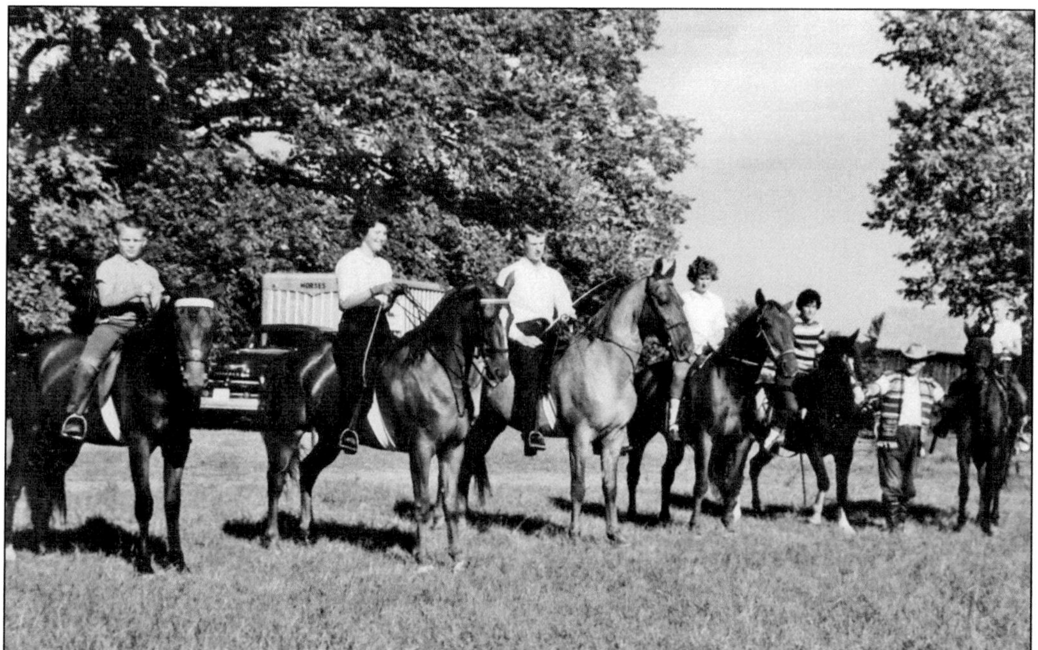

With Chase City and Mecklenburg County being one of the first homes to the Thoroughbred horses from England (*c.* 1760), horses still maintain a great popularity. The Morris Stables of the 1940s through the 1960s were a prime example. Located at the edge of town near the fairgrounds, these stables' riders appeared in almost every parade. Pictured here from left to right are Brian Haga, Susan Payne, Jimmy Payne, Annette Morris, Gloria Collins, Odie Morris Sr. (owner), and David P. Morris. Other stables around town included Owen, Edgerton, and Tharrington, each a different direction from downtown. Horses are still abundant in the Chase City area. (EM.)

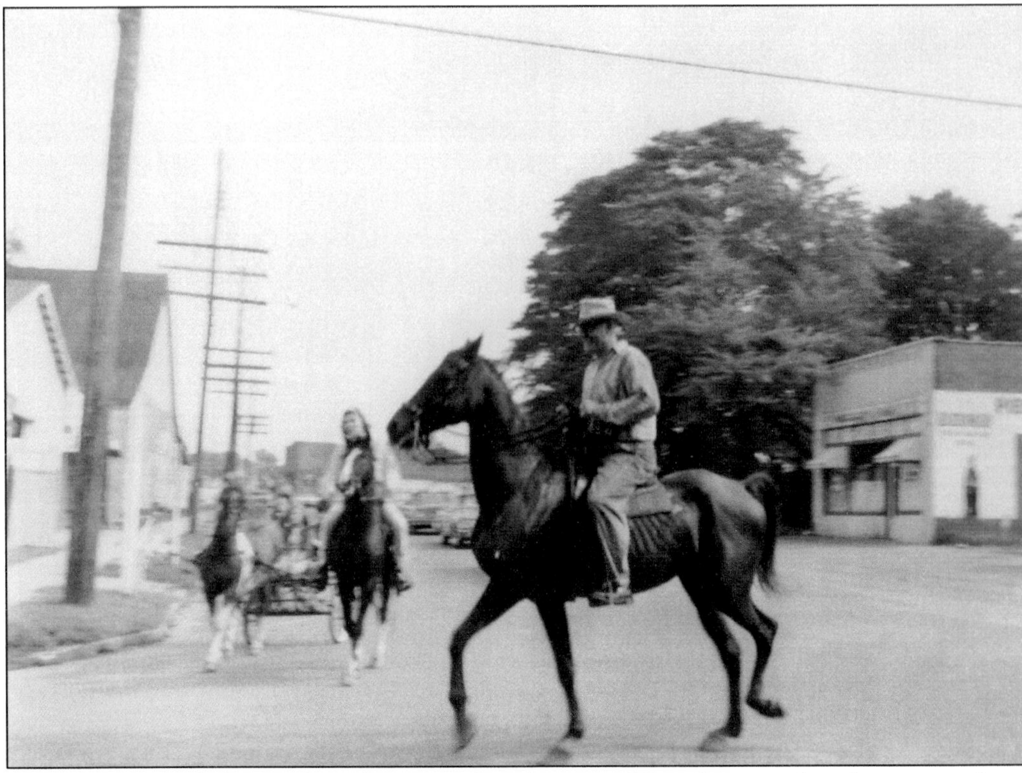

The stables provided a number of services, from livery and boarding to riding lessons, trail and countryside rides, and breeding services. Here Odie Morris Sr. finishes a parade down Main Street and will be heading out to Sycamore for the fairgrounds. He is followed by Winnie Walker Morris and the pony and cart of the stables. (EM.)

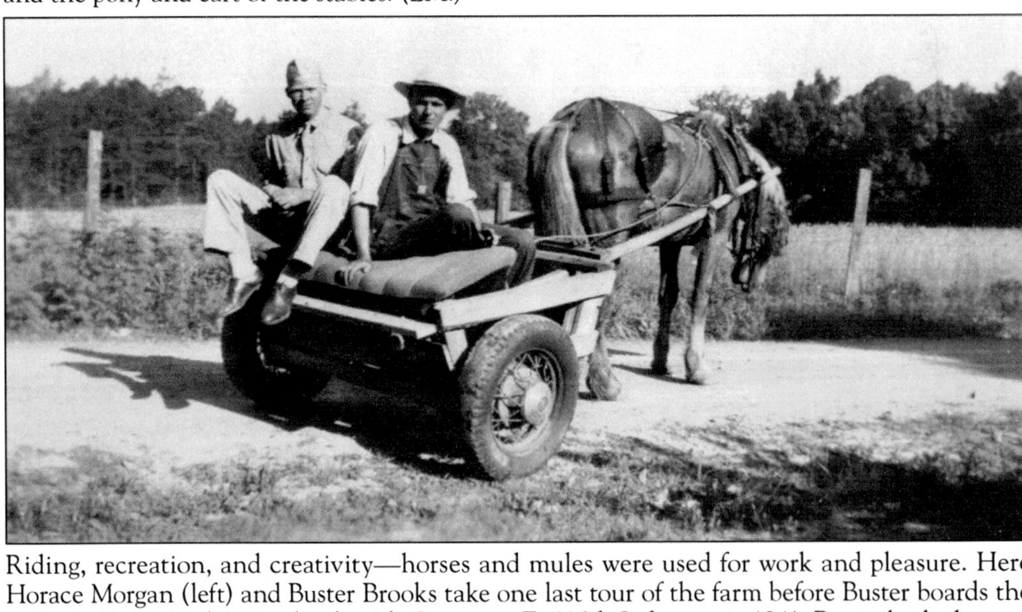

Riding, recreation, and creativity—horses and mules were used for work and pleasure. Here Horace Morgan (left) and Buster Brooks take one last tour of the farm before Buster boards the train for Fort Meade, Maryland, with Company E, 116th Infantry, in 1941. Buster built the cart himself. (IMB.)

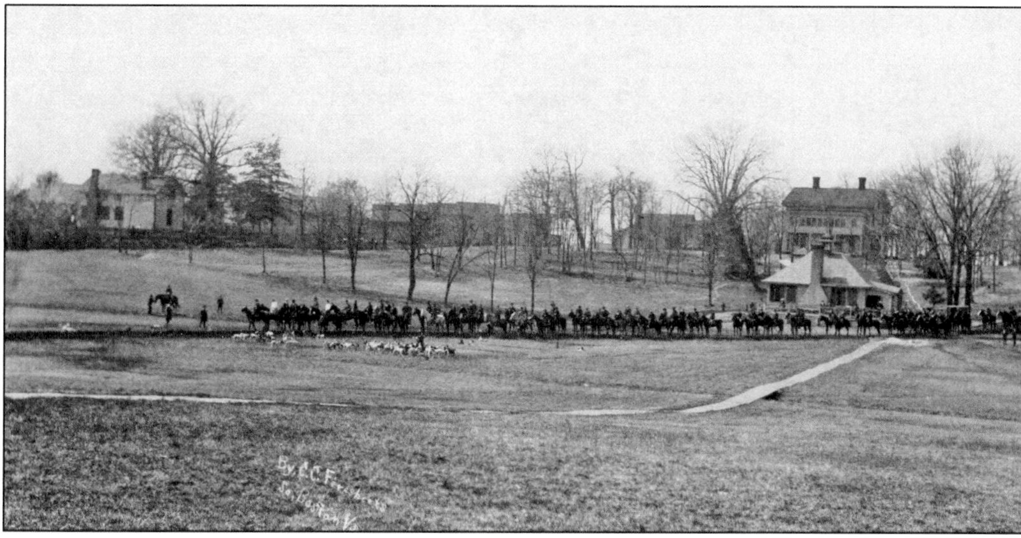

The Virginia–North Carolina Fox Hunters Association formed and held its first meeting in Chase City in 1905 at the Mecklenburg Mineral Springs Hotel. With over 20,000 acres of leased, fenced game preserves, the hotel was a desirable location for the sport. Here the hunters with their packs of dogs have returned to the springs from their hunt. The hotel also offered target and trap shooting, kennels, and livery stables. (BML/HJ.)

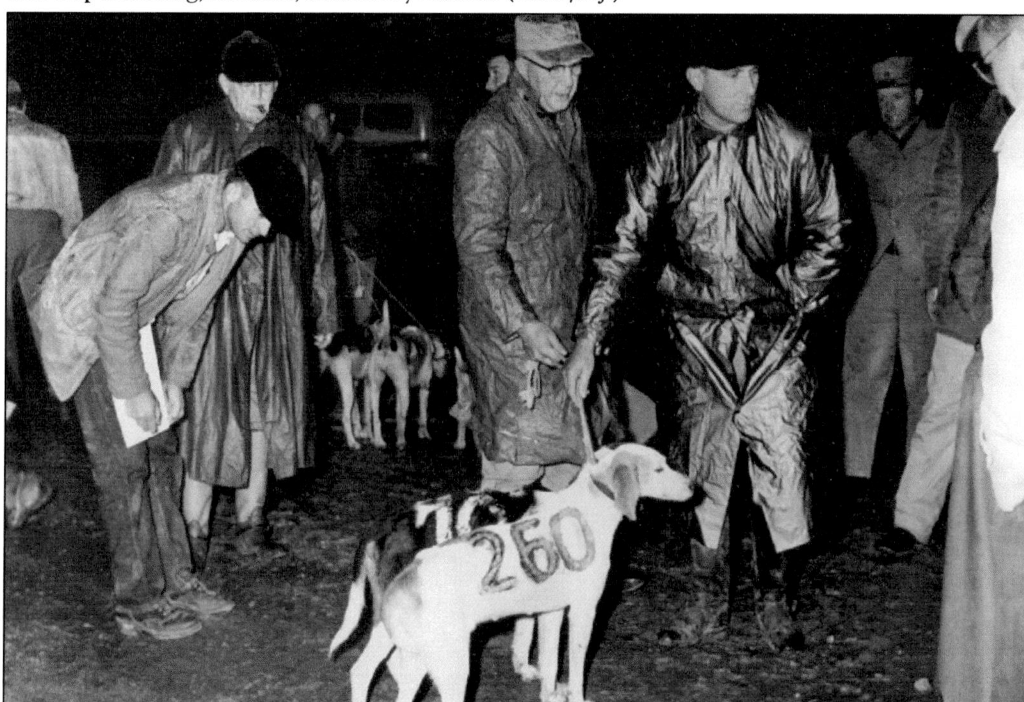

The association continued to hold annual meetings in Chase City through the 1950s, but during the Depression, they split by state boundaries. On October 3, 1946, the Virginia–North Carolina Fox Hunters Association advertised they would be in Chase City with one of their longtime members, Walter Johnson, starting pitcher for the Washington Senators. For hunts, field trials, and dog shows, Chase City was the home of sporting dogs. (Bryan Queensberry.)

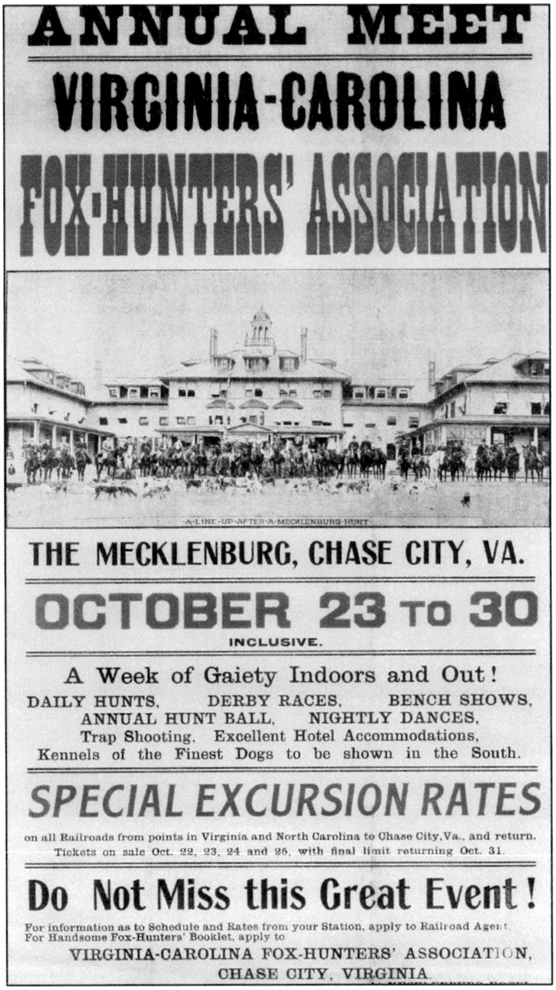

This 1906 or 1907 poster advertising the Virginia–North Carolina Fox Hunters Association meeting was widely circulated in both states. It was even spread across Maryland and South Carolina. So large was this event that special trains and fares were arranged by the railroad to accommodate guests and their animals. The photograph is of the charter meeting of the association in 1905, and because of it, these posters became extremely popular and highly sought after by collectors. (WCG.)

Fox hunting was not only a sport for men; many women participated as well. Note the women in this photograph are riding sidesaddle, rather than Western, as it was proper for the era. They are posed in front of the south wing of the Mecklenburg Mineral Springs Hotel. (WCG.)

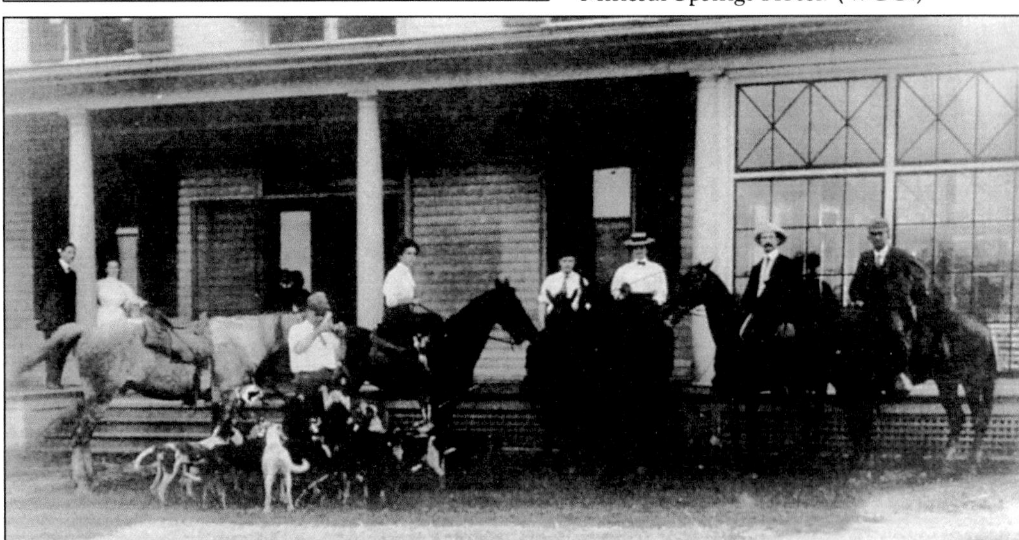

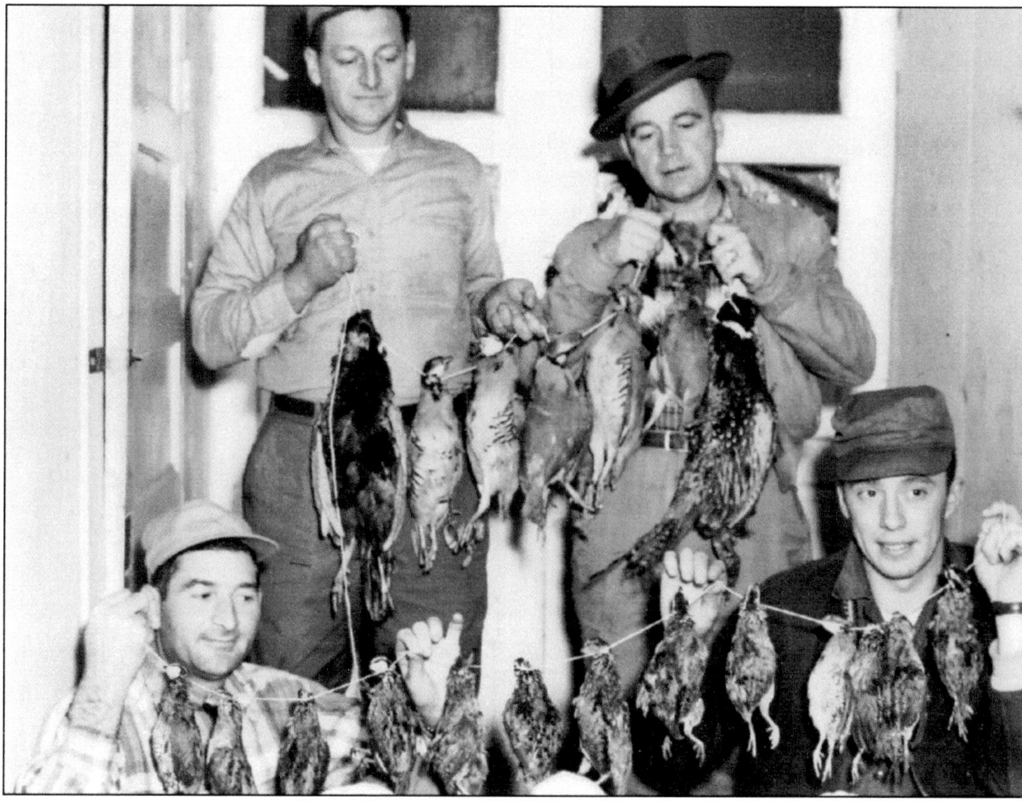

The Chase City area has always been fortunate to host an abundant variety of game and game preserves. As early as 1901 the *Chase City Progress* carried stories of successful hunts, as it was that popular. Even in 1924, there was an elk season, though they were rare. Wildlife sustained many families during the Depression, nearly to depletion, but with game management, all but the elks and pheasants rebounded quickly. The James Crump hunting party displays a successful day of pheasants, chukar partridge, and bobwhite quail. (Bryan Queensberry.)

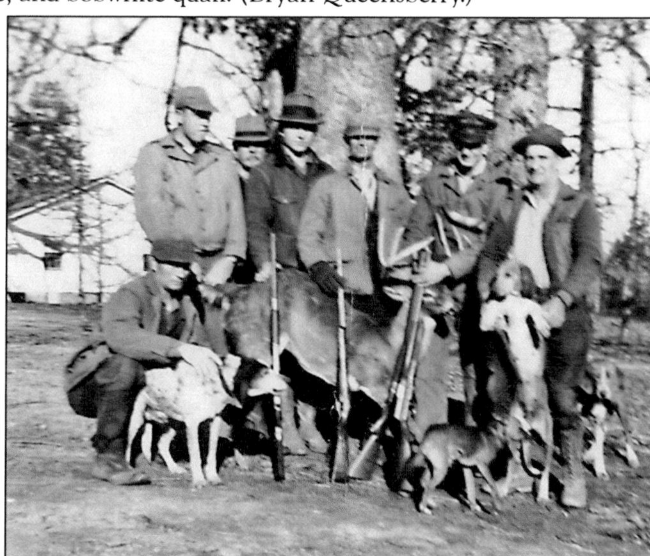

A very rare sight, this 1936 photograph of a local hunt club shows they were successful in harvesting a six-point buck with the help of their walker hounds and long-legged beagles. The early 1800s saw the extinction of buffalo in the area, and in the 1920s, the elk went away. During the Depression, deer and turkey were harvested heavily, but with management practices, these two animals' populations are larger today than ever. (Winnie Walker Morris.)

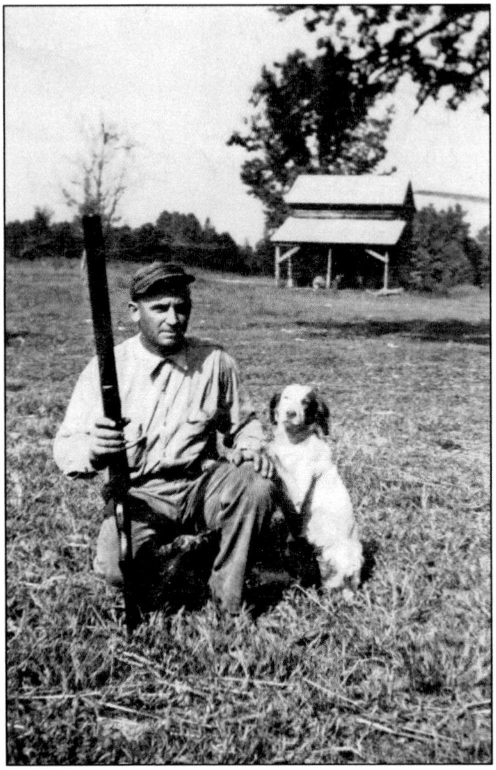

A big part of the sport has always been the dogs. Whether fox, deer, or bird hunting, each sport has dogs of a variety of breeds. The dogs engage in hunting, field competitions, and shows. Arthur Fay McKinney proudly poses with his pointer just before a bird hunt in 1942. (Betty McKinney Caknipe.)

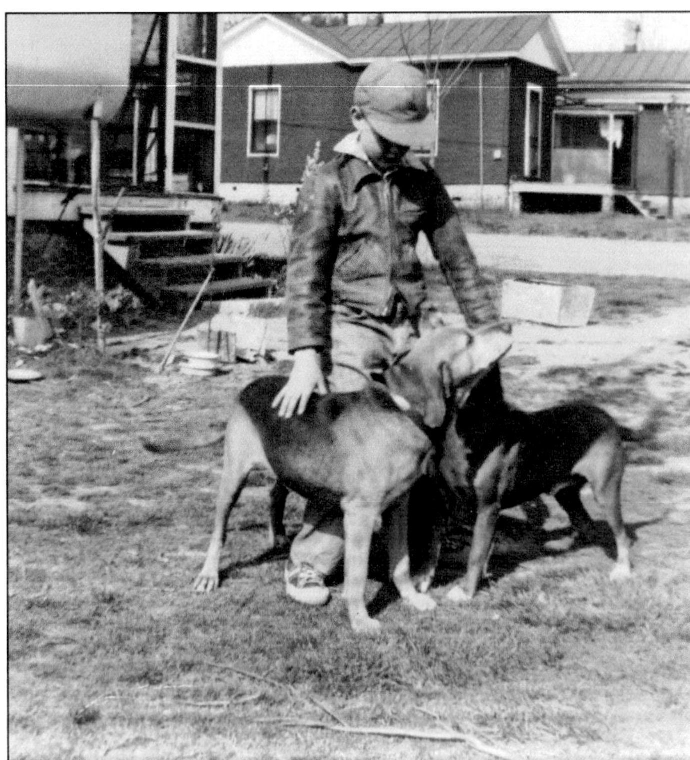

This 1949 photograph is of Eugene Morris with his two prize raccoon hounds, Blaze and Rock. Inspired by his dogs—breeding and training—Eugene entered the military during the Vietnam era to work in the veterinary medical service with service assignments at Fort Benning, Georgia, and Walter Reed Army Hospital in Washington, D.C. (EM.)

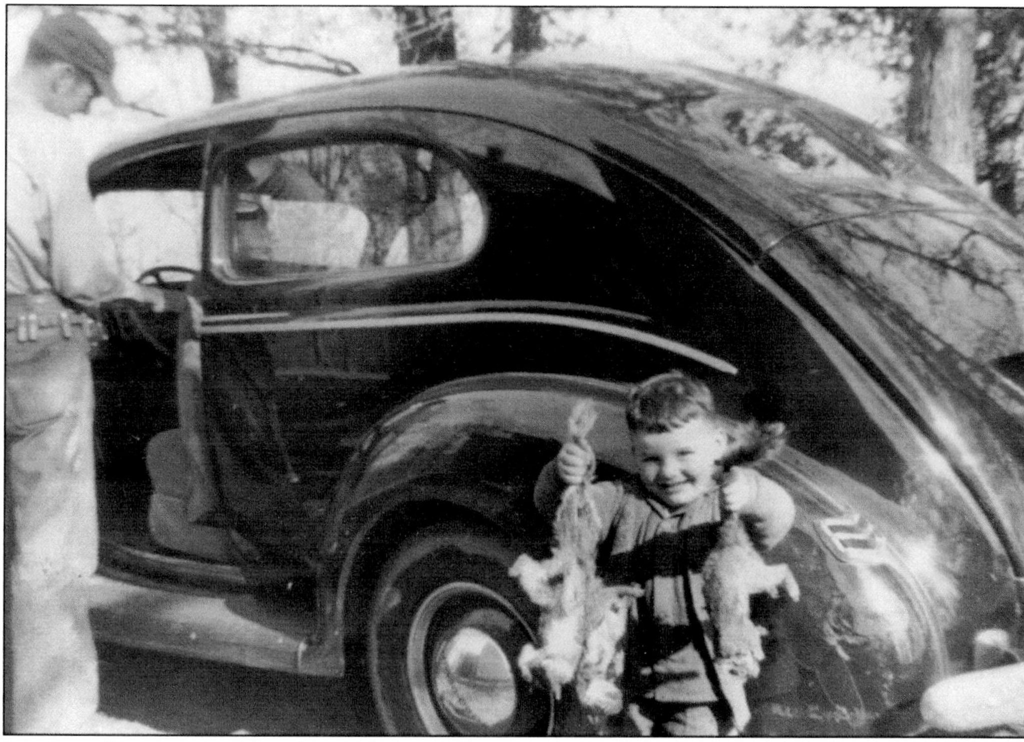

In 1949, the primary ingredient of an authentic local Brunswick stew was squirrel. These three squirrels, harvested by John Caknipe Sr. and held by John Caknipe Jr., added to a pot with chicken, potatoes, tomatoes, and corn would make at least six meals. Today beef has been substituted for the squirrel, and the meat is just not as sweet. (JC.)

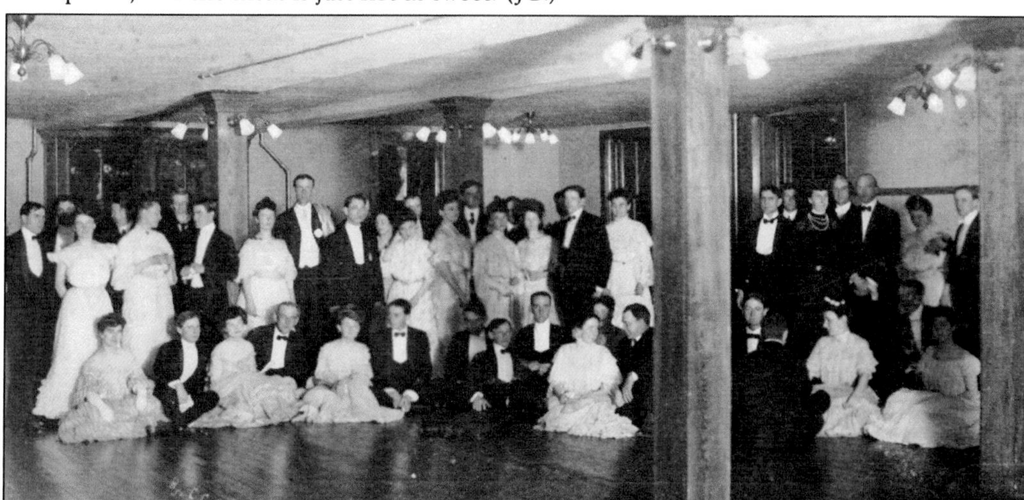

The Mecklenburg Mineral Springs Hotel also included a ballroom (pictured here), an orchestra room, and a dance pavilion. It provided a variety of musical entertainment. Many dance houses have been in Chase City since the hotel burned. Starting in 1922, Chase City had its own band. The band performed until World War II. In the off-season, several tobacco warehouses were music and dance houses drawing large crowds. The most popular dance hall was the American Legion post, which hosted dances from its beginning in 1926 until about 1990. (BML.)

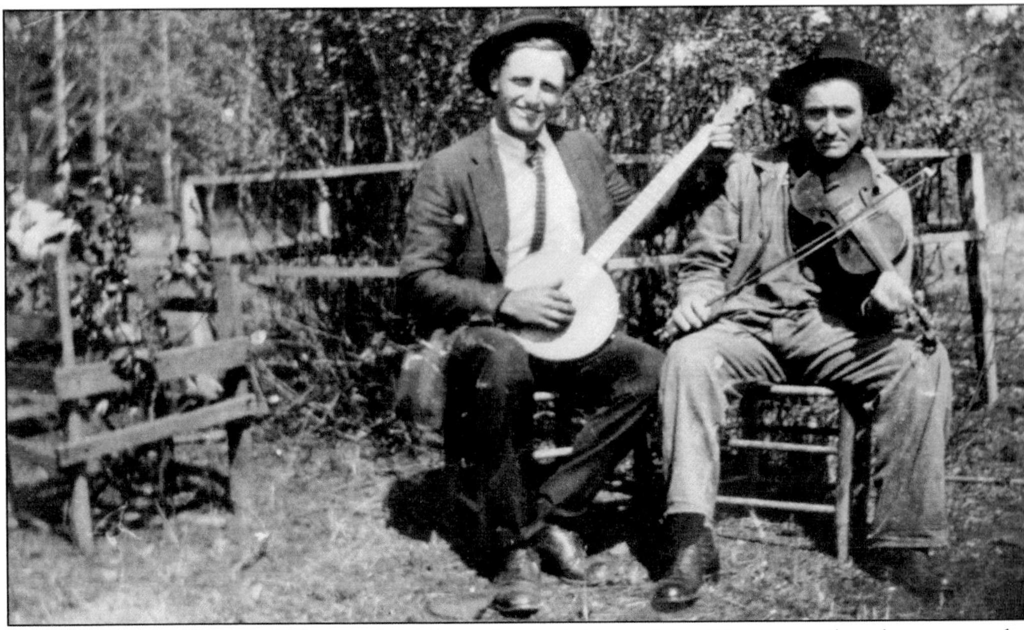

Mountain and bluegrass music evolved from the Irish jig and the Virginia reel and were popular around the beginning of the 20th century. Barn dances and warehouse dances were prevalent in the Chase City area. Here Pozie Lankford (fiddle) and Pat Holder (banjo) warm up for a performance later in the evening in 1926. (HL.)

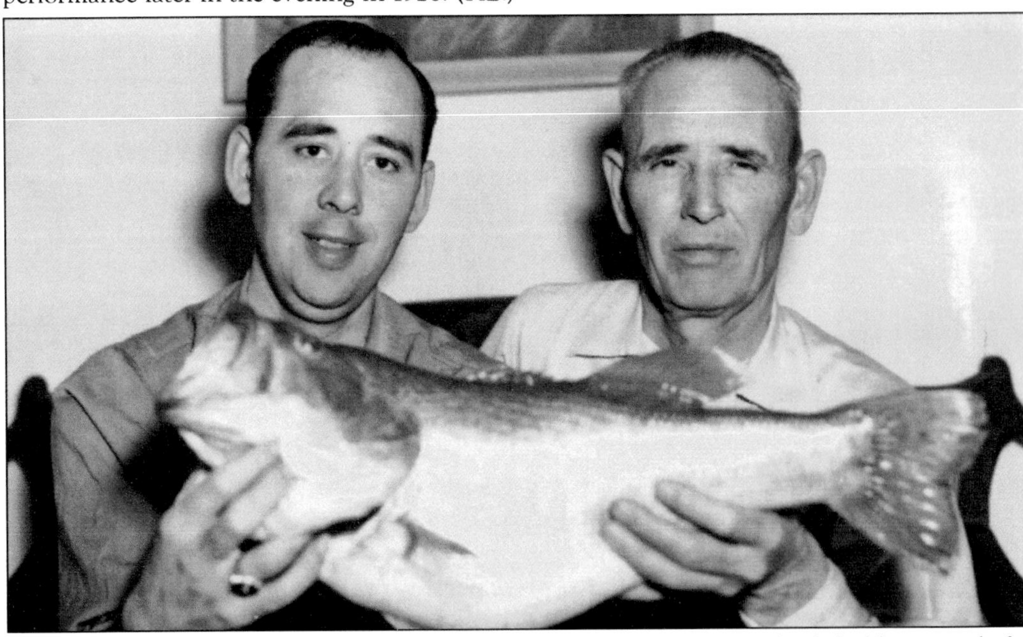

There were a number of streams in and around Chase City. Farmers built holding ponds for irrigation and livestock. These ponds were stocked with fish, and between them, the streams, and nearby rivers, fishing has been a very popular sport since the Depression. Fishing contests have been popular since the 1940s, sponsored by local merchants and country stores. Western Auto advertised a big bass contest in May 1947. Pictured here are Bernal Boswell and his father, Waverly, holding a largemouth bass that is being entered in a contest. (Bryan Queensberry.)

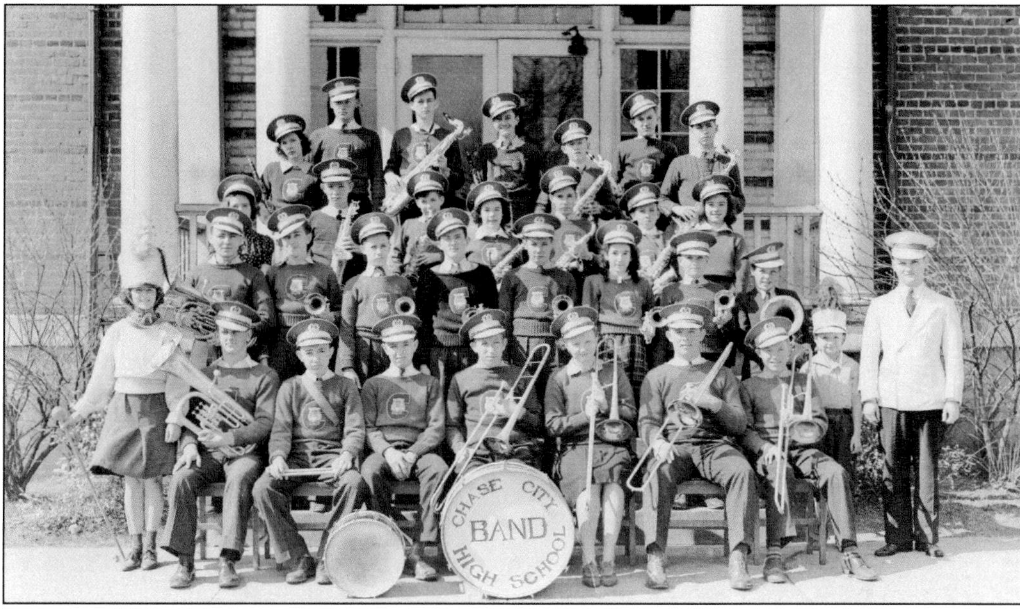

Music became popular in the schools. This is a photograph of the Chase City High School band of 1939. The drum major is Aloise Boswell. The high school band continued until the closing of the Chase City School District in 1955 for the county consolidated schools. The new high school was located more centrally for students from the west side of the county and continues to offer band classes. (Glen and Tina Wood.)

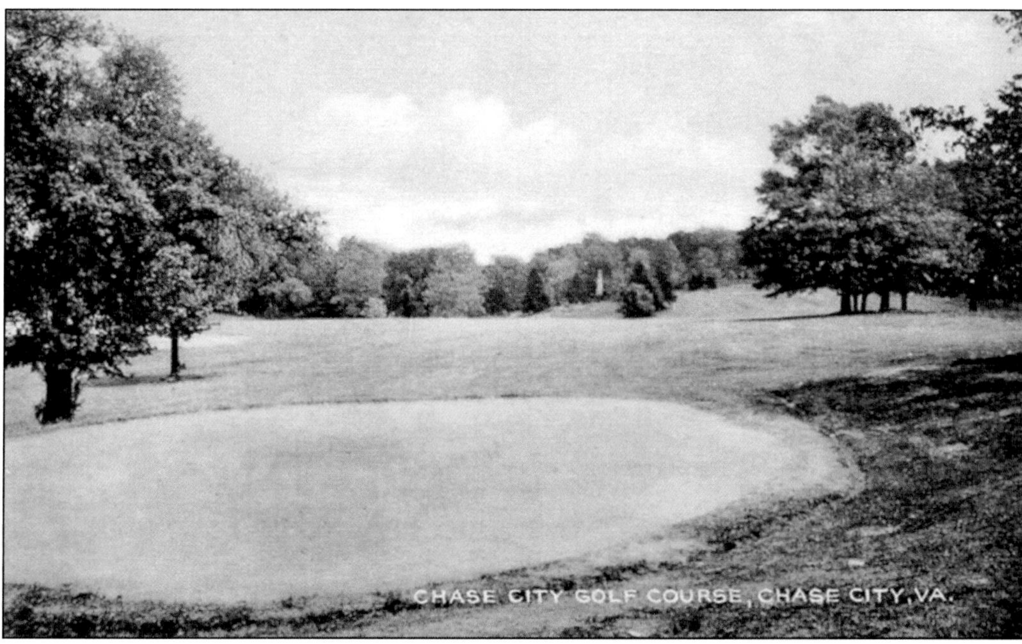

As early as 1903, golf was a major sport. The Mecklenburg Mineral Springs Hotel had a nine-hole golf course as part of the front lawn. When it burned in 1909, Mecklenburg Mineral Springs Company continued to operate until 1927, when it was platted to be sold. The Depression postponed the auction until 1946, and the golf course continued to operate until that time. (MWC.)

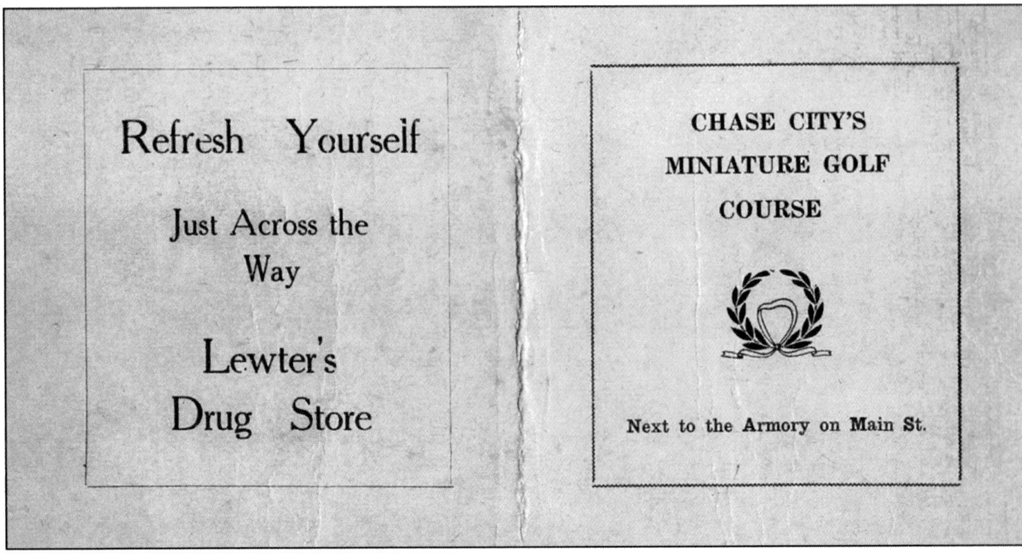

This scorecard is from the Chase City miniature golf course. The course was developed on the site of the old Barnett Hotel by Hilda Lewter around 1942, but with a lack of success during the war, it closed in 1946. (GLG.)

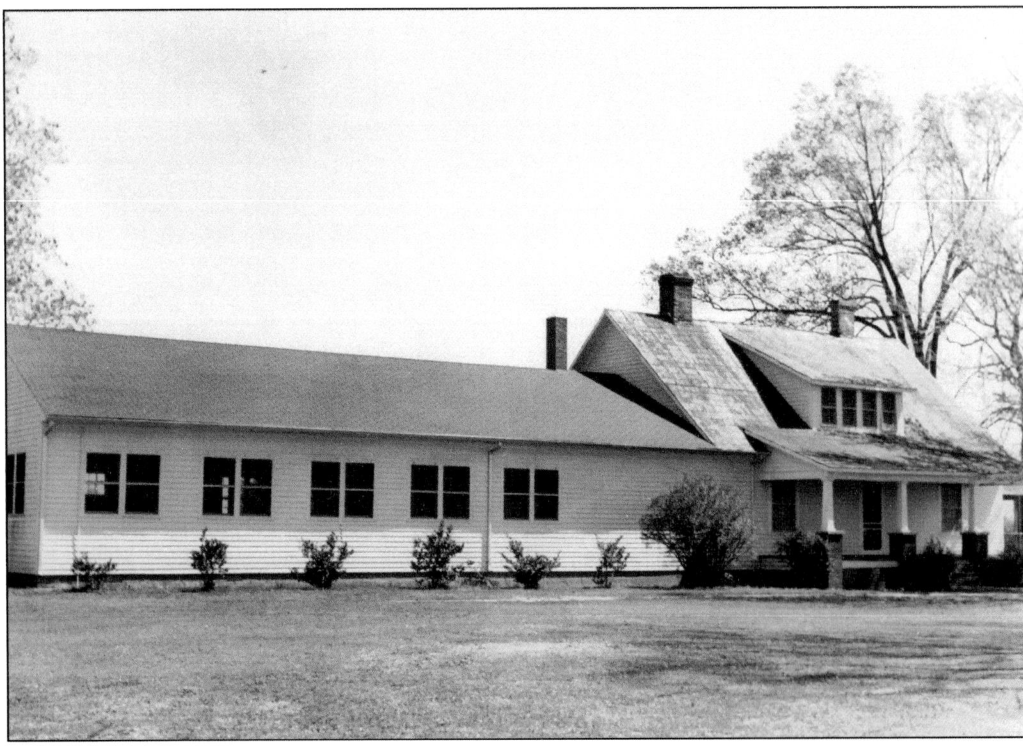

In 1946, with the nine-hole golf course now closed, a number of residents formed a corporation to purchase the Hicks Farm outside town and build a Mecklenburg Country Club with a new nine-hole golf course. The original governing board was Dave Liptz, president; Hon. Frank C. Bedinger, vice president; Arthur Greene, secretary; and John Cunningham, treasurer. (Mecklenburg Country Club.)

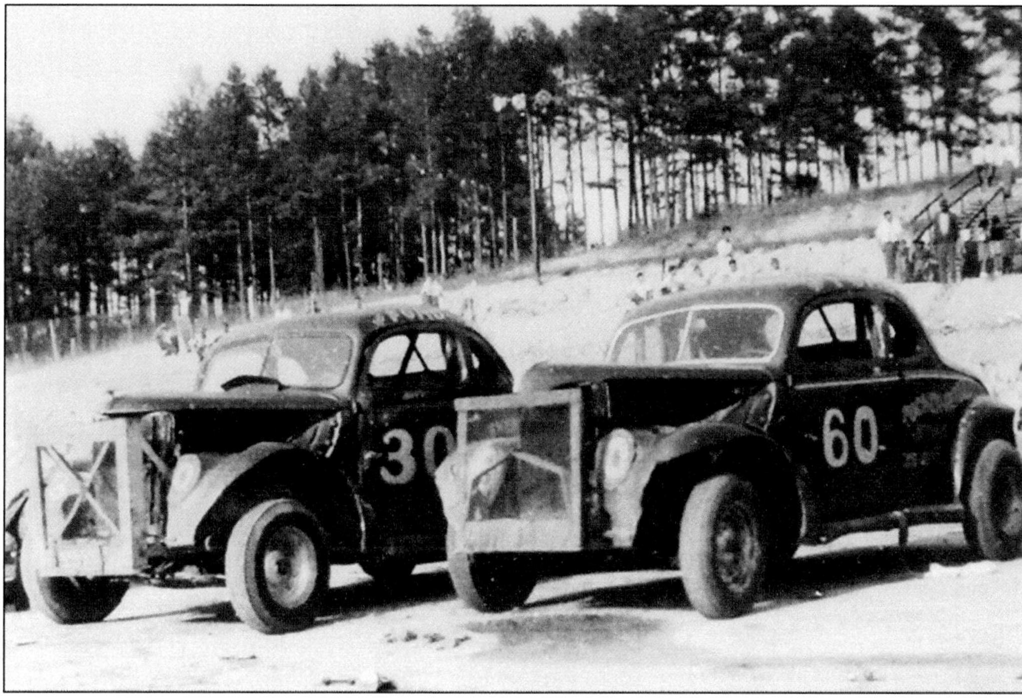

With changing technology came changes in sports and new sports. This is a photograph of 1950 Tucker-Bevell Motors race cars. Cars 30 and 60 are on the Daytona Beach track with the sand dunes as a grandstand in the background. Both cars completed the race, and it is reported that about a month later, Tucker-Bevell received it share of the purse: $35. (HL.)

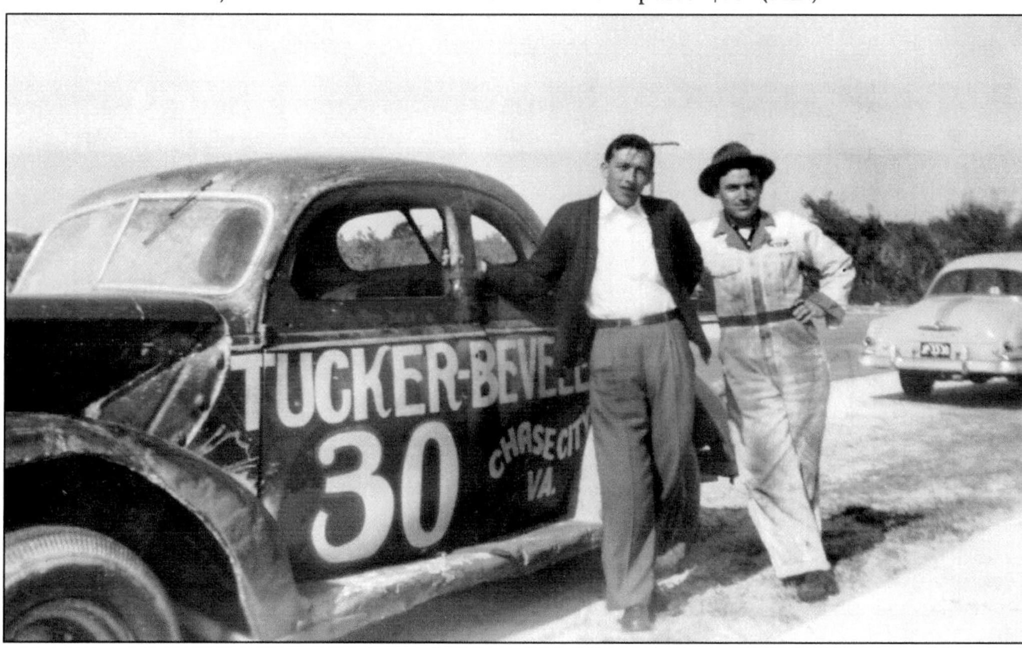

Readying for the race, car 30 is pictured here with its driver, Buford Wood of Martinsville, Virginia. The lead mechanic for the race team (right) was Hugh Lankford, a mechanic and employee of Tucker-Bevell Motors in Chase City. (HL.)

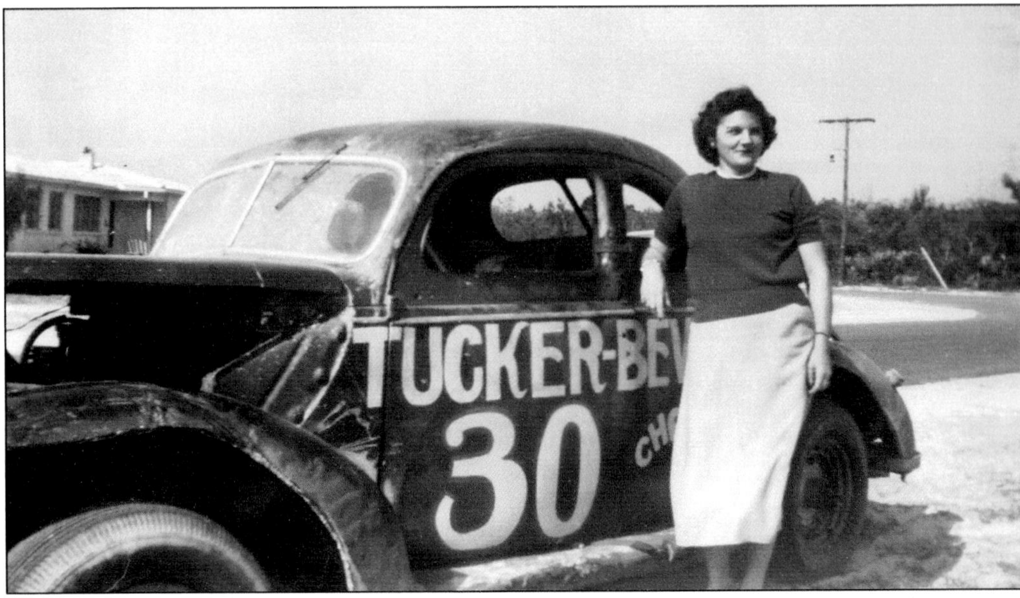

This is a photograph of car 30 at Daytona Beach with Carrie Tucker posing beside it. Upon marrying Clarence Tucker, Carrie took a great interest in the business and is said to have been the inspiration behind many of the creative marketing strategies. (HL.)

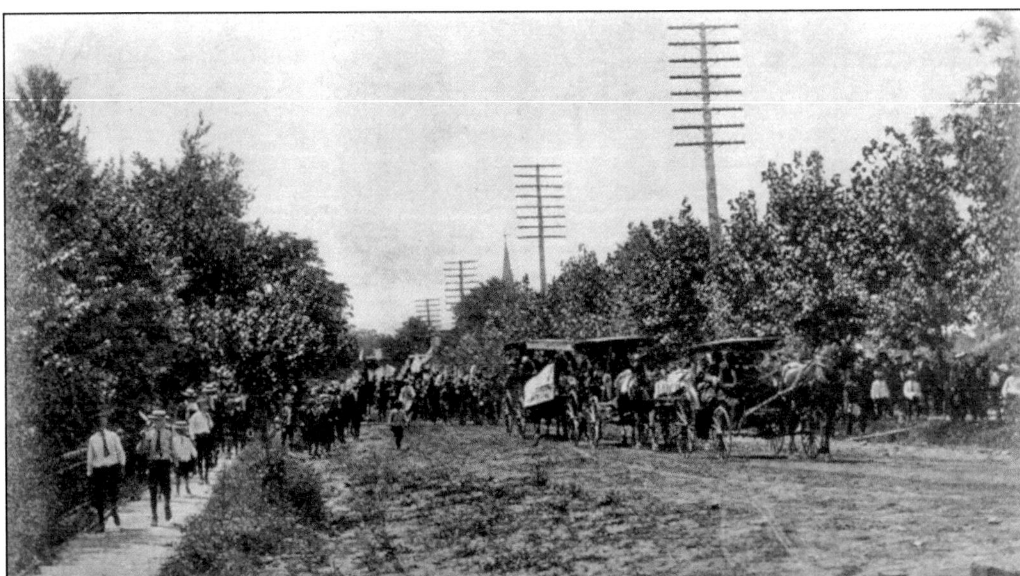

Chase City has always been a parade town, hosting as many as five or six per year. This is the earliest documented parade from July 4, 1906, welcoming Virginia governor Claude Swanson to the celebration to be held on the grounds of the Mecklenburg Mineral Springs Hotel. During Reconstruction, Virginians did not celebrate Independence Day. After many attempts to get the citizens to past celebrations had met with little success, this was seen as a perfect opportunity to unite the old and new settlers of Chase City. (SVHP.)

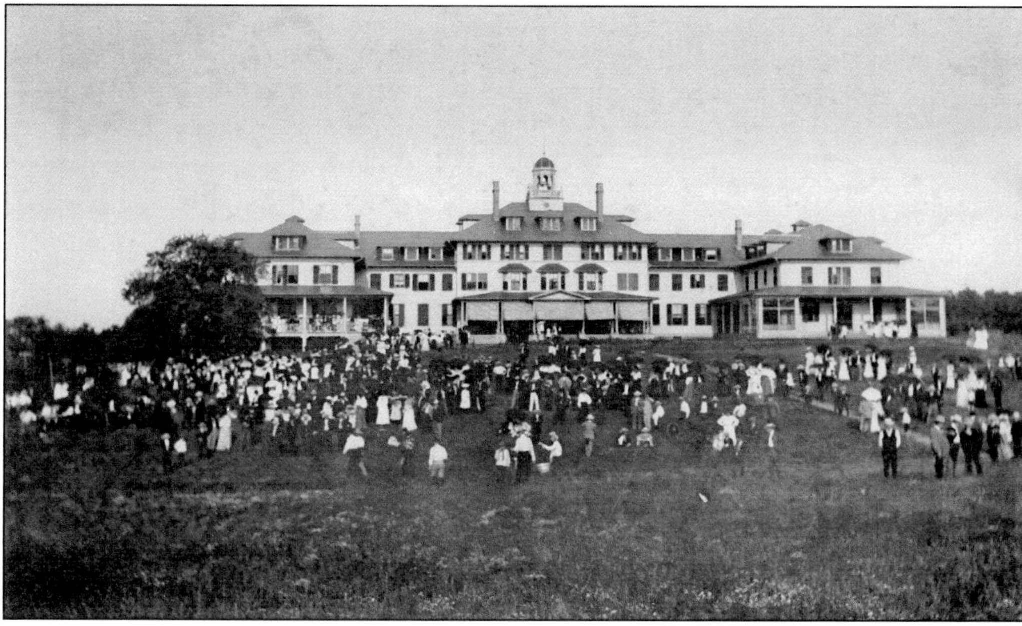

This is the famous picnic on the hotel lawn in 1906. In the front center of the crowd, W. H. Willis sells lemonade from a bucket. In the afternoon was a military reenactment, and at dusk was a powerful fireworks display said to have lasted until after darkness had fallen. Much of this was for the governor and his entourage of distinguished guests, as well as many notable guests in the hotel, but it seemed to unite the town citizens for the first time since 1866. (Polly Ward Bruce.)

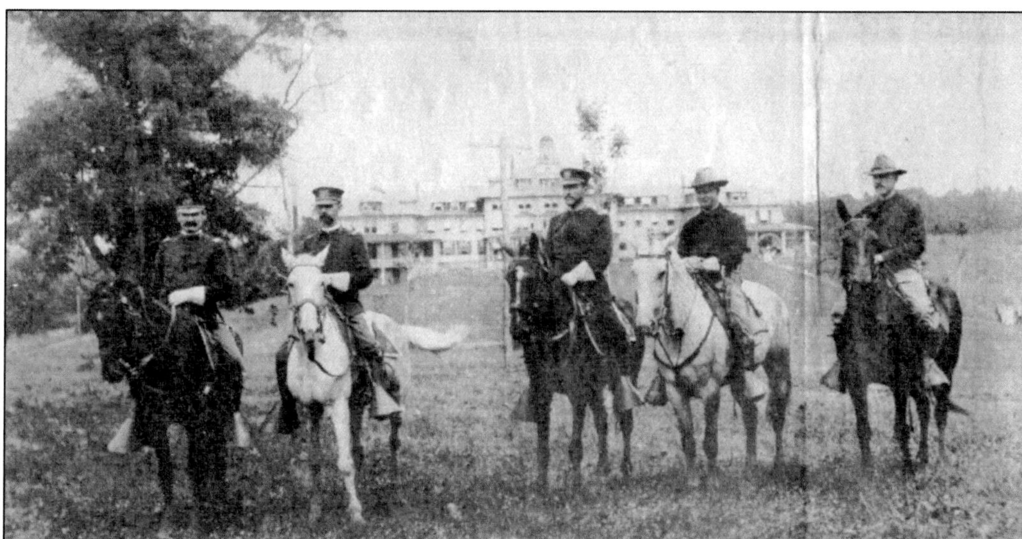

The reenactment performed on the grounds of the hotel was actually performed by a group from Richmond, Virginia. There are conflicting stories of which battle was reenacted, but the most commonly accepted is the charge of the light brigade at San Juan Hill during the Spanish-American War—at that time, a more contemporary and less emotional reenactment than one from the Civil War. (*News Progress*, Lisa and Glen Gillispie.)

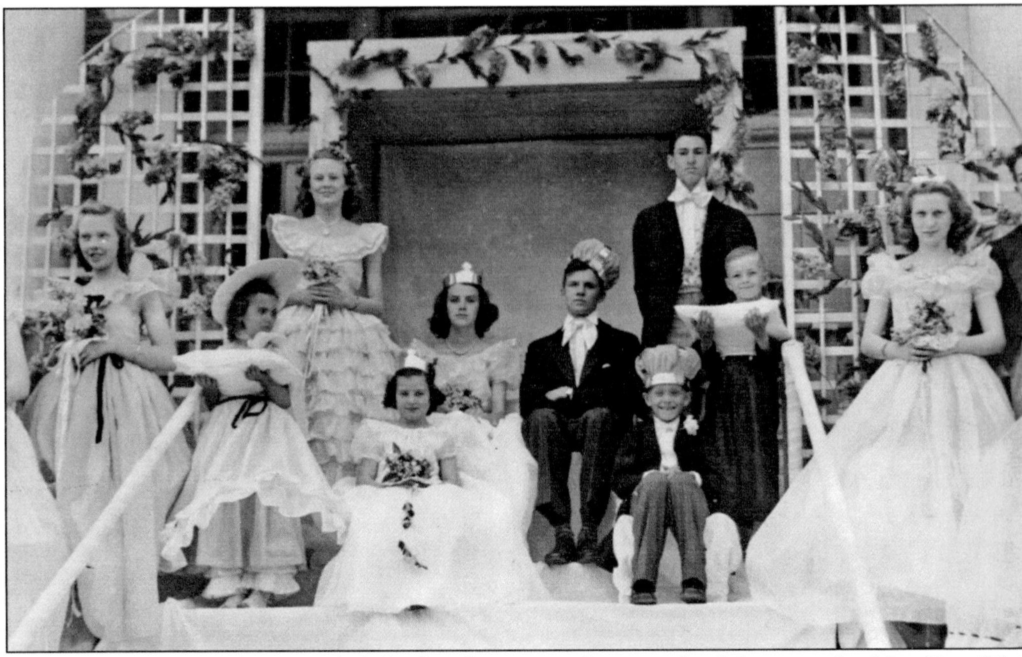

Parades and picnics also attended the local, state, and regional celebrations for May Day. This is the 1940 queen and her court from Chase City High School. As May Queen of 1938, Elsie Edmunds Broocks of Chase City went to Durham, North Carolina, and was voted the regional queen of May Day, which was of course followed by a parade there and in Chase City. (Jo Anne Wortman Andrews.)

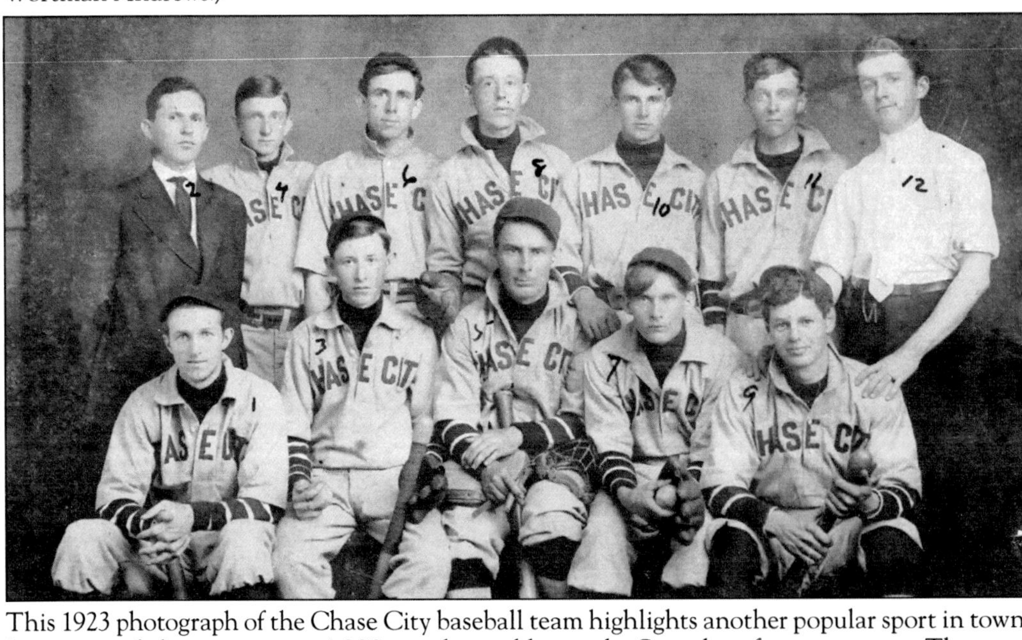

This 1923 photograph of the Chase City baseball team highlights another popular sport in town. It is reported that as many as 1,000 people would attend a Saturday afternoon game. The team consists of, from left to right, (first row) Hiram Moss, Whitt Greer, Marshal Geoghegan Sr., Perry Ozlin, and Dr. R. A. Dodd; (second row) Eddie Wilmouth, David Lipsitz, Jack Goode, Arthur Robertson, Frank Bedinger (attorney), Dr. Adam Finch, and unidentified. (WCG.)

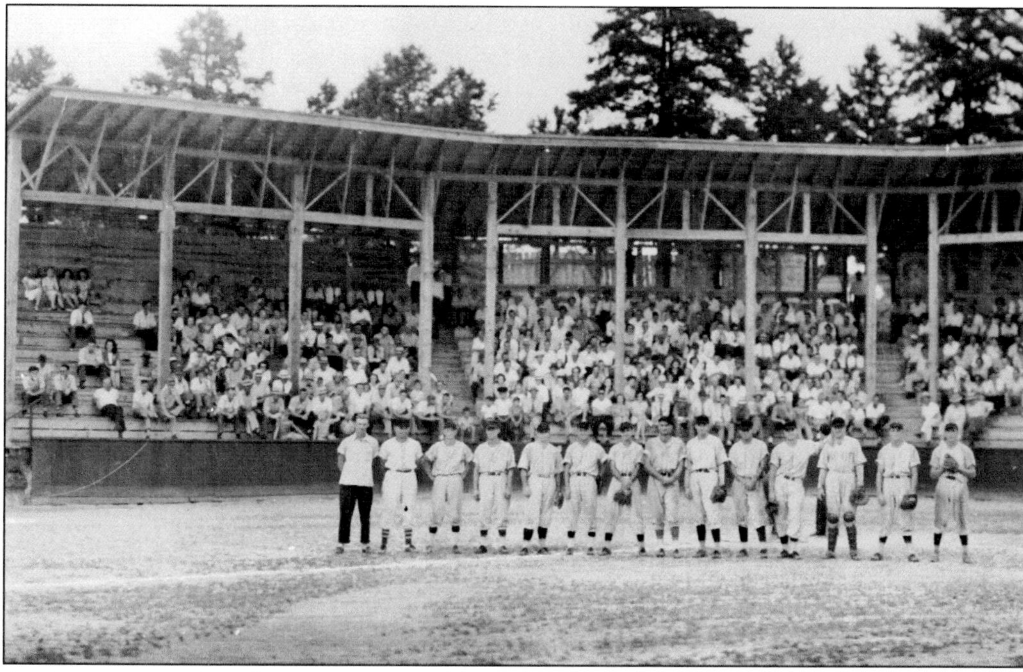

As the team continued to grow in popularity, they built a field behind the American Legion post (Victory Field) in 1946, the year of this photograph. During World War II, the team was renamed Fireman's Team, but after the war, the name changed back to Chase City Team on April 4, 1946. The team is shown on Victory Field in front of the new grandstand. In 1947, an announcers' box was added to the grandstand, and the field became lighted to host night games. (Polly Ward Bruce.)

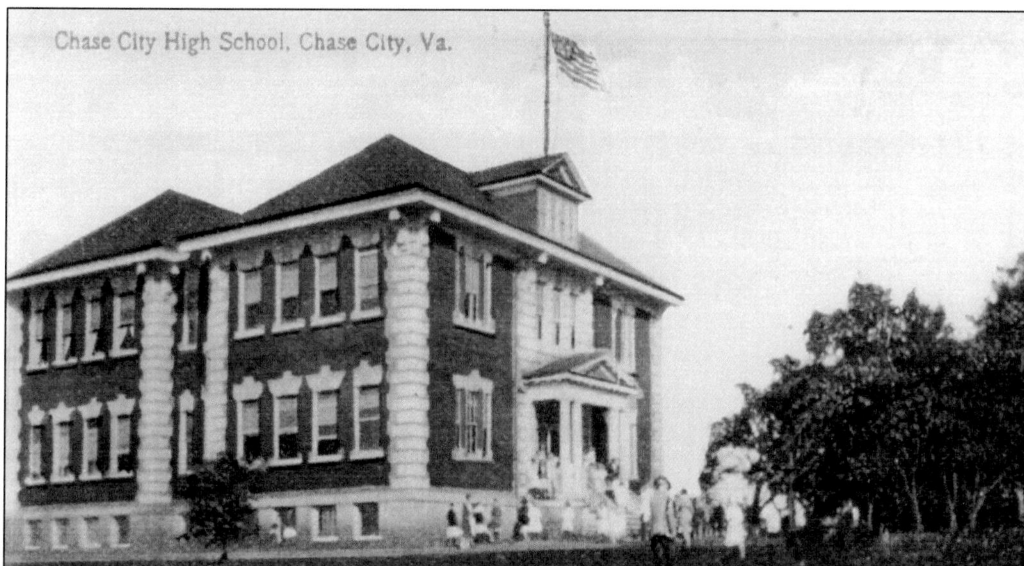

In 1909, when the new Chase City High School opened, part of the celebration was a chicken chase on the front lawn. Here the students are attempting to round up all the loose chickens, which they were able to take home after the day was done. This sport did not seem to gain in popularity, and this is the only documented time it was done. (Calvin Hoyle.)

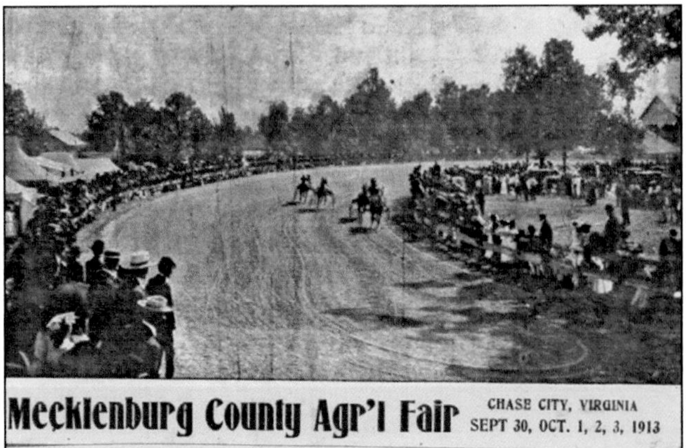

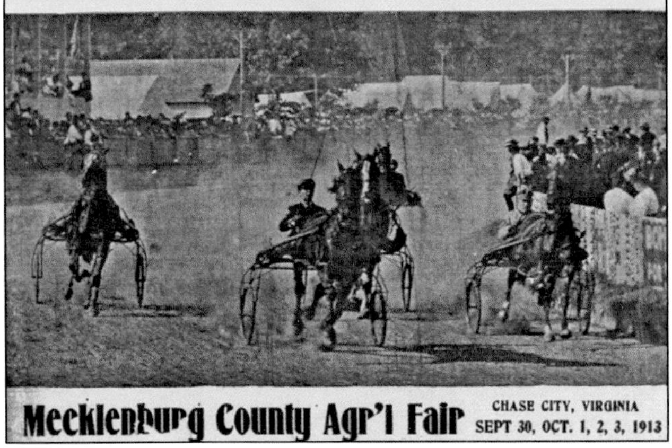

The Farmers Fair began on the lawn of the Mecklenburg Hotel in 1906. By 1911, the Mecklenburg County Agricultural Fair had purchased its own property, and in 1912, the town provided free electricity and water. This was the first and largest fair in south central Virginia. After completion of the track, horse racing, which had stopped in 1861, resumed in Chase City. Several cart and Thoroughbred races were hosted per year, not just during fair week. The races continued until 1969. (SCFA.)

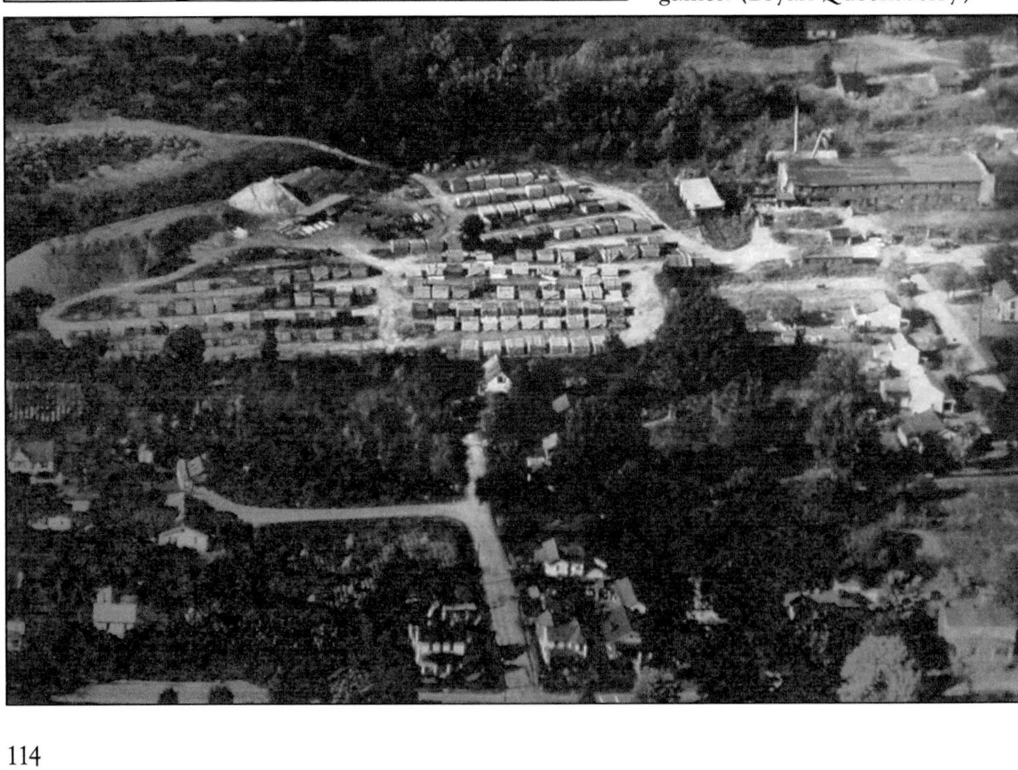

An aerial photograph of the fairgrounds in 1959 shows the racetrack and the several exhibit houses. Adjacent to the fairgrounds is Victory Field. The stadium is gone, but the field continues to host baseball games. (Bryan Queensberry.)

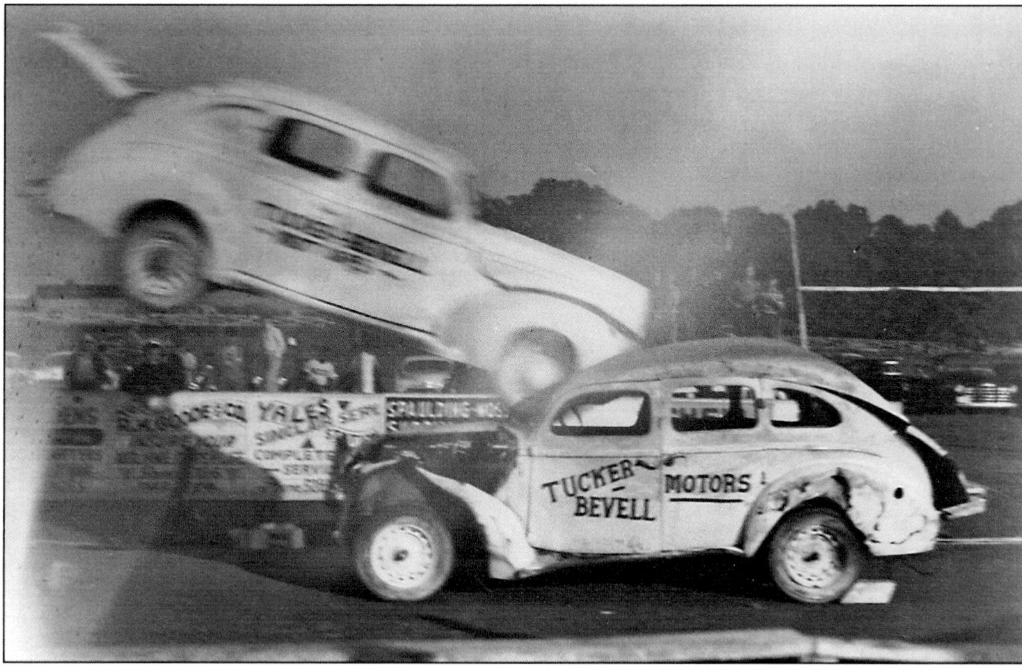

Beginning in 1949, one of the featured shows at the fairgrounds during fair week was the demolition derby. This photograph shows a whole different style of the derby. Tucker-Bevell again exercised its creativity to excite the crowds with daredevil drivers. The demolition derby continues to be a big attraction during fair week and now occupies a two-day time slot. (CDS.)

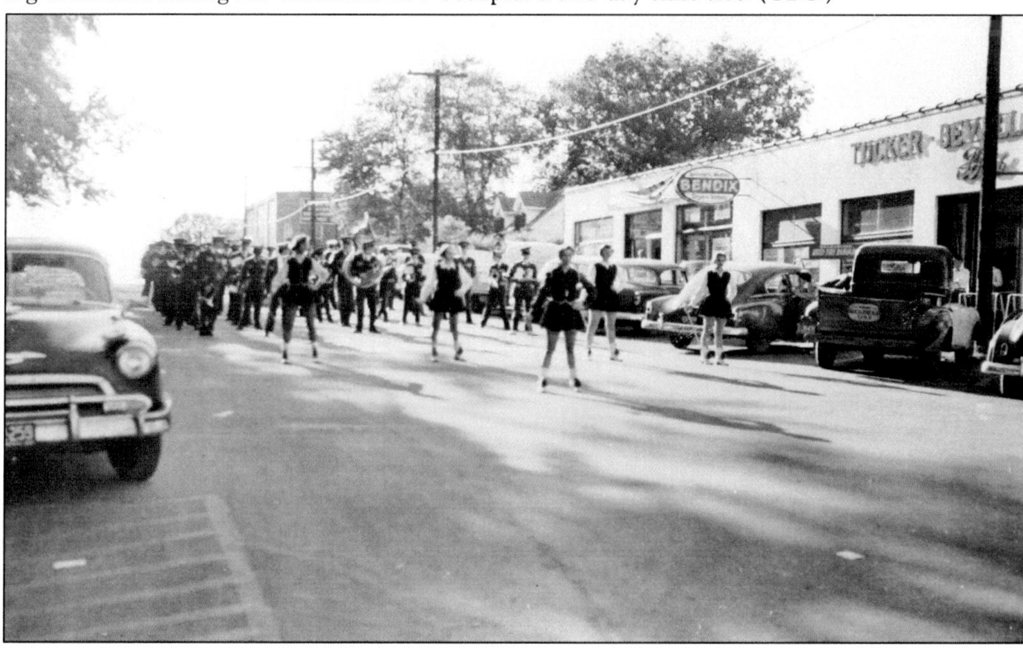

The band is lining up on Fifth Street to begin a parade in 1949. It is in front of Tucker-Bevell Motors, and in the background is the company's new wing, Bendix Electronics. Since about 1912, fair parades began on Fifth Street, turned right onto Main Street, and ended at the fairgrounds. The remainder of the parades would end at the corner of Main and Sycamore Streets. (CDS.)

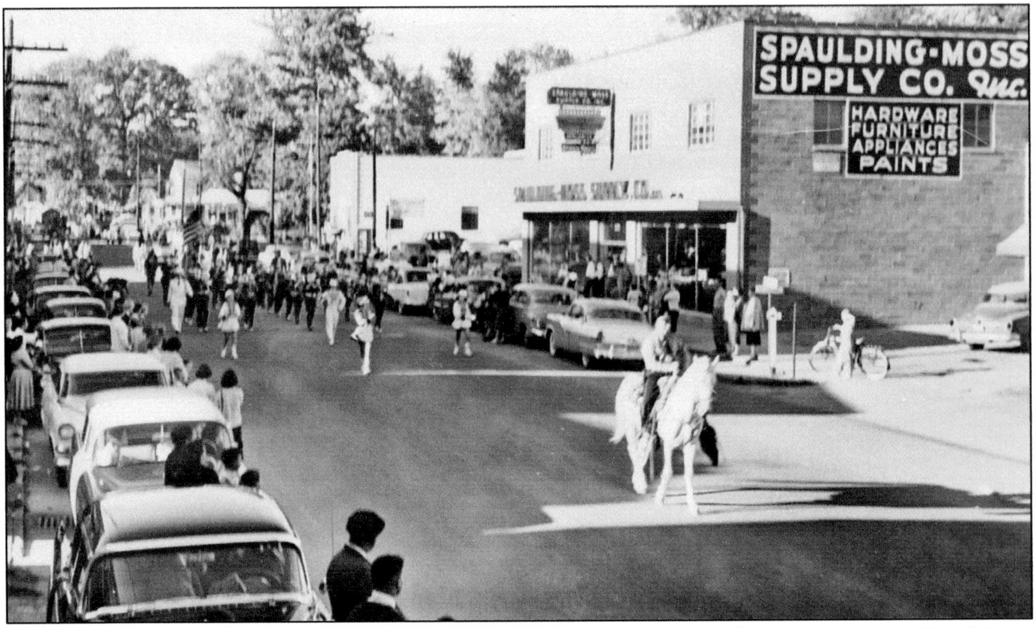

By 1956, the Garner Esso station on Main Street was gone, and in its place was the new Spaulding-Moss Supply Company, located next to the new Chase City Post Office. Above the supply company was a skating rink for several years. Leading the parade on his white horse is chief of police Harry V. Shuegart, who had over 30 years of service. (SCFA.)

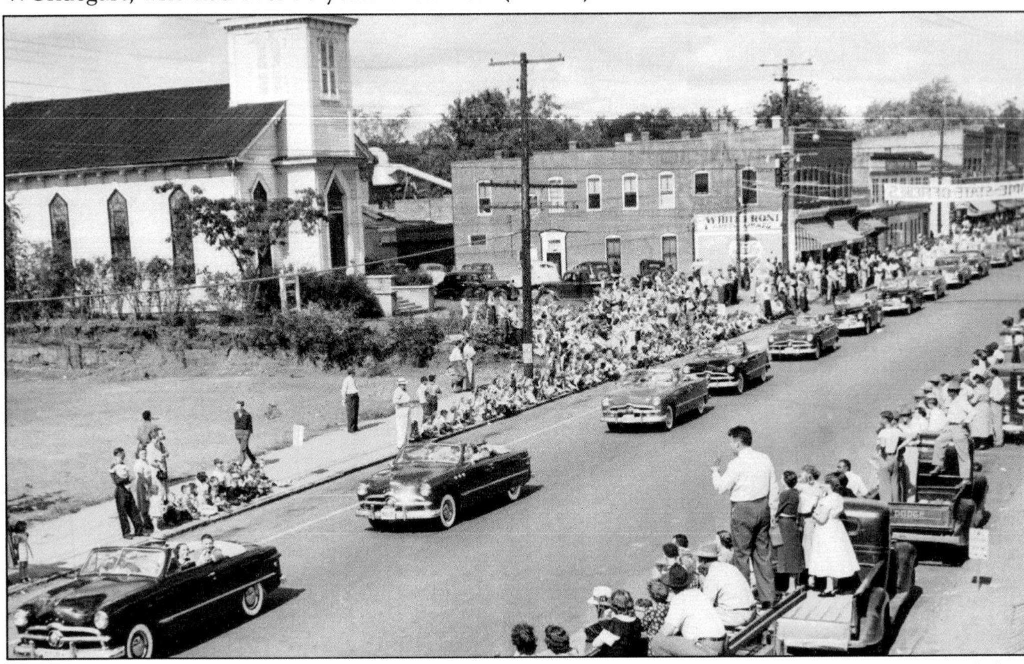

The old miniature golf course is gone, the church later moved, and the First State Bank has been White Front Grocery since 1940. Next door is J. C. Collis Grocery, then the Gregory Hotel and Craddock-Terry Shoe Company. Employees were allowed to leave their work area during parades. The 1949 Ford convertibles are being displayed for the townspeople on their way to the fairgrounds. (CDS.)

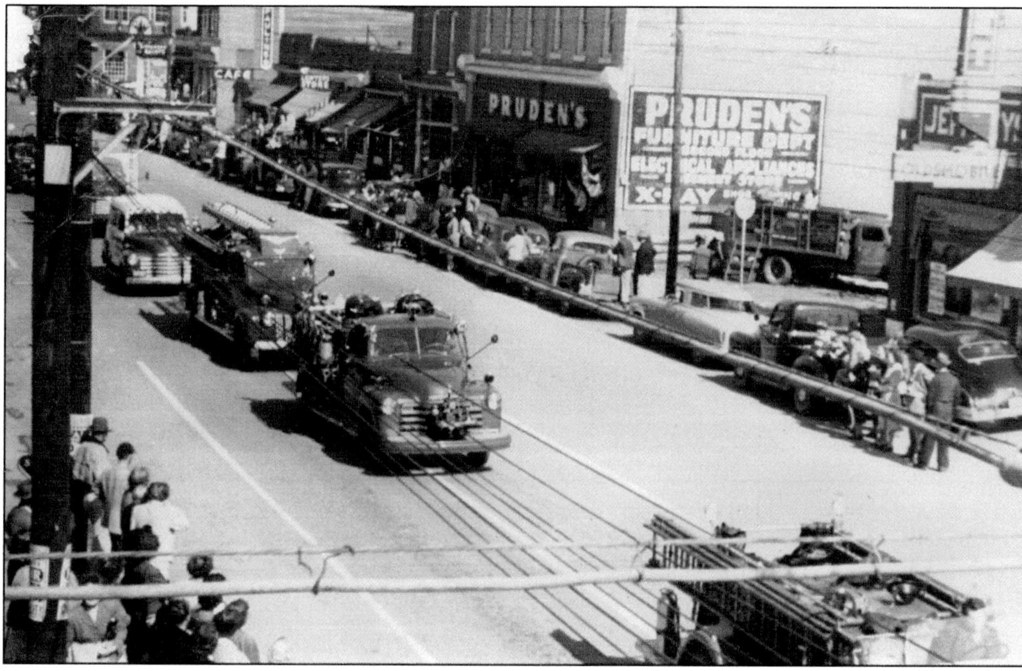

In this late-1940s photograph, the Chase City Volunteer Fire Department displays three of its trucks. They are followed by Bill Pennington's checkerboard van. Across the street is Pruden's (formerly Pruden and Hutchinson, with an undertaker's office and caskets in the basement). At far right is Jeffreys Motor Company. (SCFA.)

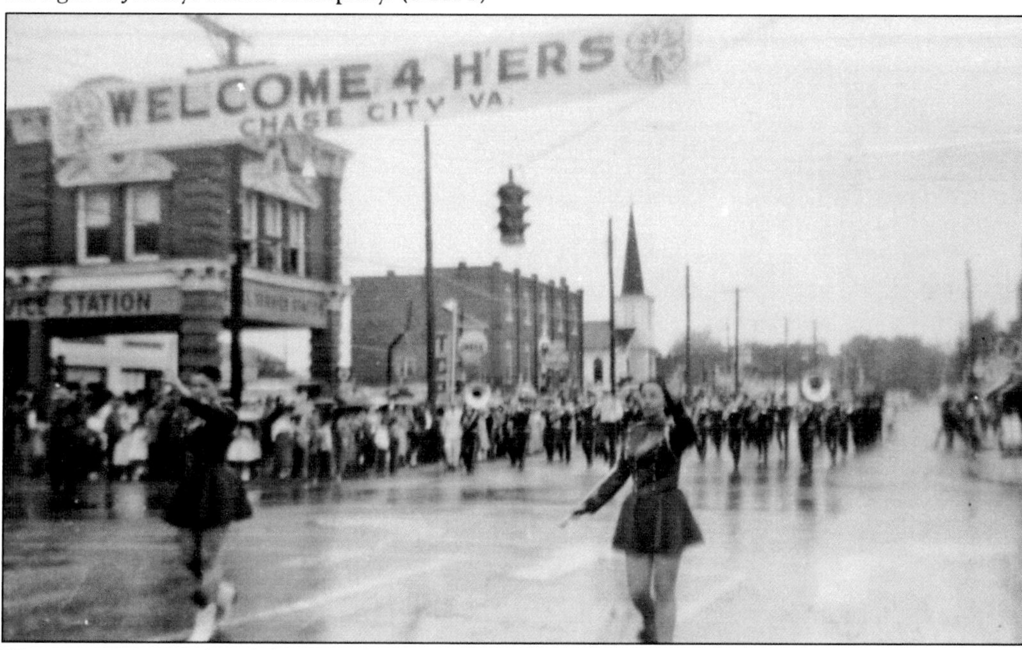

This is a 1949 parade celebrating the 4-H Club. This photograph, taken near the corner of Second and Main Streets, shows that the former First National Bank building is now a drive-through filling station that also offered hot carryout food. The station was originally operated by Billy Colgate. The armory and Presbyterian Church are in the background. (DT.)

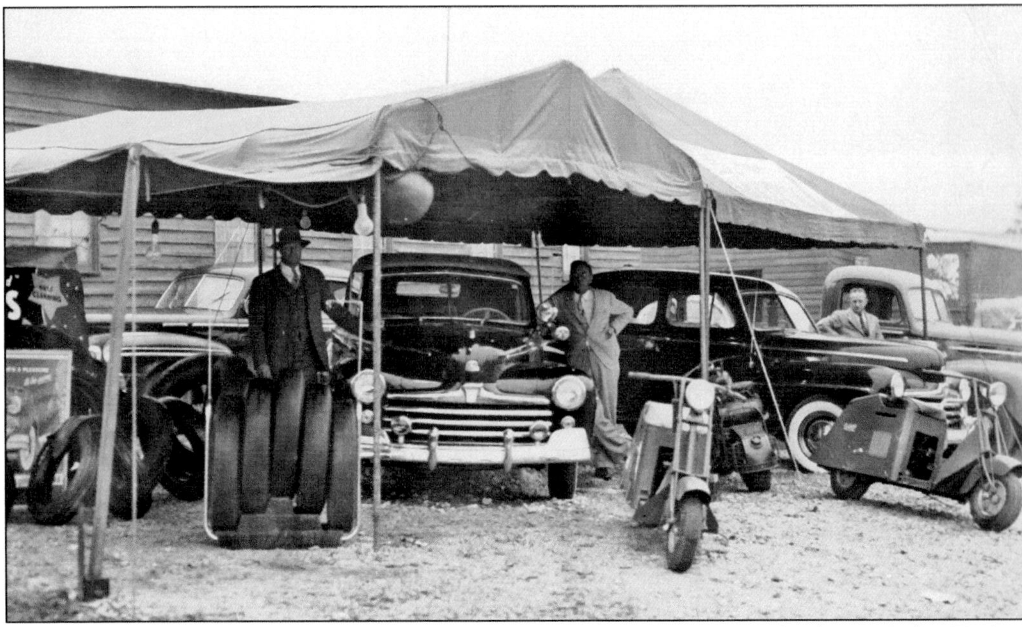

This 1947 display of Ford automobiles at the South Central Fairgrounds also includes Tucker-Bevell Motors' new line of motor scooters for leisure cruising about town. The new line of tires and automobile accessories are also on display. Under the tent are two unidentified people and Allen Bevell (center), ready to answer questions and write up sales. (CDS.)

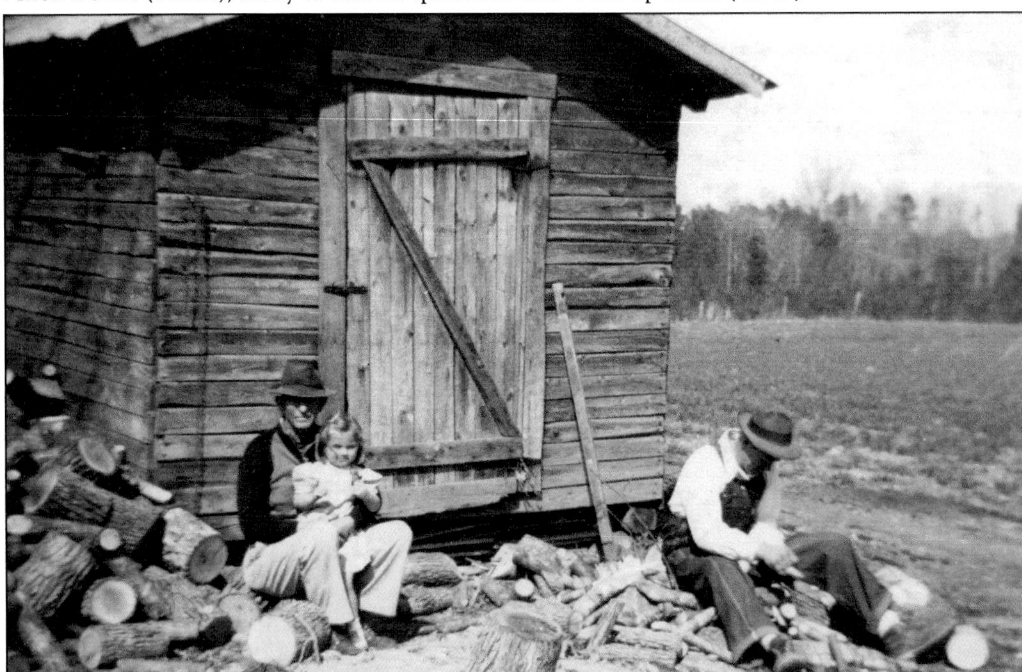

When the sports, recreation, parades, and excitement subsided, it was common for Chase City residents to return home for rest and relaxation. Often relaxing meant the pursuit of their favorite hobby, such as going out back to the woodpile and whittling. Here Will T. Morgan is pictured whittling, watched by Buster Brooks and daughter Jane Brooks, in 1948. (IMB.)

Six

Chase City
Then and Now

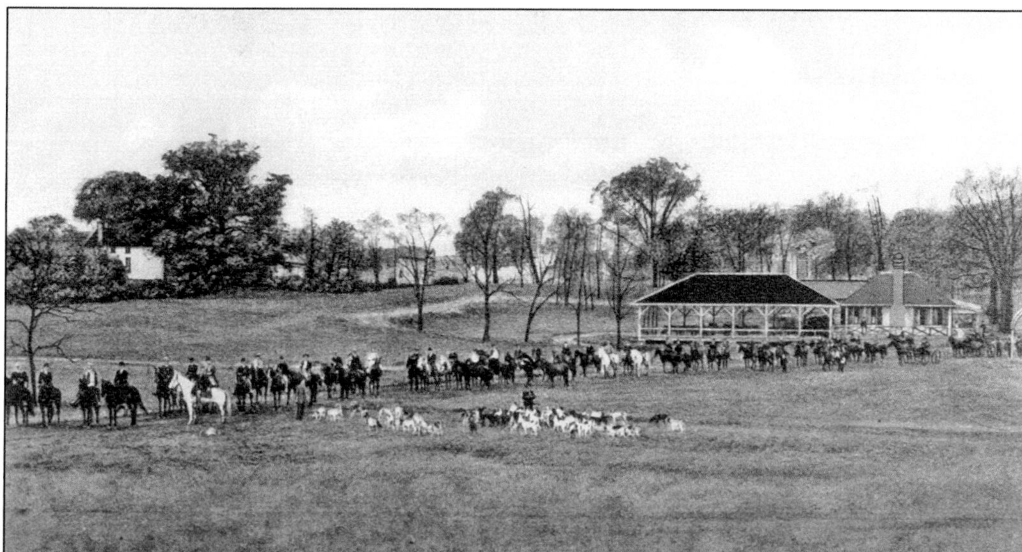

The Mecklenburg Mineral Springs Bottling Company (pictured in the 1890s) operated until 1915, when it was taken over by Coca-Cola Bottling Company, managed by Ed Williams. The company achieved such a reputation that it appeared in the *Philadelphia Inquirer* on May 4, 1911: "At the dinner to be given in honor of President Taft tonight at the Bellevue-Stratford Hotel by 300 prominent physicians . . . the Mecklenburg waters have been selected . . . in preference to all other waters. . . . The President partook liberally . . . at a recent banquet at the Astor, in New York." The little bottling company also bottled and sold Mecklenburg Ginger Ale, Sarsaparilla, and Lemon Soda made from the Mecklenburg waters and "put up in sterilized bottles." Coca-Cola Bottling only operated the plant for about six years, when it moved to temporary, then permanent, plants on Fifth Street. (SVHP.)

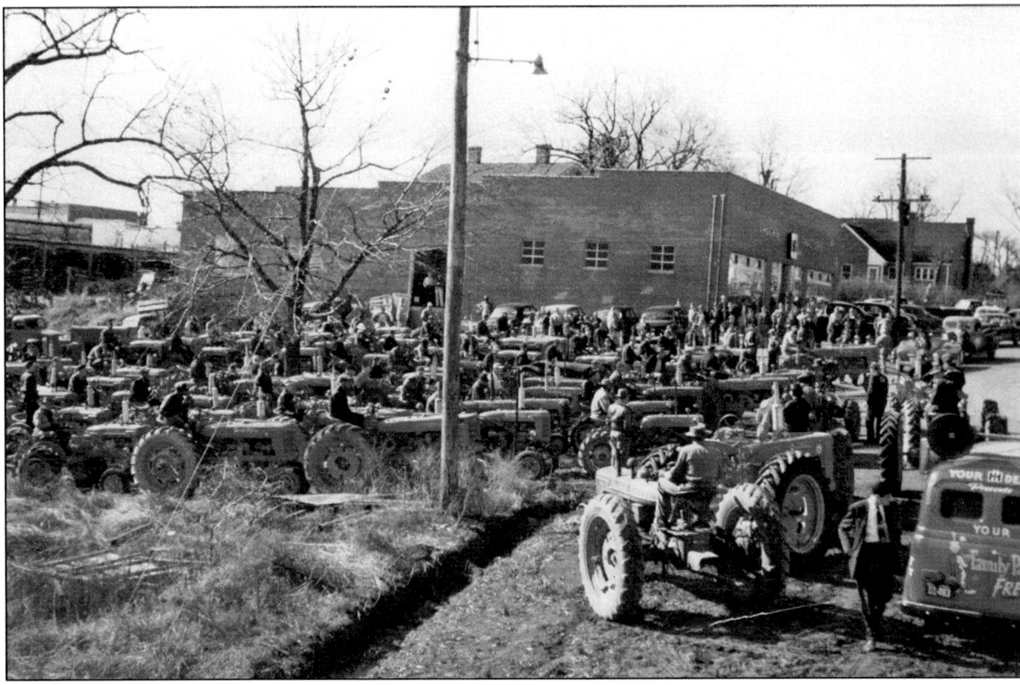

The bottling plant became the new home to Spaulding Equipment Company in 1949. In this photograph is a full compliment of Farmall tractors and International Harvester trucks and equipment. In the background is Shadow Lawn, remodeled again. (Robert Tucker.)

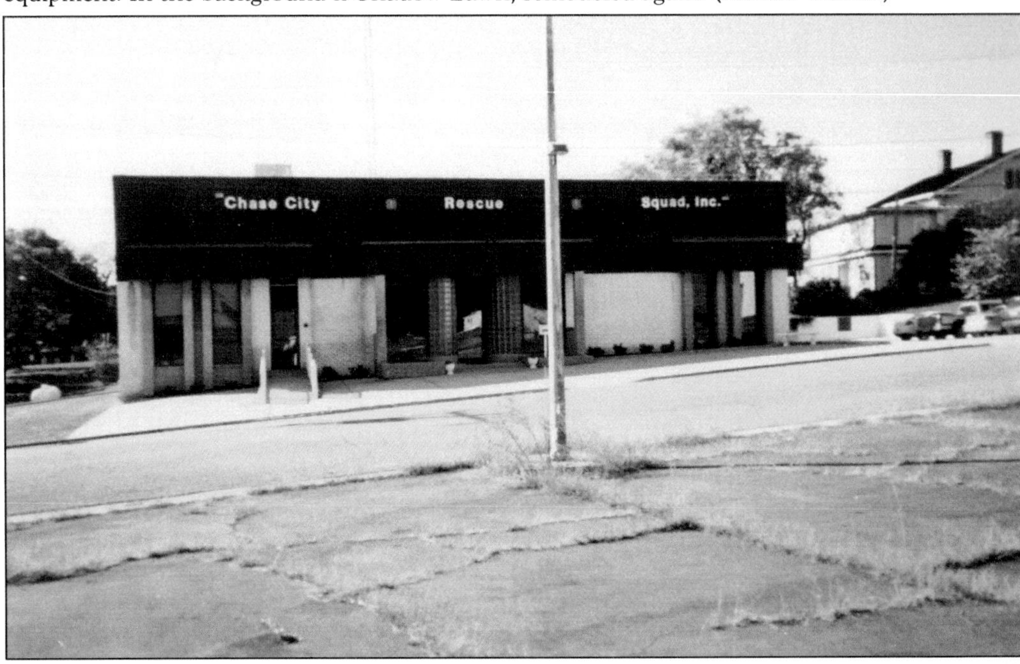

Having moved much of the business to the west side of town, Spaulding Equipment eventually moved its entire operation to the new site. The building became the new home of the Chase City Rescue Squad in 1985. With extensive remodeling and additions, this is how the building appears today. (JC.)

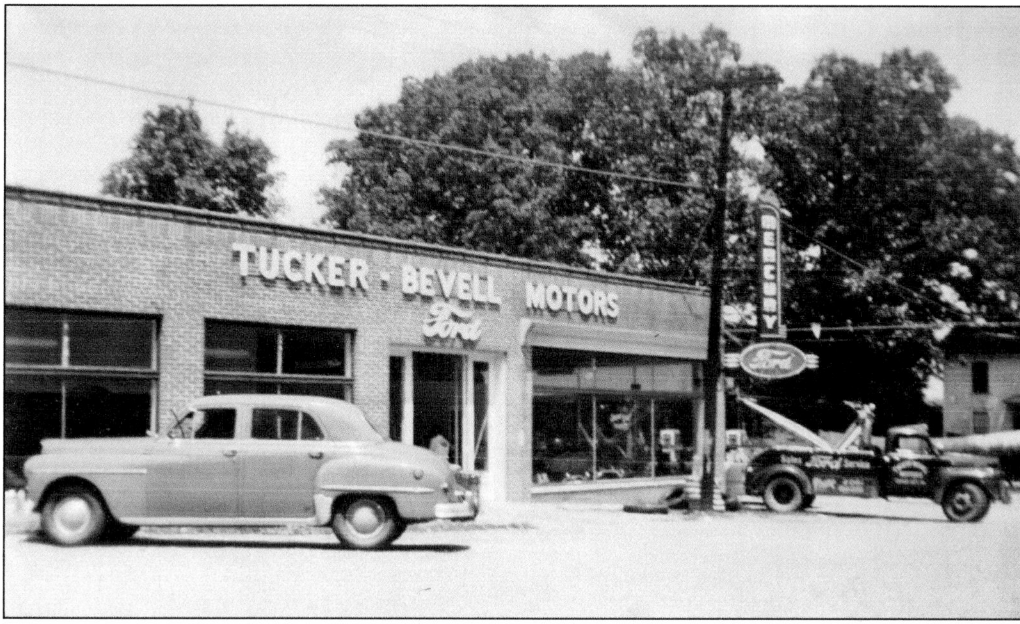

Tucker-Bevell Motor Company, which dominated Chase City from 1946 until the late 1970s, was closed. All the buildings were cleared, and a new Skatz drive-through took its place. The restaurant only lasted a few years before it too closed. (HL.)

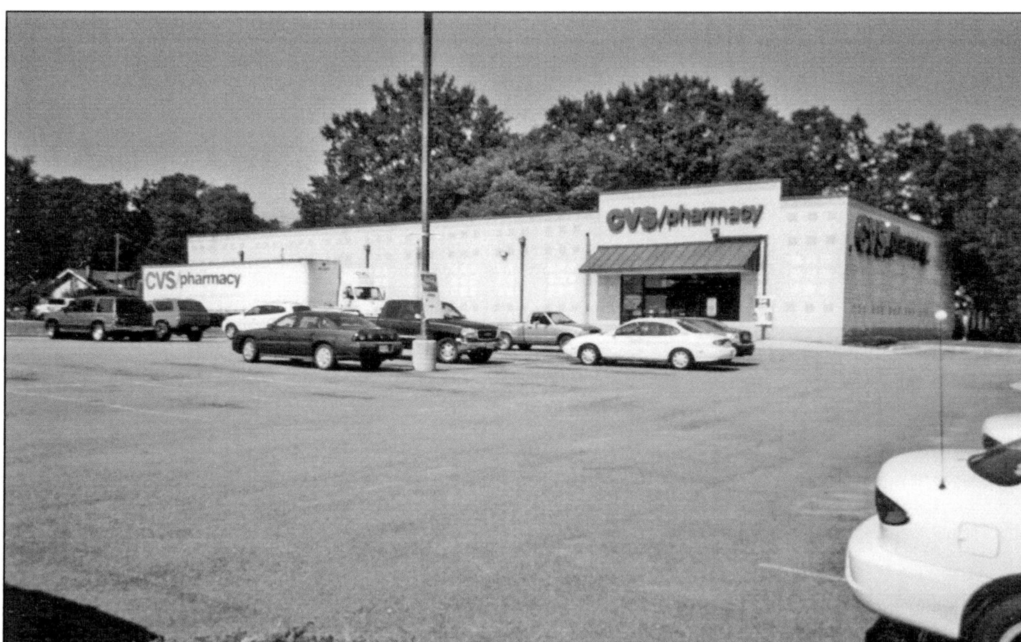

Again the corner was leveled, and all of Skatz was hauled away to make room for the new CVS pharmacy, which still occupies this spot today. (JC.)

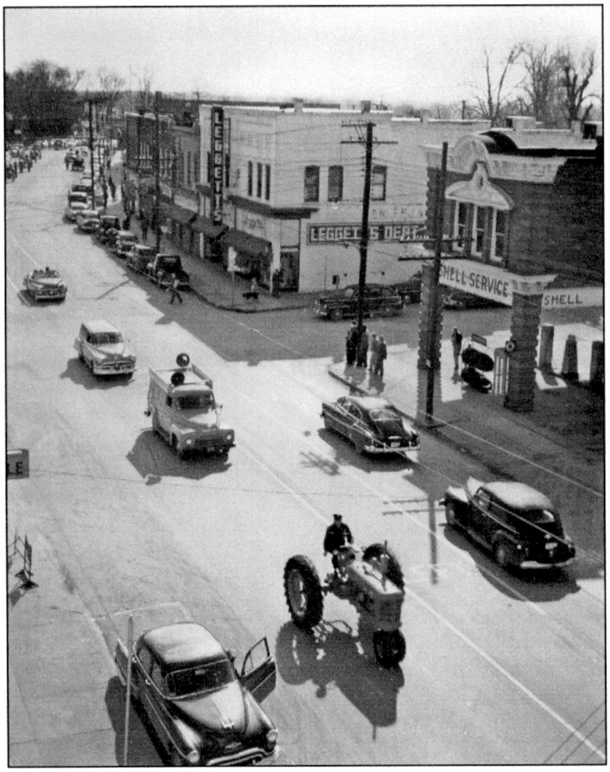

The First National Bank building became the Shell Service Center in 1936. Shown here is a 1953 parade of Spaulding Equipment Company's new products from Farmall and International Harvester. In 1936, Spaulding was managed by Billy Colgate, who kept a vault filled with beer in the basement. In the 1940 snowstorm, he was stranded in the station for three days but had plenty to eat and drink. Virginia blue laws required that businesses close at midnight; Billy would close at midnight and reopen at 12:15 a.m. (Ann Wagstaff Dembrowski.)

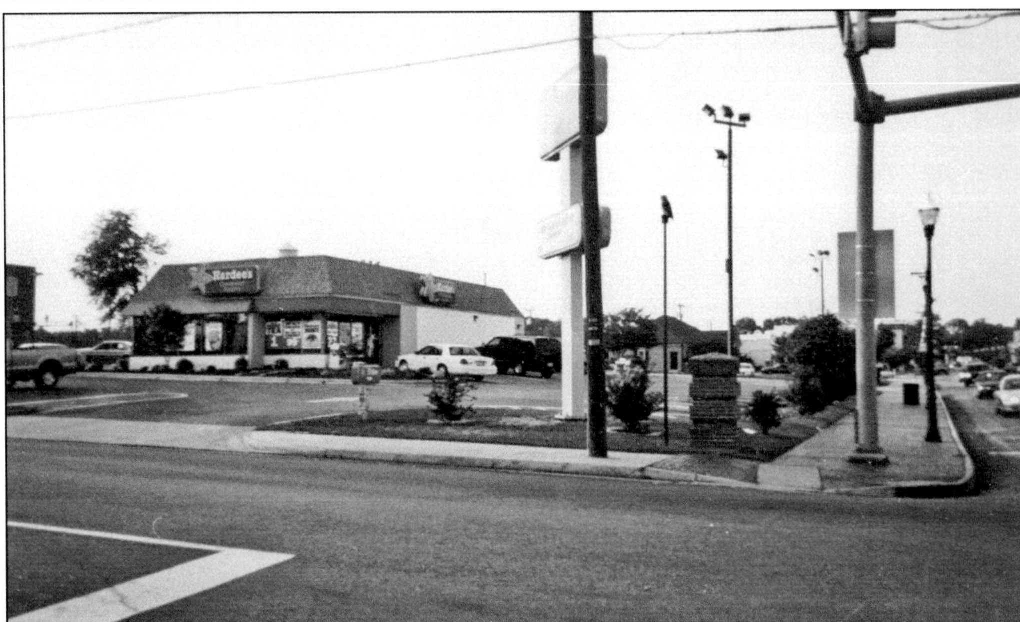

The gas station closed, and the building became a produce market. In the late 1950s, Jackson purchased Jeffreys Motor Company and the gas station. The building was leveled, and the lot became D. C. Jackson Motors used car lot. In the 1980s, the lot was purchased and became a Hardee's, which still operates today. (JC.)

In 1903, the Bank of Mecklenburg was taken over by First State Bank, which closed in 1930. During the late 1930s, the building became White Front Grocery, managed by Harry Midciff. In the 1950s, it became Spain and Weston Grocery, owned by Spats Spain and Berkley Weston. Later it became BonFabrieque, and in the 1990s, it was Ann's Consignment Shop. In 1998, it was torn down to make room for the Estes Center and YMCA club. (JAY.)

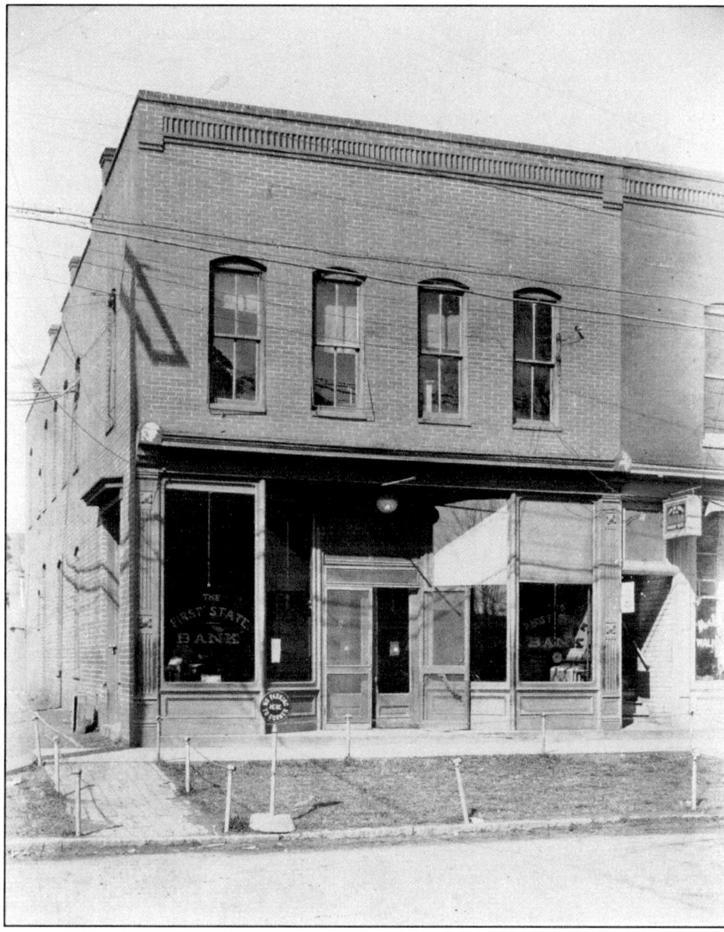

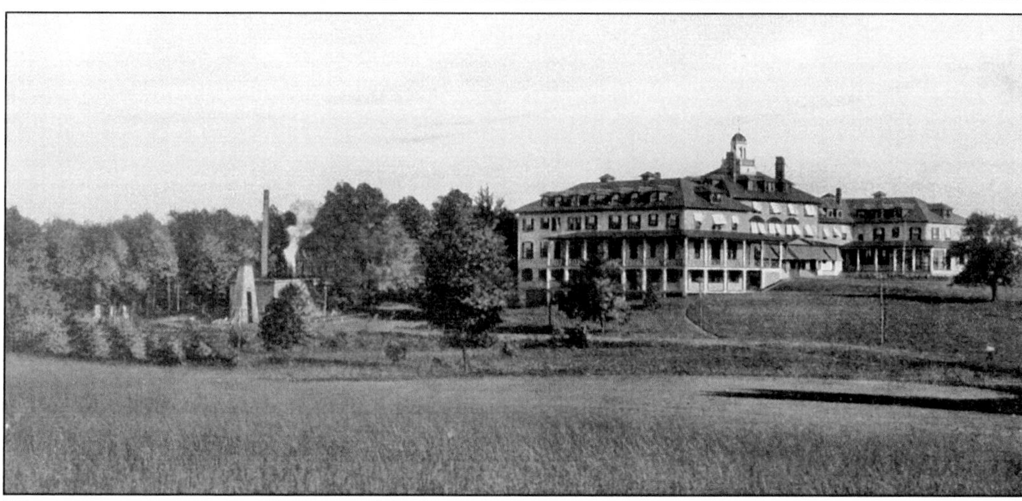

The 1901 power plant of the Mecklenburg Hotel was very much like the early power plant of Chase City, built in 1903. Although valiant efforts were made by Col. W. C. Hudgins to have Chase City purchase the power plant after the hotel burned, Chase City decided to build a new and modern facility. (SVHP.)

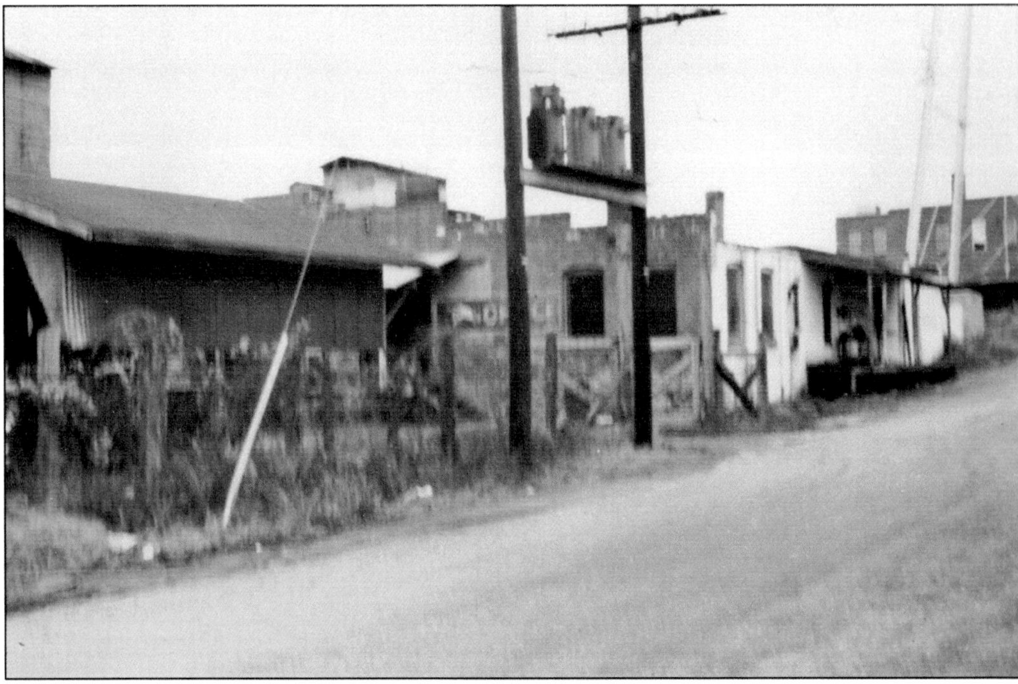

Construction began on the new power plant in 1911, but it did not operate until late 1912. Located in the old cannery building at Fourth and Boyd Streets, it operated until 1925. In that year, Halifax Power Company began supplying the town with electricity. (LLE.)

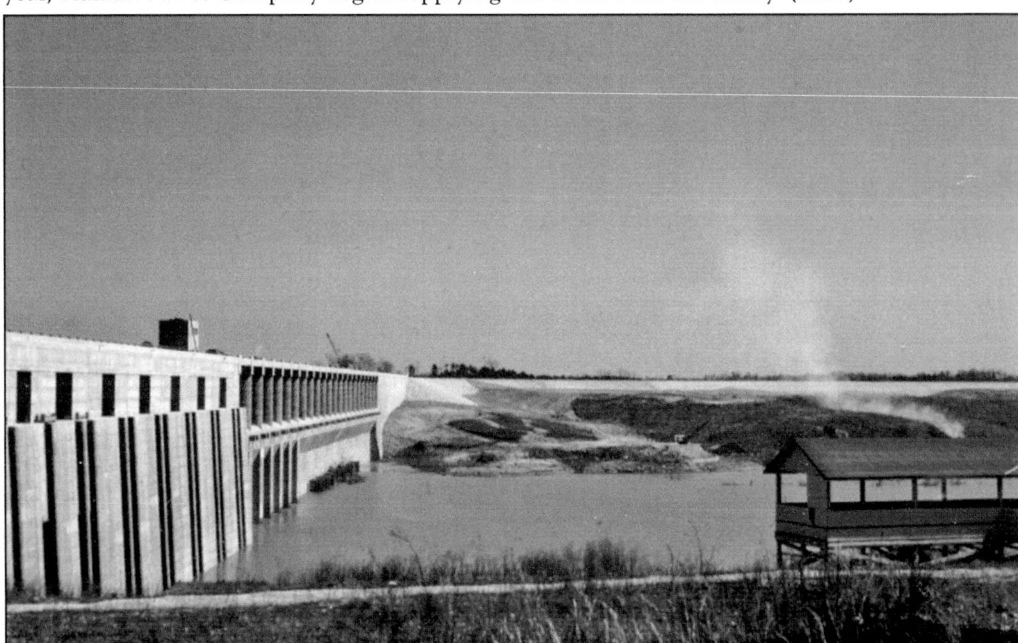

The John H. Kerr Dam was completed and operational by 1952. Developed for flood control, the dam also provides power to much of eastern Virginia and North Carolina. The Buggs Island reservoir east of the dam, called Lake Gaston, also provides water to many of the cities in eastern Virginia and North Carolina. (Mecklenburg Electric Cooperative.)

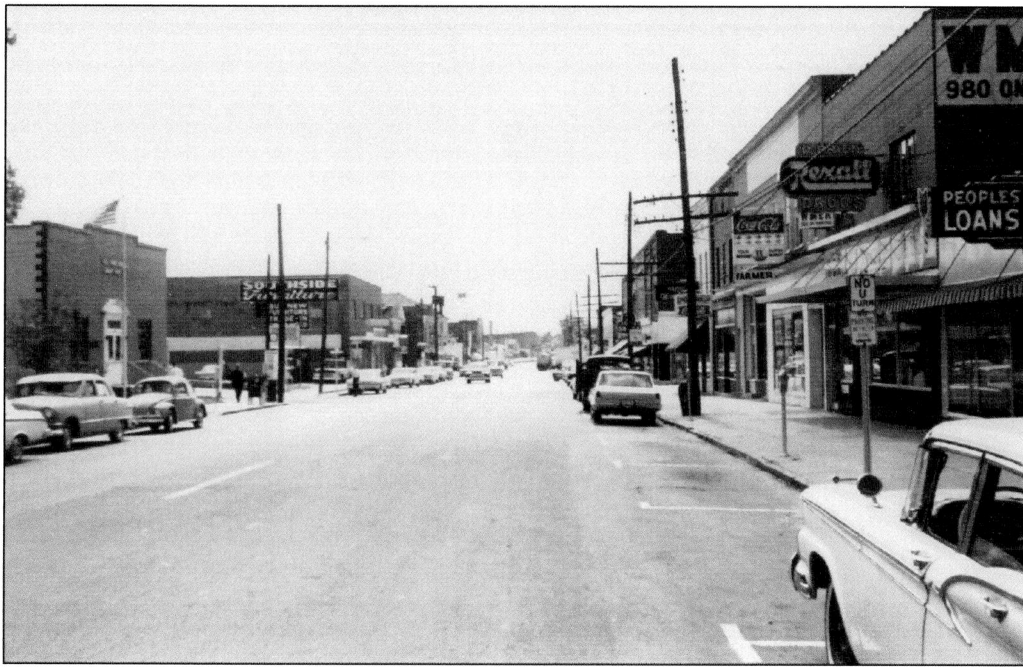

In the late 1940s, C. E. Geoghegan's wholesale was closed. In 1951, Hugh O'Brien opened a drugstore and sundries store advertising Rexall Drugs. Quickly this shop became one of the favorite locations on Main Street, especially for high school students after school. This store has closed, and the building is now occupied for the short term by Cornerstone Baptist Church. (Bryan Queensberry.)

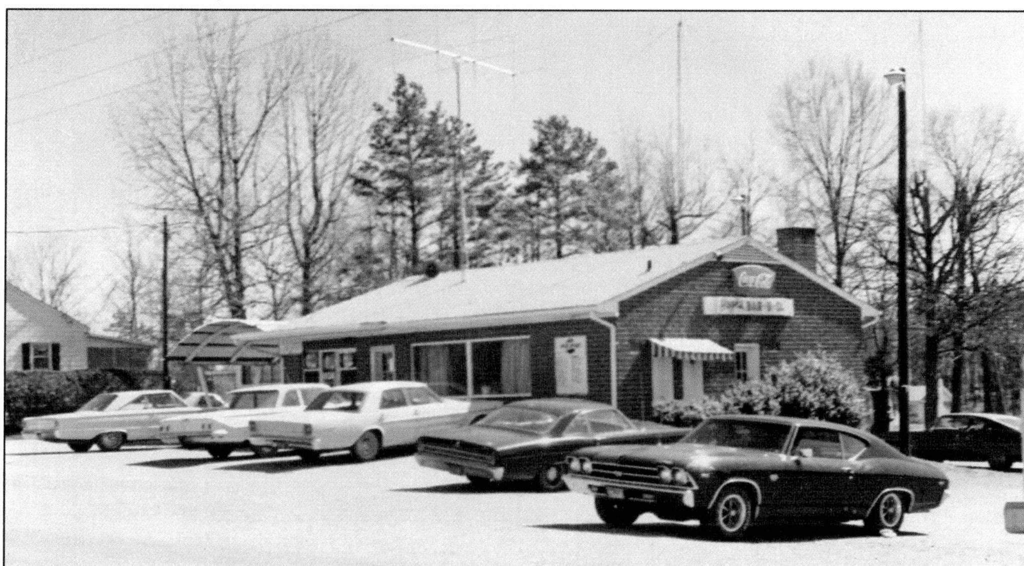

One of the favorite places in Chase City, for young and old, is Hugh's Sandwich Shop, which was remodeled and renamed Hugh's Barbeque. After the consolidation of Chase City High School, many students drove to school. Hugh Lenhart capitalized on this. By 1957, he had remodeled his shop as a modern facility with drive-up service where waitstaff met customers in the parking lot. The barbeque restaurant was considered the best in the state. (Charles Magann.)

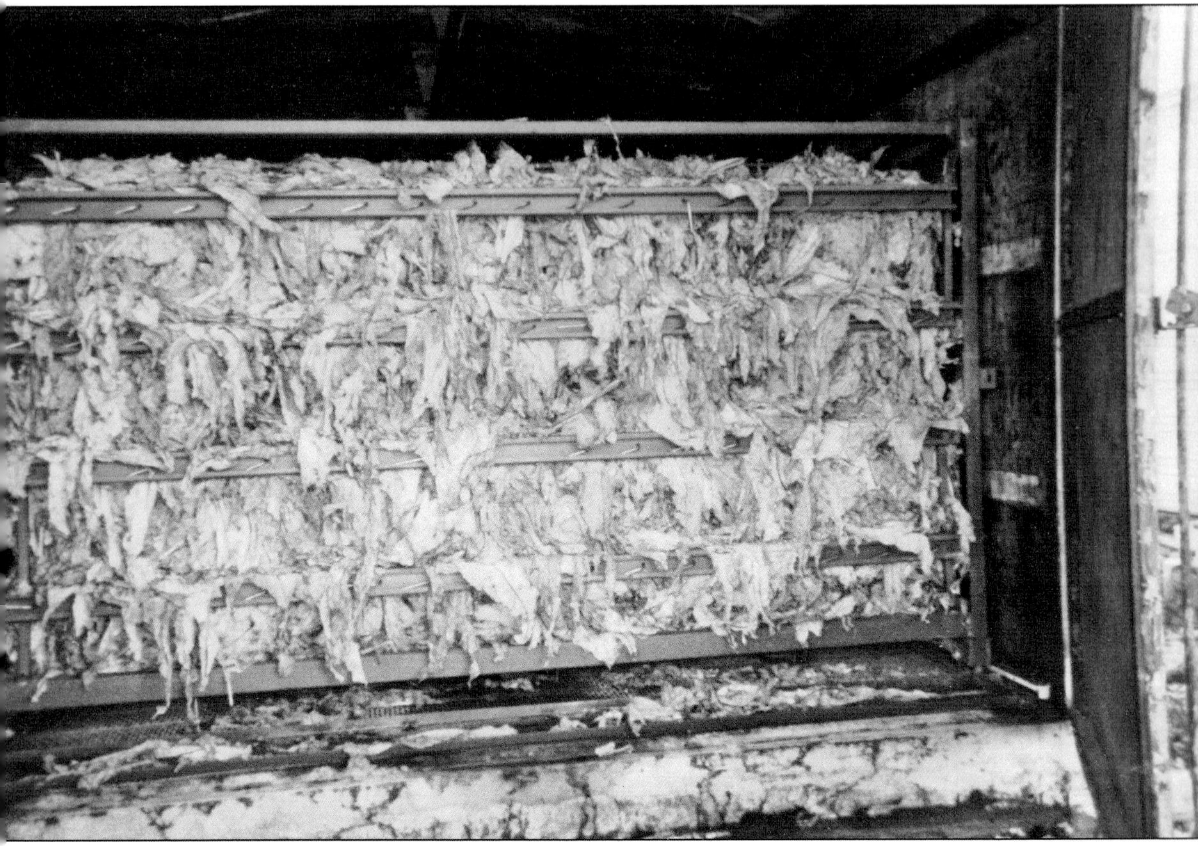

Enough could be written about Chase City's history to fill at least two more volumes, but "yellow gold" is still the staple part of Chase City's history. Shown here in the new 2005-mandated, propane-gas-fired bulk barn, the yellow gold of yesterday continues to maintain the economy of Chase City. (JC.)